READING
PUBLIC
OPINION

Studies in
Communication,
Media, and
Public Opinion

+

A series edited by

Susan Herbst

and

Benjamin I. Page

READING PUBLIC OPINION

How
Political Actors
View the
Democratic
Process

Susan Herbst

THE UNIVERSITY OF CHICAGO PRESS

Chicago and London

SUSAN HERBST is associate professor of political science and communications and director of American studies at Northwestern University. She is the author of *Numbered Voices* (1993), also published by the University of Chicago Press.

The University of Chicago Press, Chicago 60637
The University of Chicago Press, Ltd., London
© 1998 by The University of Chicago
All rights reserved. Published 1998
07 06 05 04 03 02 01 00 99 98   1 2 3 4 5
ISBN: 0-226-32746-9 (cloth)
ISBN: 0-226-32747-7 (paper)

Library of Congress Cataloging-in-Publication Data

Herbst, Susan.
    Reading public opinion : how political actors view the democratic
process / Susan Herbst.
        p.   cm.—(Studies in communication, media, and public
opinion)
    Includes bibliographical references and index.
    ISBN 0-226-32746-9 (alk. paper). — ISBN 0-226-32747-7 (pbk. :
alk. paper)
        1. Public opinion—United States.   2. Journalists—United States—
Attitudes.   3. United States. Congress—Officials and employees—
Attitudes.   4. Political activists—United States—Attitudes.
I. Title. II. Series.
HN90.P8H49   1998
303.3'8'0973—dc21   98-5160
                                                                                    CIP

For Daniel and Becca

Contents

Acknowledgments

To my mind, the proper study of public opinion demands truly interdisciplinary work, which is very challenging. If I have come at all close to shedding any light on this enduring and troubling concept, it is because a large number of colleagues from diverse disciplines have inspired me, supported me, badgered me, and even scolded me about particular ideas or approaches employed in this book. I am indebted to several groups of faculty and graduate students who listened to versions of this project during seminars at the University of Chicago, the Joan Shorenstein Center on the Press, Politics and Public Policy at Harvard University, the Annenberg School for Communication at the University of Pennsylvania, and the Schools of Journalism at Indiana University and the University of Wisconsin. Thanks especially to the following people for their insights and critiques: Bob Boatright, Mark Hansen, Lynn Sanders, Tom Patterson, Rick Sobel, Pippa Norris, David Weaver, Andy Rojecki, Joe Cappella, Oscar Gandy, Michael Pfau, Lewis Friedland, and Jack McLeod.

Near the end of my analysis I was fortunate to present preliminary findings at several conferences where I received enormously helpful feedback. Particularly instructive was a discussion among political scientists, media specialists, sociologists, journalists, and historians that was organized by Christoph Conrad and held at the Free University of Berlin's Center for Comparative Social History. Many thanks to Christoph, to the Center, and also to Loïc Blondiaux, Bob Luskin, and others who participated in that wonderful meeting. A variety of other scholars—Kathy Frankovic, Doris Graber, David Whiteman, and Kathleen Hall Jamieson—reacted to ideas in this book at other meetings, and their comments were very useful to me. Right alongside Max Weber, my own charismatic leader is Elihu Katz: He encouraged me from the start and is for me the ideal-typical intellectual.

The research in this book was supported by grants from the Shorenstein Center and the Northwestern University Graduate School. It would have been impossible to complete the project without these generous and much appreciated awards. I am grateful to Chris Marsh who handled the data input and coding for the delegate study in chapter 4 without losing his sense of humor. Noreen Sherwood helped me schedule scores of informant interviews, a tedious task that she approached with cheerfulness and efficiency throughout. Special thanks to Robert Eisinger of Lewis and Clark College. He and I designed the delegate study together, and I am grateful for his collaboration, his historical sensibility, and his repertoire of hilarious stories.

Many thanks to Bob Shapiro, Larry Jacobs, and Michael Delli Carpini for slogging through the entire manuscript and giving me scores of useful suggestions. Lance Bennett took time out from his hectic schedule to read the manuscript very quickly and gave me several good ideas for revision.

I am grateful to my students and colleagues at Northwestern who have so generously offered both ideas and support over the eight years I have been here: Dennis Chong, Fay Cook, Jim Ettema, and David Zarefsky (what a wonderful dean!). I owe many a debt to Ben Page for his friendship, his insights, and his persistent attempts to make me reflect on normative democratic theory. I am grateful to Becky Laurent for her terrific copyediting. And I must thank John Tryneski for all of his interest in my work over the years as well as his all-around good judgment, patience, and balanced perspective. To those who complain that the era of knowledgeable, intellectual editors has passed, I offer John as evidence to the contrary.

The informants in this study were not "data points" but fully engaged collaborators in my eyes. I cannot go far enough in expressing my gratitude to the legislative staffers, journalists, and political activists who spoke to me at length. I hope I have been true to their views of the political process, and I finish this book with renewed respect for their energy, their sincerity, and their commitment to democracy.

Finally, thanks to my close friends here in Evanston and elsewhere for listening to me ramble on, yet again, about my "public opinion book." In an act of great collegiality and friendship, Sarah Maza took a break from her own historical work to read this very contemporary manuscript, and gave me both helpful feedback and much-needed encouragement. My ever supportive husband, Doug Hughes, always believes I will finish a project and always thinks it will turn out just fine, even during my own periods of doubt. I am grateful to my parents for their good humor, German translation skills, and patience with small children. Speaking of whom: This book is dedicated to Daniel and Rebecca Hughes, the collective "vox" I most often heed.

Introduction

What do we mean when we speak of "public opinion"? Twentieth-century academics have struggled to define the term, yet even the most cursory reading of political theory reveals that intellectual angst about the concept began well before this century. The ancient Greek philosophers did not use the phrase "public opinion" but they grappled with many of the questions contemporary researchers still ponder: Is citizen opinion rational? Under what conditions can the people represent themselves, and when do they need more sophisticated or professional representation? Is public sentiment stable and difficult to sway, or can a leader with a knack for strategic communication mold popular feelings to his or her liking? Last, and perhaps most problematic: How are we to gauge the public will, and to whom should this responsibility fall? These questions are vital ones for all students of democratic theory. They were at the heart of public opinion research in the early years of polling and are still addressed by political theorists. With a few exceptions, however, opinion *researchers*—those who go out into the field and assess the public will—have tried their best to avoid the messy philosophical debates over the nature of public opinion that were sustained in earlier periods by Francis Graham Wilson, Paul Palmer, Wilhelm Bauer, and other thoughtful scholars.[1] In political science, sociology, and communications, three disciplines with lengthy histories of intense interest in opinion research, we have our quotes about and euphemisms for public opinion that underscore its nebulous character—Walter Lippmann's "phantom" or V. O. Key's oft-mentioned "holy ghost." But these are not just witticisms. They reveal public opinion assessment to be one of the most frustrating and challenging aspects of democratic practice.

I have posited elsewhere, as I will in this book, that the meaning of public opinion is *contingent:* The social climate, technological milieu, and communication environment in any democratic state together determine the way we think about public opinion and the ways we try to measure it.[2] The ever fluctuating meaning of "public opinion"—across historical periods and across continents—is what draws many scholars to the field of opinion research, but defining public opinion is an exceedingly difficult and complex task. Even though many of us recognize in our writings that "public opinion" is defined differently by different parties at different times, we secretly hope that our own preferred definition (the one we base our data collections on) might eventually be adopted by all. A collective definition seems necessary at first: How can we engage in a productive dialogue about the character of popular beliefs if we do not agree on the meaning of public opinion? I believe that developing such a shared definition is unlikely and probably impossible, so I hope to shift the theoretical discussion altogether: We should study how the entity of public opinion is created in the minds of political actors, as well as the sorts of very real effects this entity can have. Murray Edelman made this point in a somewhat different way years ago, but I hope to develop it much further by bringing in new evidence and by linking macro-level theorizing with micro-level study.[3]

My central argument is that public opinion is a contested and malleable concept, and that the processes of "constructing" public opinion have vital implications for democratic theory and practice. America is a democracy where public opinion is highly valued—but it is badly conceptualized, poorly measured by important political actors, and sometimes ignored entirely. Often "public opinion" is a symbol, a rhetorical being referred to by legislative professionals and journalists in their conversations with each other. Public opinion may be undertheorized by academics, but in the chaotic, day-to-day world of politics, public opinion is frequently left out of the policy-making process altogether or defined in ways that seem to be at odds with democratic ideals. The picture is not wholly negative, as we shall see in the chapters that follow. Some conceptions of public opinion we find among political actors—particularly among partisan activists—are quite inspiring from the standpoint of participatory democracy. I shall try to navigate among the multiple meanings of public opinion I found among the highly knowledgeable professionals and activists I have studied here, in hopes of expanding inquiry about public opinion and democratic process.

Public opinion is shaped by the complex and idiosyncratic cultural forces of any era, as Jürgen Habermas and so many others have documented.[4] Yet we need to retreat from macrohistorical-level trends at least temporarily if we are to understand the fundamental dynamics of working democracy: How do the players in our democratic drama conceptualize public opinion and the public sphere more generally? Researchers can read into the minds of individuals by studying the institutions they build and the documents they leave behind, but direct queries posed to citizens are just as valuable and important. This study is rooted in micro-level phenomena: How do those who need to evaluate and shape public opinion (journalists, legislative staffers, and political activists) define this rather slippery entity and measure it on the contemporary political scene? How do they understand the mechanics of the political process—the relationships among public opinion, mass media, and policy—so that they can act in the most effective ways they know how?

The most important concern of this book, touched on in most chapters but serving as the cornerstone of the concluding chapter, is the relationship between democratic theory itself and political professionals' and activists' "theories" of the political process. Which models of democracy do our legislative staffers, journalists, and political activists ascribe to, and what are the implications of these choices? In this study I have queried informants quite directly about the meaning and measure of public opinion, but asking them to expound on their models of democracy would have been far too difficult an interview task. In fact, many political scientists would have trouble elaborating on this question if asked without warning. So here I must try to construct informants' notions of contemporary democratic process from their ideas about some key *components* of that process—phenomena like public opinion, media bias, ideology, and the like. In views elicited during my discussions with legislative aides, journalists, and activists, as well as in responses to a large survey of partisan activists, there is much to applaud—from the perspective of participatory theories of democracy: Legislative staffers and journalists are very cynical about the political process and how media shape this process, but they still act in the best ways they know in order to serve the public. These professionals, as well as the activists in the study, do what they do for little or no (in the case of activists) financial reward, and they are quite clearly driven by rather idealistic motivating forces. Yet their views of public opinion—how to conceptualize this phenomenon and how to evaluate it in the context of ongoing policy debates—are also disturbing, from this same normative perspective of democratic theory. The "public" appears very much like the phantom Walter Lippmann claimed it was. Lippmann went a bit further than most democratic thinkers, of course, arguing that a concrete and measurable public opinion was empirically absent from the policy process but also that it *should* be. His elite theory of democracy may feel somewhat outdated and even absurd in an era where the rhetorics of inclusiveness and multiculturalism thrive. But regardless of how distasteful these elite views may seem, they need to be taken seriously by those of us intent on understanding relationships among public opinion, media, and policy making. We need not accept Lippmann's normative guidance to find his insights useful and provocative.

These grand concerns plague us later in the book after all the data are in, however, so let us first turn to the less abstract and less normative theoretical frameworks that guide research. One of these is "political cognition," a thriving and fascinating subfield in political psychology. Much of the research in this field is experimental in nature, and it has taught us a great deal about the way citizens reason about political parties, candidates for elective office, and particular issues. Work in this area progresses, yet it does not often enough use qualitative or interpretive methodologies that allow researchers to probe informants and give them the chance to introduce their own phrases and ideas. Many political cognition studies are based on information processing models of the mind, which dictate a particular set of research questions.[5] What is missing, beyond methodological experimentation and diversity, though, is social and cultural perspective. How, for instance, do citizens incorporate the perspectives of others or the language of institutions (e.g., the mass media or the legislature) into their own political worldviews? Experimentation has its place and its value, but if we are to understand how people think about politics, we must also identify links between the lives of our informants (e.g., their political and social roles) and the dynamic, often contradictory perspectives they hold. This book is far closer in methodology and general outlook to the work of Robert Lane than to the newer field of political-information processing, but I hope that those who normally choose experimentation will find the approach of this book useful and challenging.[6]

In addition to ideas from psychology, a variety of mid-range theories about public opinion itself are threads that run through much of the data and analysis in the chapters that follow. In particular, I draw on writings about the meaning of public opinion from the late nineteenth and early twentieth centuries, a period when many scholars struggled with the definition and measure of public opinion.[7] This work is enormously valuable to us since it was produced at a time when modern survey research was not yet available (sampling was not employed in surveying until the mid-1930s), so scholars were unencumbered by methodological concerns and therefore devoted massive attention to conceptual work. This theorizing in part laid the groundwork for methodological innovations to come, but much of it has been lost with shifts in academic culture, the excitement generated by the new sample survey, the availability of computer technology for data analysis, the need to compile longitudinal databases, and the like. These phenomena have been vital to the development of public opinion as a field, but we have now arrived at a juncture where earlier theorizing might be useful to us in assessing the contemporary scene. As a result, work by early sociologists and political scientists like Robert Binkley, Carroll D. Clark, and other rarely cited scholars implicitly shapes much of the text.

This study highlights the experiences of working political professionals and citizen activists, not average voters or college students. My informants have sophisticated opinions and ideas about the policy process—opinions and ideas that underscore for me just how complex peoples' mental models of the public sphere really are. And I asked difficult questions that demanded considerable time and patience on the part of forty-four busy individuals who participated in depth interviews (another 528 political party activists completed a survey). These men and women provided me with an enormous amount of material that gives us some keen insights into the central concern of this book—the meaning of public opinion. How these people think about the phrase "public opinion" and the connections they make among opinion, media, and policy making are not easily summarized. We can, however, discern some fairly distinctive cognitive arguments about the public sphere. These models are highly contextual: They are connected to informants' work as journalists, as legislative aides, and as highly partisan political activists.

I expected, at the start of this project, to find a linguistic and ideological morass when I asked informants to define and discuss public opinion. And the complex answers I received were indeed confusing at times. Yet several things were clear. First, for many people deeply involved in politics, the phenomena of public opinion and mass media are largely conflated. In other words, these two institutions or forces are difficult to pull apart, either theoretically or practically, in political work. Academics might write this off by claiming that we often understand distinctions and divisions that lay people do not: We are trained to direct an objective gaze toward the political sphere, to define concepts with precision, and to tell those in politics why they think and act as they do. The problem here is that policy elites—people who understand the mechanics of the process and indeed "make it happen"—see an extraordinarily close connection between public opinion and media that we tend to ignore. Following the formal depth interview, I talked with a few of my particularly curious informants about the sorts of research on public opinion and mass media we find in our academic journals. They were baffled, needless to say, by experimentation in political cognition (the mapping of decision-making processes in fictional campaigns and elections, for example) and troubled by the various "agenda setting" models that populate the literature. None could understand how media coverage of public opinion and public opinion itself might be separated for analytical purposes, or how we could talk about media and public opinion as acting in a causal order (e.g., media coverage of X issue yields public opinion Y, which then reshapes media coverage of X, etc.). We cannot dismiss the views of these knowledgeable individuals by saying "we know better" because we are still unsure about the relationship between public opinion and media ourselves. Indeed, opinion and media research are relatively new fields, and the communication environment shifts constantly. Political scientists have always learned—via survey research or depth interviews—from people who actually practice politics. Their thoughts on the mechanics of democracy are, as I hope to demonstrate, inordinately valuable to us.[8]

Beyond making me aware of the conflation of public opinion and how the media describe it, many informants pressured me to think about *groups*—how it is that interests and lobbies, in particular, try to represent public opinion. The belief that groups *represent* public opinion is not uncommon in political science, but some informants went one step further than most scholars by arguing that interest groups actually *are* public opinion. We certainly have a large body of academic literature on interest groups, so we have by no means ignored the role of such activists. Yet the public opinion literature and our theory and research about interest groups have increasingly diverged. Alexis de Tocqueville, James Bryce, Arthur Bentley, David Truman, Herbert Blumer, and other nineteenth- and early twentieth-century observers of American politics believed that group opinion and public opinion were one and the same: Groups funnel nebulous opinion into the entity we recognize as public opinion.[9] Contemporary scholars have moved away from this group-oriented model, thinking about public opinion as mass opinion (measured by sample survey techniques) and regarding interest group politics as an entirely different animal. When public opinion researchers think about groups, in fact, they are most often referring to groups created artificially through the analysis of survey data: They are not thinking about groups as interests or lobbies with strong ideological cohesion, dues, newsletters, meetings, and more generalized feelings of identity.[10] This book grapples with the links political professionals make between group activity and the nature of public opinion itself. Their ideas are instructive and demand that we go back again to reread some of our best political theory.

One of the most interesting findings distilled from my interviews is that people do not simply spout definitions of "public opinion" in dictionary style (e.g., "Public opinion is the voice of the people"). They may begin with such banal statements, but as they flesh out their definitions, it becomes clear that their meanings of public opinion are in fact *arguments* about both representation and democracy. As Michael Billig and Deanna Kuhn—two psychologists who come from very different perspectives—have both noted, people think about the social world in terms of argument, not problem solving.[11] This is not to say that people do not stretch their cognitive capacities in order to solve personal, occupational, or social problems. They do. Yet individuals also engage in constant internal argumentation about their worlds, as they explore, rationalize, interact, and generally go about their everyday routines. If we think of thinking as argument, we can better understand what it means to have political cognition.

A problem that occurs with many opinion research methodologies—survey research, experimentation, and simulation of public opinion, for instance—is the diminution or omission of contextual factors. Michel Foucault, for all the controversial things he has said and written, has taught us at least one very valuable lesson: Power and politics are very much about local environments and context.[12] Candidates running for office, legislators deciding how to vote, activists planning a mobilization of their followers, and all other political actors are very much concerned with *particulars*—the tenor of the times, recent history and events, key players, financial problems, journalistic tendencies, and so forth. These contextual factors or variables are crucial and, unfortunately for the academic observer, constantly shifting. The dynamic nature of politics, and the various factors that make it dynamic, can at times be "controlled for" or may be studied directly. Here I do the latter, asking informants to tell me as much as they can about their political work in hopes of interpreting their intricate narratives. This is a labor-intensive task, but it helps us understand how a myriad of contextual variables matter as people try to make sense of the public sphere and their actions within it. In this book political professionals speak very often through examples, anecdotes, and incidents that guide their perspectives and actions.

Much theorizing about public opinion in academe takes place either at the macrostructural level (e.g., models documenting the relationship between mass opinion and policy making) or at the microindividual level (e.g., experimentation in political cognition), yet researchers have always had trouble bridging the two levels of analysis. We can mediate between levels by studying interest groups, evaluating the dynamics of collective action, or analyzing the various institutions that lie somewhere between the processes of individual attitude formation and policy making (e.g., legislatures). Another approach is to prompt individuals to reveal their models of the public sphere—how they understand the macro-level concepts (e.g., "public opinion") and phenomena discussed regularly by academics, journalists, pundits, and leaders. One of my goals is to locate political professionals' models or "lay theories" and then identify links between an individual's model of the public sphere and the individual's actions. This is difficult, of course, because while we know a tremendous amount about citizens' and professionals' *beliefs* on a variety of topics, we know next to nothing about the ways they view representation, public opinion, media influence, and many other components and abstract concepts vital to democratic theory.[13] (On a terminological note, in this book, *lay theories* are the nonacademic, nonscholarly theories articulated by people outside of the university.[14])

But why do the mental models or lay theories of legislative workers, journalists, and political activists matter? There are several reasons. First, these are the people who influence the nature of policy making, and their conceptions of the political world affect the decisions they make. Second, the individuals interviewed here are such sophisticated actors in the system that they know a thing or two about democracy we do not: They "tip us off" in ways that may eventually enable us to develop general theories about public opinion, media, representation, and policy. Perhaps they see certain processes more clearly than we do. As it turns out, these informants lead us to pose difficult questions, the most vexing of all being this: If public opinion has varied identities and manifestations, how exactly are we to situate it in grand democratic theory? Third, if we can begin to understand how important actors in the system view the system they have created, routes to changing democratic process begin to emerge. For instance, journalists—who are currently engaged in intense discussion about the norms and goals of their profession—might find this study to be a constructive critique of their approach to news reporting.[15] Fourth, and last, we will see in the chapters that follow a clash in definitions of public opinion: Informants disagree about the nature of public opinion because of their experiences in politics and their varying locations in the social matrix. The existence of such conflict is important because it indicates a fundamental difference in conceptions of democracy across groups of citizens and may explain certain kinds of institutional and rhetorical strife.

This book describes the views that staffers, journalists, and citizen activists have about public opinion, the media, and politics more generally, but I am exceedingly cautious throughout the book *not* to valorize or celebrate any particular view of public opinion these informants provide. I am not applauding certain views and dismissing others. All the responses I received seem both constructive and destructive in complex ways, functional and dysfunctional at the same time. I *do* need to occupy my informants' cognitive positions, though very temporarily, and try to sympathize with their worldviews if I am to do these perspectives justice. Yet I do not believe any of the informants in this book are "correct" or "incorrect": On the contrary, the point of this book is that one's role in the world of politics is often correlated with particular views of public opinion. So I try to describe the views of the political professionals and activists but also analyze their lay theories, focusing on the important implications of their views about public opinion.

Developing a research design for this study was a struggle, and I made choices along the way that have, of course, significantly affected the nature of my results. Some things were clear: If I was to understand important actors' models of the public sphere, I must include media professionals and citizen activists. They are vital players on the contemporary scene, which is shaped so profoundly by the press and the parties. I knew that voices from the legislature mattered as well, though, and decided to interview legislative staffers instead of representatives themselves. I was greatly influenced early on in this study by legislative research on "enterprise models." These models demonstrate that, while it is the legislators who cast the votes, they do not come to these decisions alone. Advisors and staffers form a cohesive enterprise or subsystem around legislators, supporting them and leading them to their final decisions. The literature on enterprises convinced me that legislative staffers would be both knowledgeable and honest "reporters" about the policy-making process. I found them to be both sophisticated and blunt, which made the long hours of interviewing a real pleasure.[16]

In addition to choosing informants, I had to choose an environment for understanding lay theories about the political world. I chose state government in Illinois, the journalists who cover it, and activists engaged in its politics. I might have chosen national politics, interviewing congressional staffers, Washington journalists, and lobbyists. Yet I chose state government for several important reasons. First, it has an even more tightly knit network of legislative aides, journalists, communication directors, and activists than does Washington. While this is not a network study in the contemporary sociological sense, studying a smaller community enables a scholar to focus efficiently on particular bills and legislative debates. All the respondents in this study knew about many of the same issues, actors, and events. As a result, I could begin to map out shared opinion among groups of professionals and figure out how different players in the state interact with each other. They spoke the same language and spoke about many of the same issues or problems, so this made my work easier. Second, I was influenced by recent literature in political science on the close connections between public opinion and public policy at the state level. In national politics, these links are more difficult to draw: With state politics, as several scholars have demonstrated, we can detect connections between public opinion and representation. Third, there is little issue polling at the state level. In fact, I often think of Springfield, Illinois, as a "land without polls" compared with Washington, although recent work by Lawrence Jacobs and Robert Shapiro demonstrates that polls play a far less important role in executive and congressional decision making than we think.[17] Most legislative debates in states proceed without media- or party-sponsored polls, which clears the way for a simpler, even "cleaner" view of public opinion dynamics. Polls exist in state politics, of course, and pre-election polls are critical during campaigns, but neither issue nor election polls dominate the policy-making environment. Fourth, states are becoming increasingly important arenas for policy making—particularly in the area of health and social welfare policy—as more economic burdens are placed on them by the federal government. Last (and a lucky geographical coincidence for me), Illinois happens to be both a microcosm of the nation and a "bellwether" in terms of national election prediction, so it simulates national politics in many important regards. Illinois is home to one of the largest cities in the nation, yet it has many small towns. It has high technology industry but a substantial agricultural sector as well. Some even argue that it embodies two distinct American cultures—it is both northern and southern at the same time.

State politics is a milieu scorned by many scholars. More than once I was asked variants of: "Why study Springfield? State politics is so damn *boring.*" Or was told, "No one takes subnational-level politics seriously, at least not in academe." These are not inspiring comments to hear early in a large research undertaking. Yet despite my initial concerns with using state politics as an environment for studying general political process and cognition, I could tell it was a good choice after my first few interviews. These early interviews were the longest, as I tried to understand the rules and idiosyncrasies of the Illinois legislature and the culture of state politics. Over my seven years as an Illinois resident (before initiating this study), I had tried to keep up with state legislative matters. But when I began to focus in earnest on my state I was surprised at the sheer number of important issues—from regulatory matters and taxation to social welfare policies—that are considered and debated in each legislative session. And, despite the fears of some of my colleagues, these policy debates were not boring at all: Most controversies directly and significantly affected either small or large groups of citizens in the state. The Illinois state legislature, like Congress and other large state assemblies, has its share of symbolic debates and rituals that seem meaningless to those outside Springfield. But the content and structure of most initiatives debated there do in fact determine the contours of the economic and cultural environment for all citizens, from impoverished mothers on welfare to some of our nation's wealthiest business people.

I should note, however, that those who study state politics or who care about Illinois politics in particular will be greatly disappointed by the focus of this research. I learned along the way that state politics is interesting and important, and that this environment is badly underrepresented in scholarship and in government textbooks. Yet because I am most interested in broader issues of public opinion and the perspectives of important actors in the democratic process, I do not explore any policy debates or political institutions found in Illinois in any depth. Instead I used state politics as a means for finding political professionals who might reveal truths about policy work more generally. So, my apologies to scholars with an interest in the important details of state politics, and state legislatures in particular.

The use my informants make of public opinion polls is an issue in this book, and I pursue this topic in different ways in several chapters. So, before I describe the structure of the book, past experience tells me I should offer a brief (and I hope not gratuitous) note of clarification about my own approach to opinion polling. While there exist multiple critical tracts about polling in the United States, my own previous work questioning the authoritative nature of survey data in American politics was interpreted by some as an antiquantitative, even Luddite assault on the practice of polling.[18] From a normative perspective, I believe that polling has too much legitimacy in the public sphere and that as a populace we tend not to criticize surveying in light of democratic theory. Yet it was not my intention then or in the present work to argue for the elimination of surveys as a research method in academe, in government, in campaigning, in journalism, or in the commercial world. In fact, chapter 4 of this book contains a survey with the sort of open-ended questioning I prefer. Survey techniques clearly have valuable uses when employed with thoughtfulness and with caution. In this book I am sincerely quite agnostic about the value of surveys, and avoid normative debate about polls themselves. Instead I allow my informants to tell us how they conceptualize public opinion and when they use aggregative methods of opinion assessment.

With these qualifications behind us, let me briefly outline the structure of this book. Chapter 1 explores some of the larger philosophical and theoretical issues at stake in the field of public opinion. What does it mean to say that public opinion is "socially constructed," for instance? This term is in vogue, certainly, and is often used inappropriately, so I hope to demonstrate why it is very useful in the study of the public mood. In this chapter I also discuss the meaning and value of "lay theory," in contrast to other cognitive psychology frameworks. I rely most directly on concepts and research introduced by Jerome Bruner, Clifford Geertz, and Michael Billig. Here I also introduce my informants and explain why Illinois is a useful microcosm for understanding American politics (methodological details can be found in Appendix A). Chapters 2, 3, and 4 report on the interviews I conducted with the three very different groups of informants—legislative staffers, journalists, and political activists. Chapter 4 contains both a small depth interview study of political activists from Illinois as well as data from a larger survey of more than five hundred 1996 Democratic and Republican national convention delegates representing states across the nation.

Chapter 5 brings together theoretical concerns about public opinion, mental models of the public sphere, and the interview data. I present some comparisons among groups that are, I hope, instructive to those interested in public opinion, the media, policy, and political representation more generally. Here I draw on micro-level research to reevaluate the notion that public opinion is "constructed": How might data collected at this level of analysis inform midrange and even grand theory about the nature of public opinion, ideology, and the public sphere? It is my firm belief that thoughtful people enmeshed in government and campaign work can in fact guide some of our theorizing. This is not to say that our best theorists, who observe the political realm from a distance, are naive or badly informed about *real* political life. It is the case, though, that extended and personal contact with the politically engaged does greatly enhance our understanding of political communication dynamics in America.

1 The "Construction" of Public Opinion: Looking to Lay Theory

[P]ublic opinion gets its form from the social framework in which it moves, and from the social processes in play in that framework. . . . If public opinion is to be studied in any realistic sense its depiction must be faithful to its empirical character.

HERBERT BLUMER, "PUBLIC OPINION AND PUBLIC OPINION POLLING" (1948)

WHAT DO WE MEAN when we say that public opinion is socially or politically constructed? Or, as Herbert Blumer argued, that public opinion "gets its form from the social framework in which it moves"?[1] On the most fundamental level, positing public opinion as social construction is an admission that, like almost all concepts and phrases, the meaning of the term is subject to the ever shifting forces of culture. By bringing together and synthesizing a number of important scholarly works on the subject, this chapter explores just how institutions, technology, and political culture come to determine the nature of public opinion. Most of this work—theoretical and empirical—has been conducted on the macro level, and so I deal first with the higher, abstract levels of analysis. Yet my central goal here is to argue that the construction of public opinion happens also in the minds of citizens: People tend to define public opinion as part of an *argument* they make—to themselves and, at times, to others—about political life more generally. We can think of political cognition as the study of problem solving or the use of heuristics.[2] But political cognition is also very much about argument, rhetoric, and even rationalization. Here I view political cognition and political psychology as it resonates with the social world: When people compile their beliefs and definitions about political life, how do they integrate the ideas, discourses, and imagery generated by our large institutions—the press, the government, and religion, among others? Some very thoughtful scholars, working outside the political cognition area, have posited and demonstrated that one's thinking patterns often take the form of large and complex arguments about one's local and distant environments. Let us begin however, with macrostructural-level arguments about the social determinants of the meaning of public opinion.

13

Public Opinion, Social Forces, and Institutional Behavior

That public opinion is a social construction is in many ways quite obvious. Researchers, whether inside the academy or out in the world of electoral or pressure politics, know that their methods for detecting public feeling shape the sorts of results they get. And candidates and legislators certainly understand that meanings and descriptions of public opinion are very malleable and very fluid. Yet despite this shared knowledge about the uncertain nature of public opinion, researchers, politicians, activists, and citizens pick and choose "reliable" indicators of public opinion in order to make the most effective arguments they can. Members of Congress, for example, are expert in choosing particular forms of data about public opinion over others in order to bolster their case for a favored policy. We can see this selective defining of public opinion most clearly in the use of polls. As Lawrence R. Jacobs and Robert Y. Shapiro have demonstrated through their extensive archival research, twentieth-century presidents often selectively used polls (and pollsters themselves) to boost their own public standing.[3] And there is evidence about selective use of polls from a variety of other realms in American politics—even from the nonmainstream world of alternative politics. A leftist political activist once told me that her organization ignored or argued against media or other public polls when they did not fit her organization's rhetorical strategy. She stated, however, "We use [polling] when it's to our advantage. I think all [activist] groups do."[4] In fact, these groups often—like many political organizations and actors—argue against the entire *notion* of polling, but later turn around and use polls in their advocacy of particular public policies.

The macro-level social construction of public opinion is driven by a variety of forces, but four are most important:

1. the model of democracy shared by members of a community or nation;
2. the types of technologies or methodologies available for opinion assessment;
3. the rhetoric of our leaders; and
4. the evaluation of public opinion by journalists.

What is our shared model of democracy in contemporary America? A difficult question, and certainly an abstract one, that those outside of academe and politics tend not to think about it. It is safe to say, however, that there are particular features of democracy that we celebrate publicly and that are promoted by almost all institutions. Many of these features are succinctly outlined in theorist David Held's *Models of Democracy*, a rigorous and thoughtful study that explicates a variety of ideal-typical structures and cultures associated with democracy in the West. Perhaps contemporary American democracy comes closest to what Held describes as "protective democracy." In this model, citizens want government to protect them from others and enable them to pursue their own personal interests. Held summarizes the key features of his protective democracy as follows:

> Sovereignty ultimately lies in the people, but is vested in representatives who can legitimately exercise state functions
>
> Regular elections, the secret ballot, competition between factions, potential leaders or parties and majority rule are the institutional bases for establishing the accountability of those who govern
>
> State powers must be impersonal, i.e. legally circumscribed, and divided among the executive, the legislature and the judiciary
>
> Centrality of constitutionalism to guarantee freedom from arbitrary treatment and equality before the law in the form of political and civil rights or liberties, above all those connected to free speech, expression, association, voting and belief
>
> Separation of state from civil society, i.e. the scope of state action is, in general, to be tightly restricted to the creation of a framework which allows citizens to pursue their private lives free from risks of violence, unacceptable social behaviour and unwanted political interference
>
> Competing power centres and interest groups[5]

This model stands in contrast to other possible models, Held posits, such as classical democracy, which is characterized by more direct citizen participation in the legislature, a lack of status distinction between citizens and elected officials, and brief terms in office. The classical model is the ancient Greek city-state, despite its small size, slave economy, and restricted citizenship. The protective democracy model also stands in contrast to the more elitist ("competitive elitist") models of democracy presented by Max Weber and Joseph Schumpeter.[6] In the elitist model, rival individuals and parties compete to run a strong centralized government with an independent and highly efficient bureaucracy. Citizens select "a skilled and imaginative political elite" who make what they believe to be just policy decisions.[7]

No matter which model of democracy best describes contemporary American political culture, these ideal types do—with or without our conscious knowledge—tend to determine the ways we think about public opinion. If one believes that we do in fact have a very powerful bureaucracy and our democracy does look most like an elitist one, one is likely to view public opinion as both uneducated and irrelevant. This sort of link, between an elitist form of democracy and a skeptical view of the nature and value of public opinion, was probably best developed by Walter Lippmann.[8] In contrast, Aristotle's notions of direct democracy and the sovereignty of the citizens' assembly are intricately tied to his more respectful attitude toward public opinion.[9] The point is obvious: Conceptions of public opinion are tethered to models of democracy. The social construction of public opinion is rooted in and derives from our choice of ideal-typical democratic models.[10]

The second social force that determines the nature of public opinion is technology—the methodologies we use to assess the popular mood. I have argued elsewhere that meanings or constructions of public opinion are inextricably intertwined with our measurement tools.[11] Opinion polling, for example, assumes public opinion to be the aggregation of individual opinions recorded by trained, objective interviewers. Opinions are expressed within the strictures of confidentiality, so the citizens who participate in the typical professionally conducted national survey are never identified and most certainly (in a mass society like our own) will never have contact with one another. Public opinion expression, in this case, is categorical in nature (individuals may choose among two or more options), unattributed, statistically representative of the populace, and directed by the survey researcher and his or her choice of survey form. Alternatively, public opinion may be measured by letters to newspaper editors or public officials. Here, public opinion is most often attributed, and the form the opinions take tends to be dictated by the citizens expressing those opinions. Tabulating such letters or scrutinizing the text of these letters does not enable the analyst to generalize to a larger population with any certainty, but one can evaluate the nature of involved citizens' arguments on issues. So, the forms employed or available for opinion expression most certainly determine what public opinion looks like.

The third, and far more complex, factor that can construct public opinion is the rhetoric of our leaders. Presidents, members of Congress and of state assemblies, candidates for high office, interest group leaders, and others in legitimate policy-making roles often try to conceptualize the nature of public opinion for citizens and for their own colleagues. Fortunately, we can cite a long and impressive history of rhetorical studies in this area, which illustrate how and why our leaders knowingly and unknowingly define public opinion.[12] Presidents, for example, quite naturally select among definitions of public opinion in order to bolster policy arguments, as part of their general rhetorical strategy. A recent and quite typical example is drawn from Bill Clinton's 1994 address to the National Governors' Association. After noting that fifty-eight million Americans were without health insurance coverage, and that eighty-one million Americans had "preexisting" medical conditions that prevent them from changing jobs, he said:

> Now, those are the facts. They can be seen in the million letters, almost, that the First
> Lady has received since we started this whole effort to deal with health care. On the way
> in, I was describing briefly to Governor Campbell a letter I got from . . . Jo Anne
> Osteen of Sumter, South Carolina, who owns a small business, works 6 days a week,
> raised three children by herself with diabetes and arthritis. . . . But her insurance rates
> went up to $306 a month, even though she was only taking home $305 a week from her
> business. Her doctors told her that the answer was to quit and go on disability. . . . Well,
> I think we ought to heed her call for help.[13]

In other speeches, Clinton cited poll data supporting health care reform or news broadcasts and articles along these lines. But here he turned to one of the more vivid and textured forms of opinion measurement: citizen letters. And Clinton is by no means the first president to cite his mail and use these letters in his speeches. Franklin Roosevelt was very interested in his mail, for example, and used it as one form of public opinion assessment.[14] What is important in Clinton's speech, from our perspective, is that he is simultaneously making an argument about the nature of public opinion toward health care reform and legitimating letter analysis and counting as a means for understanding public opinion. Public opinion here is constructed as idiosyncratic and personal reports from citizens out in the electorate. Murray Edelman sees the invocation of "public opinion" as a form of manipulation by rhetors: "The term connotes a force independent of government, but a large part of it echoes the beliefs authorities deliberately or unconsciously engender by appealing to fears or hopes that are always prevalent."[15]

The fourth and perhaps the most significant molder of public opinion is the press. The news media are, as scholars since Lippmann have noted, the key force shaping our conceptions of public opinion. This shaping is accomplished in subtle, and most often unconscious, ways by journalists who are trying to report as best they can on public affairs. At times, journalists seem in thrall to polling, and use surveys to make arguments about the true nature of public opinion.[16] In other instances, journalists may both report on and discount polls at the same time, as in these quotes uncovered by Roderick Hart in his comprehensive look at presidential speechmaking:

> Our poll is unscientific but interesting. (David Brinkley)

> Any opinion-sampling like this is necessarily arbitrary. But of the more than thirty blue-collar workers questioned here, the ratio was 5 to 1 against the president. (Virginia Sherwood)

> From our unscientific sampling, a higher cost of gasoline will not affect driving habits here. (David Henderson)

> I hesitate to apply the word typical to any group, but . . . (Frank Reynolds)

Hart argues that, "These disclaimers function not unlike the minute warning from the surgeon general on a package of cigarettes: it protects the product [polling] without cutting into sales of the product."[17]

Yet beyond polls, journalists report on popular sentiments in a variety of other ways that legitimate or condemn particular meanings of public opinion. Journalists are attracted, for instance, to vivid stories of individuals just as President Clinton was in his 1994 speech to the governors. Shanto Iyengar calls these sorts of stories examples of "episodic framing": Many news reports focus on the plight of a particular person (e.g., a teenage mother on welfare or a struggling illegal immigrant) or are keyed to an event.[18] Journalists often take the statements or narratives of individuals featured in episodic stories to be *representations* of public opinion and use the language of generalization. Skilled reporters utter phrases like: "Person X, portrayed here, is not alone. He, like millions of Americans feels that . . ." And journalists must, in fact, underscore that this particular person is representative of some sizable segment of the population. Otherwise, why should the viewer care?[19] W. Lance Bennett provides some strong examples of how media can construct public opinion by broadcasting the comments of individuals *claiming a distinct insight into public opinion*. During the 1992 Los Angeles riots set off by the Rodney King beating, a *New York Times* reporter quotes a citizen as saying, "All of this [rioting] is a statement of unity. This is about the black community coming together."[20]

On the macro level then—the realm of democratic culture, technological trends, rhetorical strategy, and the content of mass media reports—the meaning of public opinion fluctuates. At times public opinion is represented by poll data. At other times it is represented by personal anecdotes. And sometimes, public opinion is quite clearly the Lippmannesque projections of our leaders and of influential journalists. The critical notion that public opinion is constructed by the mass media has growing empirical research behind it. [21] Much of this work was inspired by Edelman and by William Gamson, who dubbed this a "constructionist approach" to media and public opinion. Gamson argues that people are in constant conversation with the mass media and with each other. In conversation, they draw on their experience, but they also draw heavily on mass media frameworks that can tell them what public opinion is and how best to evaluate it.[22] And so Gamson, by reminding us that conversation is also key to our understanding of what public opinion *is*, forces us to jump down a level of analysis to political cognition. It is the media that link micro- and macro- to a great extent: Our conversations with friends, neighbors, and coworkers inevitably incorporate the images and the language found in the institutional, group project we call "news."

Mental Representations of Public Opinion

The formalized study of what is now called "political cognition" is a relatively new area, but students of politics have always been interested in how people think and act in democratic settings. From the ancient Greek philosophers up through Machiavelli, Rousseau, and Tocqueville, writers have speculated about the thoughts of the common citizens: Are they rational? Can they understand the issues of the day and articulate their feelings about such issues? Under what conditions are people holding minority opinions afraid to express these opinions? Take, for instance, the passage from *The Politics* in which Aristotle discusses the relationship between citizens and their constitution. In exploring the notion of a constitution and its connection to the polity, Aristotle must consider how men see themselves. He argues that the citizen has his own personal goals but also thinks about his role in the larger community in which he lives. Citizens capable of democracy realize the ultimate importance of the collectivity over their own interests. So here, among other places in his work, Aristotle nods to psychology, linking micro-level cognition to macro-level concerns about the formation of the state:

A citizen is one of a community, as a sailor is one of a crew; and although each member of the crew has his own function and a name to fit it—rower, helmsman, look-out, and the rest—and has therefore his goodness at that particular job, there is also a type of goodness which all the crew must have, a function in which they all play a part—the safe conduct of the voyage; for each member of the crew aims at securing that. Similarly the aim of all the citizens, however dissimilar they may be, is the safety of the community, that is, the constitution of which they are citizens.[23]

Building democratic theory was and still is, of course, impossible without serious focus on political psychology—the ways citizens think about their own participatory functions.[24]

Though I am most certainly working in the shadow of ancient and modern speculation about political psychology in democratic practice, I draw here on twentieth-century sociology, psychology, and anthropology for guidance in building theory about political cognition. My particular interest is the conceptions individuals have about public opinion, the mass media, and the workings of the public sphere more generally, but there is much relevant theorizing that speaks quite directly to the general interface between the individual and his or her construction of the social world. One key twentieth-century text on consciousness and the perception of the social world is Peter Berger and Thomas Luckmann's phenomenological *The Social Construction of Reality*. For Berger and Luckmann there is most certainly a concrete reality, an external world containing phenomena "independent of our own volition (we cannot 'wish them away')."[25] Yet reality is located by people who employ idiosyncratic cognitive tools and travel in a world of distinctive social structures: A woman looks at the world in the context of her work and the institutions that set down the rules she lives by, and through the lenses of her large and varied interpersonal network of family, friends, neighbors, coworkers, and strangers. Her perceptions of what Berger and Luckmann call "objective reality" are shaped by all these forces, institutions, and people, and it is the social scientist's task to map the interplay of perceptions and concrete reality. For Berger and Luckmann, "Knowledge is developed, transmitted, and maintained in social situations."[26] In all societies, and in the political world more specifically, there is knowledge shared by many—the "common knowledge" explored by Gamson or by Russell Neuman, Marion Just, and Ann Crigler in their constructionist work in political communication. And there are other forms of knowledge—knowledge that is hidden, more controversial, or simply difficult to pin down with our somewhat crude methodological tools.[27]

In this book I argue that personal "portraits" of the public sphere—particularly the relationships among media, policy, and public opinion itself—are constructions of reality by individuals. Informants who participated in this study often noted that their ideas about public life evolved over time, with changes in their occupation or lifestyle. They frequently pointed to social structural forces, or what I refer to above as macro-level forces, noting how various social movements or perceived ideological shifts in culture affected the way they view politics. Many informants also pointed to the very mechanisms outlined by Berger and Luckmann in their discussions of politics: Several informants noted a key conversation or set of conversations that "changed the way they thought" or "got them interested" in politics and government. The mass media are also critical to us, as we figure out how the public sphere really "works"; this is clear from the interviews reported on in this book. Scholars working in the area of "lay" or "implicit" theory posit that even those who do not build formal theory for a living make causal arguments about the political world that are quite consistent. Some of this work is a variant of attribution theory in psychology. But this approach also takes issue with traditional approaches to attribution and is fortified by insights and findings from both rhetorical studies and ethnographic fieldwork.

Lay Theories and Lay Arguments about Politics

Contemporary political cognition research, as exemplified by recent journal articles and edited collections, is largely experimental and based on problem-solving tasks: Experimental subjects are asked to respond to information and stimuli of various sorts and their responses are carefully recorded.[28] There are many other approaches to political psychology, of course, that involve surveys or fieldwork, but the cognition research I refer to in this book is laboratory based and concerned with categorizing and processing information. This sort of attempt at understanding how people think and respond to politics is problematic, as those who endorse it acknowledge: All thoughtful scholars in the area of political psychology have pondered limitations on external validity, the narrow characteristics of experimental stimuli, and the difficulties of capturing long-term effects of stimuli when laboratory testing is over. My goal here is not to attack experimental or traditional positivistic work in the diverse field of political psychology, but to broaden and enhance the study of political cognition. Although findings in political cognition studies have been interesting, there is often something rather artificial about them: They do, in fact, seem to ignore the powerful and dynamic processes of culture and interpretation. External validity problems haunt this research, though many political cognition practitioners seem to have accepted this limitation. I contend here that people think about politics in particularistic terms that are very much a product of media exposure, conversation, and internal dialogue. These are complex processes, and from my point of view, slippery and difficult to isolate in the laboratory. When it comes to the meaning of public opinion and articulating the relationships among media, public sentiment, and policy, people tend to have complicated and textured ideas that they express through narrative, through lengthy multi-faceted examples, and through symbols. If we are to begin to understand how citizens and policy professionals view the public sphere, we must at times depart from dominant "information processing" models.

But let us ponder, at least momentarily, the "cognitive revolution" cited by so many social and political cognition scholars. In one recent volume, the editors note that their starting point for theorizing is Walter Lippmann.[29] Lippmann argued that individuals—from all parts of the political spectrum and all levels of political sophistication—carry around in their minds "stereotypes" or "pictures in their heads" that enable them to make sense of a rather chaotic public sphere. Lippmann viewed these stereotypes as tools for simplification of reality—ways to make it easier, in Berger and Luckmann's terms—to cognitively "take over" the world. Yet to argue that Lippmann's thoughts on the subject lead directly to an information processing approach is not quite accurate, because it slights the phenomenological, interpretive dimensions of Lippmann's work. Lippmann understood that meaning shifts and evolves, and that people make *arguments* about the world around them. Stereotypes are not simply vehicles for information processing: They are, in fact, structures of argumentation that are tied to one's experience in political culture. If we think of stereotypes as arguments and not just tools for processing stimuli, we begin to see how they are linked to media representations, to partisanship, to economic self-interest, and to the symbolic world more generally.

Was the original cognitive revolution in academe about information processing? One of the founders of this movement has concluded that it was not. Jerome Bruner, in his thoughtful essay *Acts of Meaning*, finds current cognition approaches wanting. Reflecting on "computational" models of the mind, which rely on the study of people as information processors, Bruner wonders how cognitive studies became so blind to culture and to the constant interpretive and symbolic work humans tend to do. About the roots of the cognitive revolution, Bruner writes:

It was *not* a revolution against behaviorism with the aim of transforming behaviorism into a better way of pursuing psychology by adding a little mentalism to it. . . . It was an altogether more profound revolution than that. Its aim was to discover and to describe formally the meanings that human beings created out of their encounters with the world, and then to propose hypotheses about what meaning-making processes were implicated. It focused upon the symbolic activities that human beings employed in constructing and in making sense not only of the world, but of themselves. Its aim was to prompt psychology to join forces with its sister interpretive disciplines in the humanities and social sciences.[30]

While much of cognition research is truly interdisciplinary, political cognition research has not yet been influenced by insights from the humanities or anthropology. The recognition that meaning in the world is fluid and that symbolic communication—embodied in language and experience—is necessary as people make sense of their environment seems largely absent in much political cognition research today. Bruner argues that, while the original cognitive revolution was an attempt to understand how people construct *meaning,* cognitive psychologists are now intent on understanding how people process information. Instead of focusing on the way people integrate language and perception of the social world with their own experiences, information processing models focus on categories and items (bundles of information, labels, or tasks) that are well defined and are already encoded with meaning by the researchers. As Bruner puts it, "Such a system cannot cope with vagueness, with polysemy, with metaphoric or other connotations."[31]

The meaning of political events and policies is often open to interpretation, while at the same time, people bring *particular* sets of cognitive tools to these events. Yes, many of these tools are the ones specified by our experts in political cognition—"heuristics" or "schemas." But use of these tools is quite often tied to the particular historical context in which people live: This is what is distinctly missing in the texture of contemporary experiments in political cognition. As Clifford Geertz put it in his influential book *The Interpretation of Cultures,* "We are, in sum, incomplete or unfinished animals who complete or finish ourselves through culture—and not through culture in general but through highly particular forms of it: Dobuan and Javanese, Hopi and Italian, upper-class and lower-class, academic and commercial."[32] We need a political psychology that works—in a very active and diligent way—to understand how particular occupational and political cultures shape cognition and interpretation. This is vital because the interpretation of meaning in the political world is individual and cultural *at the same time.* Bruner believes that, while anthropologists find this sort of argument banal (it has become an assumption of their discipline), psychologists resist it. Bruner, with Geertz, believes that people become themselves through culture, through the constant negotiations with the social structures and ideologies that surround them. Bruner makes a plea for the approach I take here, for the study of what is often termed "folk psychology": nonacademics' values, beliefs, goals, motivations, and causal arguments concerning the social world. And to discern folk theory, to prompt it, involves an intense and open-minded methodology. Most importantly, a focus on political folk psychology is attentive—first and foremost—to the culture and language of politics. As we shall see in this book, people can explain their views of public life only with considerable reliance on cultural icons, on certain events, and on the specifics of historical circumstance. Bruner makes an elegant argument in favor of studying folk psychology or lay theory, and he is worth quoting at length on the subject. Note the value of talk, of conversation, in his writing. Conversation shapes one's view of social reality, and conversation is in fact crucial to the methodology of this book, as I spend considerable time analyzing my discussions with informants. Bruner writes:

> To those who want to concentrate upon whether what people say predicts what they will do, the only proper answer is that to separate the two in that way is to do bad philosophy, bad anthropology, bad psychology, and impossible law. Saying and doing represent a functionally inseparable unit in a culturally oriented psychology. . . . A culturally oriented psychology neither dismisses what people say about their mental states, nor treats their statements only as if they were predictive indices of overt behavior. What it takes as central, rather, is that the relationship between action and saying (or experiencing) is, *in the ordinary conduct of life,* interpretable. It takes the position that there is a publicly interpretable congruence between saying, doing, and the circumstances in which the saying and doing occur.[33]

In summary, then, a culturally informed political psychology takes talk seriously: What people *say* motivates their actions is valuable. We cannot always tell what they do or why they do it without asking them directly and intently. A culturally informed psychology looks to individuals' conceptions of the world while making links to larger discourses and to social structure. How do informants' occupational constraints affect their mental models of political life? How are informants' theories, definitions, and ideas linked to their experiences, to social pressures, and to the greater shifts in political culture we all learn about through the mass media? This is the business of folk psychology, and it is necessarily interdisciplinary in its theoretical and methodological approach.

The Value of Lay Theory

People reason about politics, although not in the ways social scientists want them to or expect them to. First, social scientists worry about what people know and do not know about the political parties and the general workings of government and the courts. Research about what people know and do not know was in large part stimulated by Philip Converse years ago, but recent evidence of lack of knowledge is even more troubling, given how much information about public affairs can be found in old and new media (cable television, the Internet, specialized magazines, etc.).[34] Second, even when citizens or policy professionals are well informed, we wonder about their reasoning processes—whether or not they can make rational and accurate decisions about real or hypothetical problems.

Many contemporary cognitive psychologists are, unlike Bruner, highly skeptical of folk psychology. Using experimental protocols that involve decision-making and problem-solving tasks, they argue that people are very bad at making inferences. Richard Nisbett and Lee Ross, for example, note that individuals tend to make certain kinds of errors over and over again: They tend to base inferences on prior knowledge or experience and have trouble avoiding generalization to a population from data about a sample.[35] These mistakes, Nisbet and Ross argue, make people bad scientists, since scientists tend to follow formal logical and statistical rules for making inferences and attributions. Nisbet and Ross do not mean to take a superior position (that social scientists are smarter than lay people), but they do believe that cognition is characterized by information processing and the carrying out of narrow, very particularized mental tasks. They are, like many other cognitive psychologists, working in the general tradition of attribution theory, a large subfield in psychology introduced by Fritz Heider in 1958.[36] Attribution theory attempts to identify how people make causal arguments about human behavior and about the world more generally. But as Nisbet and Ross themselves admit, psychologists know little about "real-world" behavior. Despite their focus on cognition measured in the circumstances of the laboratory, they acknowledge Bruner's central critique of American psychology: It tends to ignore culture, the world of symbolic communication, and the relationship between action and thinking. Further, it pays no heed to the explanations people give for their own thinking or behavior, choosing instead to make those judgments *for* experimental subjects.

We should not dismiss attribution theory—in all its variants—out of hand, for it has its limited range of uses, and the debate over its contributions is long running and vigorous. But for the purposes of studying political cognition, it is extraordinarily problematic. Politics is a rich and complex cultural form, and it is not clear—as it is with arithmetic or logic games—what is an "error" and what is a "fact." Charles Antaki, a British psychologist who advocates studying cognition within cultural context, believes that attribution theory has led psychologists astray for three reasons. First, American cognitive psychologists have focused on the private and not the public; psychologists see reasoning as something we do by ourselves, without benefit of conversation or social pressures. Second, psychologists have implicitly agreed that we occupy one of two roles when we reason: We are either scientists (i.e., logical, cautious) or nonscientists (i.e., prone to error). There is no room in this role structure for advocates, historians, or even liars. Third, the celebration of the scientist over the lay person is a very explicit thread running through most of attribution theory—despite Nisbet and Ross's claim that they do not paint a negative picture of the ordinary person.[37]

Fortunately for those of us interested in political cognition, some scholars have left the laboratory to study folk psychology—lay theories people have about the course of their own lives and the workings of the public sphere more generally.[38] What Antaki and others engaging in this research are working toward is a rhetorical psychology. This is a psychology that links lay reasoning to occupation or social status and at the same time takes seriously people's interpretation of the public sphere. This form of cognitive psychology is very much concerned with argument, with the *contested nature* of social and political events and policies.

People Make Arguments

When individuals are presented with political information or hypothetical candidates in a laboratory setting, they make decisions and "solve problems." They use heuristics and they "compute," for better or for worse, in the ways researchers ask them to. But outside the laboratory, in conversation and as prelude to their actions, people make arguments about the public sphere. When they are asked to give definitions, as they are in this study, of "public opinion" or "media bias," for example, they do not just provide an answer. They make an argument very much tied to their place in the social matrix and the sorts of institutional discourses that interest them. To see cognition not as problem solving and decision making but as a form of argumentation makes cognitive psychology far more interesting and more socially grounded. When we view political cognition *as argument*, we are able to make the micro-macro links that we need in the study of contemporary American politics. Arguments are intra-psychic phenomena. They have their own idiosyncratic structures, surely. Yet they also echo larger cultural forces and arguments one finds in complex mass society. Argument is a social process, and if we can demonstrate that people think and *articulate* their ideas through argument, we are very much attuned to culture.

Several theorists have recently elaborated on this notion of cognition as argument. In addition to Antaki and Adrian Furnham, psychologist Deanna Kuhn has found in her empirical work that thinking looks like arguing. In her book, *The Skills of Argument*, Kuhn notes that the reductionism and the use of artificial stimuli so common in cognitive psychology have both been enormously problematic. Psychologists tend to reduce thinking to small units, and they have an interest in how these units are organized or categorized. Additionally, psychologists avoid experimental stimulus materials that embody the characteristics of real-world stimuli. She notes:

> If psychologists studied thinking involving content from people's everyday lives, so the rationale was, what people know about this content would likely become confused with their ability to reason about it. . . . A characteristic that applies to all of them [experimental stimulus materials], however, is that they are what have come to be referred to as *well-structured*, in contrast to *ill-structured*, problems. Well-structured problems have a single, well-defined correct answer and, usually, an optimum strategy for proceeding from problem presentation to solution. Ill-structured problems, in contrast, have no definitive solution.[39]

That a social problem has no definitive solution does not mean that we cannot—rigorously and with great care—study the creative reasoning people engage in. In fact, Kuhn's book is devoted largely to empirical work in which she asks people to discuss the causes of criminal recidivism, children's poor performance in school, and unemployment. She argues that her informants, 160 people from teenagers to persons in their sixties, were active and willing theorists interested in explicating their causal explanations to her and her colleagues. Like Antaki, she finds that people readily provided multiple and complex arguments about social problems, and that they were sometimes attuned to the complexity of their own argumentation and at other times unaware of the multiple propositions they presented. One of the most interesting sections of her study concerns the sorts of evidence people draw on to make *persuasive* arguments to the researchers. There is the usual covariation evidence, evidence about correlation, as well as other forms of argumentation: analogies, assumptions, discounting (the elimination of alternative explanations), and scripts of hypothetical scenarios. Kuhn's findings are complex, and she concludes that people are not as good at making arguments as they need to be. She worries that, while her informants were very certain about their causal arguments, they were not always able to generate counterarguments or particular sorts of evidence she believes make for the best kind of persuasive discourse. Interestingly, she finds that informants who were experts in the subject areas of the study (teachers and parole officers) were not any more sophisticated in their argumentation than were those with no professional experience in these areas.

Yet despite her disappointment in sophistication levels of both lay and professional people about education and penal reform, Kuhn's research convinced her that studying lay theory is the basis for attitude research. She asks: What does it mean to have an attitude? This is a question psychologists have struggled with continually over the past decades.[40] For Kuhn and her colleagues the answer is clear: Opinions and attitudes have little meaning and value unless they are informed and examined by the opinion holder. It is contemplation and the ability to understand and integrate causal argumentation that give attitudes their strength and their intensity. Attitudes that are not built on argumentation—on intra-psychic and social dialogue—are weak and uninteresting to students of psychology. She ends her book with a nod to John Dewey, one of the earliest political theorists to recognize the importance of public debate and dialogue. Dewey's familiar plea for public argument was rooted in his pedagogical concerns about citizens and his desire to create a more effective democratic state.[41]

Perhaps the most important theorist who asserts that people think in terms of argumentation is Michael Billig, a social psychologist with an interest in both cognition and rhetoric.[42] Billig has spent considerable effort integrating the ideas from classical communication theory (ancient rhetoric) with more contemporary concerns of psychology. Like Kuhn, he posits that people think through argumentation, but he takes the notion even further, concluding that people do in fact think rhetorically. In other words, cognitive structure is very much guided by one's place in the social matrix and one's attempt to be a persuasive actor in the world. In Billig's view people do not, except in a few very extraordinary circumstances (e.g., solving an arithmetic problem), follow rules when thinking about personal or social issues. And, Billig notes, an information-processing model based on categorizing and organizing information around already existing procedures is wrongheaded: It ignores most of mentality, which is very much guided by the constant and very complex negotiations we make with the social world. Taking cues from rhetorical theory and also from twentieth-century theorists like George Herbert Mead and Serge Moscovici, Billig is doing exactly what Bruner asks of psychology: making it more cultural and less computational.[43] Billig believes, as do others in this school, that work outside the laboratory is crucial if we are to understand the innovative ways people think. Yes, people at times follow cognitive rules of thumb, but these rules get bent and ignored outside the lab as people try to make sense of politics and try to influence it in their local circumstances.

In his fieldwork among a group of white British fascists (the National Front) who were viciously racist, Billig found that his informants did view the actions and characteristics of nonwhites in entirely pejorative ways. But this was not simply a matter of stereotyping and cognitive rule following, where National Front members fit new data about nonwhites into existing schemata. He notes that

> there was more to the beliefs of the National Front than being a matrix for organizing incoming information about individual non-whites. The group also possessed a bizarre ideology about world conspiracies and myths of racial blood. Such an ideology weaves strange patterns around the social world, and is itself a cognitive construction. In order to create and to maintain such beliefs, it is necessary to show a certain imagination and intellectual ingenuity (albeit of a malevolent and hate-filled variety). In addition, the beliefs of this bizarre ideology were arguments. The fascist ideology of conspiracy and racial myth was a deliberate criticism of the views of non-fascists. Not just a way of organizing information about race, it was also a self-conscious challenge to tolerance. In this sense the thoughts of the members of the National Front were not merely taking place in the interior of the individual believer's skull. The thoughts also belonged to a wider argumentative context of criticism and challenge. This dual location is not confined to the thoughts of fascists, but there is a more general point. Our beliefs and our attitudes do not merely occur in our heads, but they too belong to wider social contexts of controversy.[44]

One important point Billig makes, through his assault on information processing and his fieldwork, is that we do not simply hold attitudes or beliefs: We articulate opinions—whether we mean to or not—in order to "locate ourselves within a public controversy."[45] Thinking is a specific process, tied to the multi-faceted public debates that we find in mass democracy. Are men and women, by nature, political-information processors? Or are they rhetoricians silently or very publicly making arguments about controversial issues of the day? Ancient philosophers like Isocrates believed the latter, and while we have learned much from cognitive psychologists, it is clear that we must also reconnect the study of political cognition to a central tendency of democratic life: controversy.

Rule-following paradigms for studying political cognition are problematic from a variety of perspectives, and scholars like Bruner, Kuhn, and Billig have challenged psychologists to acknowledge the social. Here I attempt a similar inquiry: What are the multiple meanings of public opinion? And how do people make sense of an ever changing public sphere and their own shifting place within it? How can we connect the visions people hold of the political world with their own very specific locations in that world?

Michael Schudson has argued that the Watergate scandal, like a few other selected events from the recent past, is useful to "think with." For Schudson and for Americans, Watergate provides a framework for understanding the Nixon years, but also for understanding the presidency, the relationship between the president and Congress, the internal workings of the White House, and the nature of partisanship, among other things.[46] In this book I also focus on what I believe are important items in American politics—public opinion and the character of our mass media—which are useful to "think with." Asking people about such central democratic concepts and institutions forces them to articulate their larger theories of the public sphere, democratic life, and their role in political culture. Just as Schudson uses Watergate as a key to unlock some basic currents in American culture, I hope to use inquiries about the nature of public opinion to reveal folk psychology about contemporary politics.

The informants in this study—legislative aides, journalists, and political activists—are lay people with lay theories. They are not social scientists. Their notions about public opinion, media, and representation are far less elaborate than our own and are never put to systematic or rigorous testing. Yet we must keep in mind that these informants are not ordinary citizens either: They are people *accustomed* to making arguments. They like to argue, in fact, and do so within their professional environments and social circles. When individuals must *act* in the political world, by researching legislation, writing a newspaper article on a policy debate, or fundraising for a candidate, they typically carry with them an arsenal of arguments. And such arguments give us clues as to the uses of public opinion—as information and symbol—in political work on the ground level.

If we are to study the nature of politics, as viewed by those who practice it, we need willing informants. The people I interviewed have great personal and vocational interests in the evaluation of citizen opinion. Some of these men and women—journalists and legislative staffers—are paid for their work, but most of the political activists work in politics without financial compensation. Regardless of whether they are paid or not, however, the citizens in this group are different from most Americans, since they maintain an extraordinarily high interest in public affairs. Many have been politically active for long periods and come from families that were involved in local partisan politics. One informant, for example, is a seventy-one-year-old Democratic activist who came from a long line of precinct workers and captains in an Irish working-class suburb of Chicago. Others I spoke with were newer to the world of public affairs, joining staffs in the state legislature quite recently, right from the university. All the stories and indeed "theories" generated by these individuals are based on their intense experiences in legislative, local, and—sometimes—national politics. Scholars may not agree with the way these people view the public sphere, but they are key operators in it: The informants in this study draw up legislation, direct policy debate, report on policy to the public, raise money for candidates, and constantly talk politics. Cognition of such actors can reveal to us the nexus of social position, visions of politics, and the forms of argumentation people employ to bolster these visions. I made three theoretical and methodological decisions at the start of this study: I chose to study sophisticates, I focused on state government, and I employed interpretive methodologies for querying informants.

Talking with Sophisticates

Political scientists, sociologists, and communication researchers have long studied politically sophisticated individuals. In fact, some of the most interesting studies of public-opinion dynamics have centered around interviews with or surveys of legislators and activists. From Robert Dahl's *Who Governs?*, describing influential New Haven citizens, or James David Barber's *The Lawmakers*, to Doug McAdam's study of the college students who participated in "Freedom Summer" during the civil rights movement era, social scientists have taken a great interest in those most engaged in the democratic process.[47] And, in fact, some of our premier insights into this process come from students of American politics—like Tocqueville and Bryce—who spoke at length with highly placed political actors. In this book, I prefer to write about informants as political professionals or sophisticates rather than as "elites," because I find that term to be both inexact and pejorative in this particular case. It has great resonance, of course, and is entirely appropriate in many studies of politics, so I am not arguing for the elimination of the term. Yet the term "elite" does group together a variety of individuals into a sort of undifferentiated and indeed suspect class of people, and I find that a bit worrisome. I will admit that I do not have a perfect substitute for "elites" in this book, so instead I simply try to label informants in the least pejorative and most straightforwardly descriptive manner possible. They are political professionals, journalists, activists, or simply, political actors.[48]

I chose to study nonacademic sophisticates—people actively engaged and interested in politics—for several reasons. First, and most important, those who work in politics are likely to have richer and more elaborate lay theories about the relationships among media, public opinion, and policy. Although political scientists, with the exception of Robert Lane and a few others, have not focused on the textured study of lay theory, those from psychology and anthropology who have conducted such research find that those who know a significant amount about a subject area tend to have more elaborate notions about that area.[49] And this makes sense: Where we see expertise, we see elaboration and complexity. For example, the literature, beginning with Converse's work, provides us with many clues and fragments of evidence about the ability of well-educated, involved people to use descriptive labels ("Democrat" or "Republican" for example), ideological terminology, and the like. Unlike Converse, however, it is not my intention to compare lay theories to what I believe are the correct or incorrect ways to view public opinion, media, and policy making. I am, though, very concerned with the *implications* of informants' views: how their approaches to public opinion affect their work in politics—the legislation they create, the articles they write, and the candidates they support. The second reason I chose to study engaged political actors is obvious: They have some power to change their environments. The people I spoke with *absorb* a tremendous amount of information about public affairs, but they also *affect* public opinion, the nature of media content, and the character of public policy. I hope to provide not a snapshot of their attitudes on particular issues at a moment in time, but instead a more lasting picture of their political lives in motion: What sort of processes are they involved in, and how do they view their own activities and effects? Informants ranged from the extraordinarily bright and thoughtful to those who were not particularly insightful, but all can and indeed have influenced law or political campaigns at the local, state, or regional level.

Legislative Informants

The first group of people I interviewed (twenty in all) were staffers at the Illinois state legislature, which consists of a 59-member Senate and a 118-member House of Representatives. Each legislative district in Illinois is represented by one senator and two House members. In Illinois a bill can originate in either house and can be vetoed by the governor: During the typical session, between four thousand and five thousand bills are introduced, but less than half are reported to committees for review and debate. All of the legislative staffers in this study were associated with committees, although several were asked by their party's leadership to leave the state payroll every two years and work on senatorial or house campaigns. In this legislature two or more committee staffers from each of the two major parties assisted legislators on almost every committee. Seven of the staff members I spoke with served on the Republican side of the Senate, and six worked on the Democratic side of the Senate. In the House, I interviewed four Republican staffers and three Democratic ones. In keeping with promises of confidentiality, I cannot specify which staffers served on which committees, but I have listed in table 1 the committees represented by staffers in the sample. The staffers were selected randomly.[50]

Some of the staffers in this study had been in Springfield since the early 1980s, but others had only recently begun working on committees. Several informants had been attorneys or had pursued careers outside of government be-

Table 1 Committees Staffed by Study Participants

Senate	House
Agriculture and Conservation	Agriculture and Conservation
Appropriations	Appropriations
Education	Cities and Villages
Executive	Elementary and Secondary Education
Higher Education	Higher Education
Judiciary	Judiciary
Local Government and Elections	Privatization, De-Regulation, Economic and
Public Health and Welfare	Urban Development
Transportation	Revenue

fore serving at the legislature, but others had come to the assembly directly from a postsecondary legislative internship program at the state university. Most of the staffers in this sample had been working at the legislature, in some policy-making or constituent-service capacity, since the mid-1980s and were in their thirties or forties. Only four staffers were women, who are in fact a minority among committee staff.

Committee staff are critical to the legislative process in Illinois, since they help to evaluate the magnitude of various problems in the state, assess public opinion related to these issues, help to draft legislation, and influence the nature of debate among the members of the legislature. They are seen as experts in their area, and the journalists who cover the legislature remarked to me that staff tend to know more about the costs and benefits of most bills than the members, who have concerns beyond policy—particularly constituent service, party cohesion across houses, and, of course, reelection to office. David Everson, an academic and long-time observer of the Illinois legislature, has argued that the committee structure in the legislature is weaker than it should be—falling far short of the Wilsonian ideal of committees as "little legislatures."[51] This may be true, but during discussions of the committee system, staffers explained that members depend very much on their staff for analysis of bills and their impacts. One well-placed staffer noted:

> Very, very rarely does a bill go through committee and lose on the House floor. The reason why is because members in the General Assembly trust the committees to do their job. And I think that a tremendous amount of importance is placed on the committee because . . . you look at the number of bills . . . that actually failed on the floor, it's none to one. You're going to get a handful of bills in the General Assembly that are going to lose on the House floor. For the most part, the members who live in suburban districts are going to defer to the members of the Ag [Agriculture] Committee to know what's best for Illinois agriculture. The people in the agricultural communities are going to defer to the people in the suburbs on issues concerning taxes and those kinds of things because they trust their judgment . . .

It is doubtful that staffers are inflating the importance of their work: They produce key analyses of policy and guide busy members who must keep abreast of a tremendous number of bills.[52] In the next chapter, readers will get a better of sense of what committee staffers do at the legislature and how their influence is manifested in the evaluation of public opinion and the construction of policy.

Why not study legislators instead of staffers, though, if we are interested in elaborate and complex lay theories of the policy-making process? There are several reasons. First, staffers are a vital component of what legislative scholars call the "enterprise" perspective or model of legislative action: Members of a legislative body do not work alone but depend on an entire *infrastructure* of expertise and personnel as they debate and make policy.[53] David Whiteman points out that the enterprise model of legislatures is useful because it integrates the study of staff into the study of policy making. In much legislative scholarship, staff are viewed as important but are not studied directly—the enterprise perspective forces researchers to acknowledge their direct roles. In addition, in state government as well as in Congress (which Whiteman studied), the policy-making process begins long before votes are cast and is often invisible to the public. Whiteman argues that "[Pre-vote activities] include the recognition and definition of problems, the identification and interpretation of alternatives, and the search for and use of information throughout this process."[54] The scale of government is much smaller in the Illinois assembly than in Congress, in terms of fiscal issues, populations affected, resources, and staffing. Nevertheless, the Illinois assembly resembles Congress in that much legislative action of interest occurs prior to voting—a period when staffers are crucial. The enterprise model forces scholars to attend to the processual nature of policy making—the fact that policy issues have a history, that legislative bodies have a culture, and that there are continual flows of research, hearings, and discussions in the lives of all legislatures.

Staffers are a vital part of policy making in Congress and in the state legislature in Illinois, but there are other advantages of studying them. Among these is the fact that committee staff are squarely focused on issues and tend not to be distracted by elections. This is not to say that they have no interest in elections or in the changing membership of the Senate and House, for they are greatly affected by these shifts. Yet their jobs do not rely on the constant assessment of parties and candidates. When a researcher queries legislators themselves, he or she must constantly try to separate these informants' thoughts on public opinion about *issues* from their thoughts on public opinion about character and performance in office. This is certainly possible, but it is also extremely difficult because issues and performance are so closely woven together. If we study staffers, we can get a distinct sense of how those inside the legislature (and very close to the members) think about nonelectoral public opinion—the way people develop and communicate opinions on policy matters. So legislative staffers, as we see in later chapters, provide us with expansive windows into the internal workings of the policy-making process. As informants they were universally cooperative and serious. In fact, only one person on my list of potential interviewees declined to be interviewed and her refusal was tied to scheduling problems rather than lack of interest.

I should emphasize that while all staffers in the legislature are concerned about elections—which party will hold each house and by what margin—committee staff are far less election minded than the men and women they work for. Indirectly, all legislative work influences the strength or weakness of candidates as they enter the campaign field: Which bills did they introduce and how many passed? What major political initiatives did they lead, and how effective was their leadership? These are questions posed to senators and representatives by journalists, interest group leaders, opponents, and citizens during campaign season. Yet despite the ties between substantive legislative work and elections, committee staff are far less involved—in mind, body, and spirit—in campaigns than the members. Some staff are asked to leave their substantive positions temporarily to work on campaigns, but they then go back to legislative work. I came to believe that these dynamics make staffers valuable as informants. They *are* somewhat removed from the rough-and-tumble world of electoral politics. They feel the pressure of the political environment, of course. Anyone working in the capitol does. But their slightly removed position gives them a view of public opinion less distorted by electoral pressures than the perspectives one might get from legislators themselves. I am, in this book, less interested in campaign strategy and the mobilization of public opinion for *electoral purposes*. My focus is more on the policy debates themselves, and how actors who participate in these debates see such legislative activity.

In addition to interviewing full-time committee staff, I also interviewed three out of four of the communication directors or press secretaries on the House and Senate sides of the assembly.[55] These individuals serve as mediators between policymakers and journalists, and they are officially members of the assembly staff. In fact, they shield staffers from reporters, who are usually looking for "inside information" about the legislative process or about particular members. Few staffers said that they talked to journalists on or off the record, most left to communication directors the translation of policy activity into public information. Party leadership asks staffers *not* to speak with reporters, so that the party can "speak in one voice" about various important policy matters. However, journalists reported that they did occasionally speak with staffers on technical issues. Since staffers can be fired for talking to the press directly, some will use elaborate techniques to obscure their conversations with reporters, including using a member's telephone so a call to a journalist cannot be traced to the staffer (many staffers may have access to a member's office). Staffers can sneak into the pressroom to meet with reporters or see journalists in other more secluded locations. It was difficult to discern the extent of these direct contacts, since few informants would admit to them. Several journalists, on the other hand, claimed to have had direct access to knowledgeable staffers when they needed it.

Press secretaries, or communication directors (I use the titles interchangeably here), do try, successfully or not, to put the "spin" on issues for their party leadership in both the House and the Senate.[56] They normally have a background in journalism or public relations, so they understand the sorts of pressures that reporters face and their needs for particular kinds of information. These men and women, with their staffs or on their own, write press releases, appear on radio or television programs, send letters to constituents, and talk to journalists about their party's approach to legislative matters. But they do spend considerable time and energy portraying issues to journalists in ways favorable to their side. One of the communication directors told me, "I can walk around the [Springfield] pressroom in about an hour and talk to everyone, whatever the issue, to get our [party's] spin in. . . . [Because] it's so concentrated down in the pressroom it's easy to have a good friendly relationship with 'em, go out and have beers after work, build up a good solid basis of trust so I can give somebody a scoop in exchange for them not revealing their source." Communication directors are interesting because they tend to see the legislative process from two vantage points—that of the party leadership and that of the journalist, even though their loyalties are to the party. These mediators are especially interested in the ways that public opinion is evaluated and communicated, since their jobs really do depend on gaining journalistic and popular support for various policy positions, particular bills, or members.

Journalist and Activist Informants

Journalists were also informants in this study of lay theory, and eleven were included in the sample. My first inclination was to draw a random sample of members of the Springfield legislative press corps, but after my initial calls and interviews I realized that there was great variance in knowledge and influence among the group. While I did include some broadcast (radio and television) journalists in the sample, I generally focused on reporters who worked for news

Chapter One

Table 2 Journalist Informants' News Organizations

Organization	Approximate Daily Circulation
The Chicago Tribune	691,283
The Chicago Sun-Times	500,969
St. Louis Post Dispatch[a]	338,793
The State Journal-Register	66,656
Capitol Fax[b]	3,000
Copley News Service	N/A
United Press International	N/A

[a]The *Dispatch* has significant circulation in southern Illinois and therefore covers the Illinois legislature closely.
[b]*Capitol Fax* is an independently owned and operated news service which sends news to subscribers via facsimile. The publisher estimates that between 3,000 and 4,000 people read *Capitol Fax*, even though the number of paid subscriptions is approximately 400 at any time. Since entire offices and departments take only one subscription and circulate it, the precise number of readers is difficult to estimate.

services or the major newspapers in the state and on a few other journalists who were deemed by their colleagues to be important members of the corps. In the end, I conducted interviews with journalists for the news outlets listed in table 2.

Many smaller newspapers, radio stations, and television stations not listed in table 2 have reporters covering events at the legislature. Yet most of these other outlets do not devote extensive resources or coverage to events in Springfield. And, traditionally, print media have had much more interest in state government than broadcast media have had because newspapers have more space to devote to policy issues and debate than do broadcast media. It was obvious from my few conversations with broadcast journalists that they were not able to focus as rigorously on the legislature as were journalists from the major newspapers in the region (the *Tribune, Sun Times, Journal-Register,* and the *Dispatch*). The Chicago metropolitan area, by far the most populous area in the state, receives almost no broadcast news about legislative activities. Springfield stations, however, make more of an attempt to cover events at the capitol, since so many viewers and listeners are employed or connected to state government.

I felt confident that I spoke to the large majority of influential and knowledgeable journalists at the capitol—a small but fascinating group of dedicated and highly professional reporters. Like the staffers, they were young—most in their thirties and forties, with a few in their late twenties. I did not identify the gender of informants, because attaching gender to the comments in chapter 3 might reveal their identities and thus violate my promise to them of anonymity. But I will note that women journalists compose about one-third of the Springfield legislative press corps membership.[57] Journalists were cooperative and seemed to enjoy the interview: It was a chance for them to reflect on their work during a slow period—after the session ended and before the fall political campaigns began in earnest. All of the journalists were somewhat cynical about the legislative process, in sharp contrast to the staffers, but nonetheless expressed a commitment to covering the capitol in the most accurate and evenhanded ways possible. Journalists, like staff members, believed that an understanding of state governmental affairs is crucial for citizens, and they spent considerable energy thinking about the tone and extent of their coverage of policy making.

The last group of informants for the qualitative study, ten in all, were Illinois party activists. Most had been involved in local community politics and all were delegates to their party's national conventions in 1996 (some had attended previous conventions as well). Six of the informants were Republicans and four were Democrats; six of the informants were men and four were women. This group of activists was drawn randomly from lists of convention delegates provided by the state party organizations. It proved difficult to locate ten delegates by telephone because, at the time of the study, many were busy with campaign work, preparation for the convention, or postconvention activities. Those I did interview were quite cooperative and willing, but between the hectic nature of the summer and fall campaign seasons and the incompleteness of the phone and address listings I had, selection of informants was challenging. Although many convention delegates are high office holders (e.g., the mayor of Chicago, state senators, and members of Congress), none of the party activists participating in this qualitative study had then held elective office above the municipal level (one informant had received a temporary appointment to the legislature to fill an unexpected midterm vacancy, however). Seven of these party activists lived throughout the Chicago metropolitan area, and the other three were from the western or southern parts of Illinois. Using lists of delegates was a very effective way to locate a diverse group of highly experienced activists, since being selected is usually a recognition of many past efforts on behalf of the party—organizing meetings, canvassing by telephone and in person, raising money, and the like.[58] I also conducted a larger survey of delegates, discussed in chapter 4.

The forty-four informants in this study were all very much intellectually engaged with politics. Even though they were either working (in a paid or unpaid capacity) for one of the two state party organizations or covering state politics for their news organizations, all were well versed in local, state, and national public affairs. This engagement made them excellent sources for informed lay theories about the relationships among media, public opinion, and the policy-making process. While their occupational differences did cause them to have particular perspectives about public opinion and media, there were some interesting commonalities across groups that will be discussed in subsequent chapters.

The State as Milieu for Research

Political scientists have long studied states and state government, but in the last few years there has been increasing interest in politics at this level, particularly legislative policy making.[59] As states are charged by the federal government with the administration of more programs—in areas from welfare benefits to highway improvement—the importance of decision making in state legislatures becomes absolutely crucial for understanding American politics. Moreover, states *originate* new sorts of laws, regulations, and programs. State legislatures have become more active for a variety of reasons, many of them fiscal. But these days, many talented individuals with an interest in policy are drawn to state legislatures as staffers or officeholders. As Alan Rosenthal, a long-time student of state politics puts it, "Legislatures are probably the principal political institutions in the states—the guts of democracy."[60] And indeed, state law affects many aspects of our daily lives, from health services and education to the regulation of local elections and the structure of law enforcement. Carl Van Horn argues that one of many indicators of increasing state government influence (a "quiet revolution in American politics") is that effective governors are able to attain high national prominence and are often elected to high office (e.g., Jimmy Carter, Ronald Reagan, and Bill Clinton).[61]

The reasons that states have become more powerful are complex, but Van Horn posits that there are two premier causes of this increased scope of influence. The first cause of increased state legislative power was the 1962 Supreme Court decision, *Baker v. Carr,* which forced reapportionment of election districts and eventually more evenhanded representation across districts in the states. The Civil Rights Act of 1964 and the Voting Rights Act of 1965, Van Horn notes, broke down some barriers faced by minorities and made the legislatures more reflective of state populations and therefore more effective bodies.[62] In fact, the state legislatures of today look radically different, in terms of their composition, procedures, and use of staff, than they did before the mid-1960s. Due to various reforms and the more general forces of Weberian rationalization, state legislatures are complex bodies with extensive division of labor. Another real change in recent years has been the proliferation of committees with significant influence within their parties and within the entire legislature. Professional staffers provide support for committee members, translating research into advice, helping the members think about legislation, and strategizing for public hearings and floor debate. On the major standing committees in state legislatures, Rosenthal notes, chairs are "figures with whom lobbyists, executive officials, legislators, and legislative leaders must reckon. Ten or twenty standing committees, each in its own domain doing its own thing, constitute a formidable centrifugal force in a legislative body."[63]

In one of the most comprehensive and rigorous studies of the relationship between public opinion and state policy making, Robert Erikson, Gerald Wright, and John McIver find state government to be highly responsive to public preferences: One does find more liberal policy in liberal states and more conservative policy in conservative states.[64] Like other researchers who have recently begun to take state policy and public opinion processes seriously, Erikson, Wright, and McIver see states as "laboratories" that enable us to look closely at relationships among partisanship, opinion formation, and the legislative process. One interesting point about their study, which matches state-level opinion survey data with legislative ideologies and positions, is that it demonstrates how much public opinion matters, even when people know very little about state politics and indeed, about their own representatives. The authors argue, as did V. O. Key before them, that while there is no "one-to-one" correspondence between public opinion and public policy in the states, public opinion does set the wide boundaries within which legislation is developed and enacted: Public feeling sets limits on what policymakers can and cannot do. In one—albeit very modest—study of state lawmakers, state representatives were deemed to be fairly good at summarizing public opinion and predicting the outcomes of policy referenda. Politicians based their predictions on far more indicators of public opinion than did voters (also included in the study), which is what we would expect from lawmakers and those running for elective office.[65] So states are interesting arenas for exploring public opinion issues, because there is a demonstrable relationship between public sentiment and policy, and because representatives do make concerted efforts to understand public opinion dynamics, if for no other reason than their desire to gain or maintain high office. We should not be overly confident about "matches" of public opinion (measured by surveys) and state policy, of course, but these research projects are extraordinarily important and provocative.

One last advantage of focusing on states in a study of public opinion con-

[handwritten margin note: PO sets limits (boundaries) to policy]

ceptions and processes is that opinion polls and surveys play a much smaller role in the discussion of the public mood than they do at the federal level. While we are quite far from understanding whether and how much opinion polling matters in national policy making (nonelection polling, that is), polls produced by parties, the media, and consulting firms are an omnipresent force in many important national policy debates. This is not the case in state legislative politics, where issue polls are much less likely to be conducted. On very high profile issues in Illinois, such as proposals to bring casino gambling to Chicago, polls have appeared in major dailies and are circulated through the legislature. But on the vast majority of policy initiatives, polls are absent from public debate. This absence of survey data makes states a particularly useful milieu for studying the nature of public opinion, because polls are seen—by legislative staffers, journalists, and party activists—as *one of many* ways to evaluate public opinion. Without the omnipresence of polls, which are often controversial and of limited value even in national policy debates (when the issues are complex), we can get a clearer picture of how the people who need to understand public opinion get a sense of this very slippery entity.

The interviews that constitute the empirical basis for this study were conducted with legislative committee staffers, journalists, and political activists in Illinois. Illinois is an appropriate setting for studying the discourse and dynamics of public opinion, since it is both a microcosm of the United States and a "bellwether" state. One of the largest states in terms of population (well over eleven million), Illinois is very diverse, with urban and rural areas and varied industrial and commercial interests. Moreover, the composition of Illinois' population resembles that of the country as a whole. In terms of racial diversity, for example, 15 percent of Illinois residents are black and 78 percent are white, while 12 percent of Americans are black and 80 percent are white. Likewise, 74 percent of Illinois residents live in cities and 15 percent live in rural locations, while 64 percent of Americans live in cities and 25 percent live in rural locations. Beyond these crude population breakdowns, though, some have argued that Illinois has proven to be a trustworthy political microcosm of the nation. David Everson notes that Illinois culture is both northern and southern, that it has both agricultural and industrial bases, and that it is a premier exporter to foreign markets. He notes that, "If Illinois were a nation, it would be the 14th largest in Gross National Product."[66] Furthermore, the state has a strong, competitive two-party system that makes it useful as a predictor for national election outcomes. Citing a study by James Pryzbylski, Everson reports that, since 1928, Illinois has never been more than five percentage points away from presidential vote outcomes. Using other indicators of a state's predictive power, such as how the population is "swinging" from one election to the next, Illinois also fairs extraordinarily well.[67]

Interviewing and Understanding

As noted earlier, I took as my guide to this research the interpretive interview tradition exemplified so well by Robert Lane, but also by other scholars attempting to understand—simultaneously—some of the psychological and sociological dynamics of democracy. Examples of this research abound in recent years, but earlier models such as *Beyond Adversary Democracy*, Jane J. Mansbridge's now classic study of community self-government, are still some of the best guides for conducting this sort of research.[68] One key characteristic of this earlier work is that scholars consciously or unconsciously worked very much in the spirit of *verstehen*, Max Weber's term for research methods that force students of social life to (momentarily) take the perspectives of the actors they study. In these times, seventy years after Weber wrote *Economy and Society*, his statements about the ease of assuming alternative viewpoints of current or historical beings seem a bit naive (Weber notes: "One need not have been Caesar in order to understand Caesar"), but some of the general guidelines Weber provides are quite useful to those of us interested in links between political psychology and social action.[69] Furthermore, what is it to "understand" someone else's behavior from his or her own point of view? How do we verify that we have, in fact, understood? These questions and problems raised about *verstehen* are well known and have long been debated in sociology.[70] Semantic debates about Weber's multiple categories for types of understanding aside, what is most useful are two points now taken for granted in interpretive sociology: Complete understanding of an action cannot be reached through observation alone, and context of action is all-important in determining meaning of those actions.

Since Weber wrote before sociologists (and certainly before political scientists) realized the vital importance of language and rhetoric for understanding action, he badly underconceptualized language in his methodological tracts. Yet Weber provides much of the intellectual motivation and indeed justification for interpretive sociology, and he foregrounds my study very well in the introductory chapters of *Economy and Society*. In my study I am very much interested in conceptualization of "public opinion"—the meanings people assign to it and the way it is thought to interact with mass media content and policy-making processes. Although Weber focused on historical explanation of individual and institutional behavior, he was concerned with how *verstehen*-inspired interpretive methodology might help us clarify the way individuals use *basic political concepts and terms*. Take, for example, this note Weber makes about the way we use the word "state":

> [T]he subjective interpretation of action must take account of a fundamentally important fact. These concepts of collective entities [such as "state"] which are found both in common sense and in juristic and other technical forms of thought, have a meaning in the minds of individual persons, partly as something actually existing, partly as something with normative authority. This is true not only of judges and officials, but of ordinary private individuals as well. Actors thus in part orient their action to them, and in this role such ideas have a powerful, often a decisive, causal influence on the course of action of real individuals.[71]

Weber speculated in this discussion that the word "state" had particular meanings in sociology but had different and interesting meanings in the judicial, political, and social realms beyond the academy. From my perspective, Weber did not go far enough with his own important insight: that definitions of terms vary across cultural context and that they drive social action. Perhaps it is our late-twentieth-century sensitivity to the power of language and rhetoric that makes this problem in Weber's work so obvious, but it seems particularly odd coming from the originator of the idealist "Protestant ethic" hypothesis.[72]

The interviews in the present study were semistructured. In other words, there was an interview protocol (set out in appendix B), but because it was critical to use extensive probing, each of the interviews had its own unique characteristics. Since the informants were very knowledgeable about politics, and usually very opinionated, they often guessed the next question or took the conversation off on an interesting tangent. This is sort of openness and "negotiation" with the interview protocol is entirely intentional, and it is what makes the method different from conventional survey research or experimentation, where opportunities for respondent commentary are usually quite restricted. I got the sense, in fact, that these informants were relieved that I was not conducting a survey composed of closed-ended questions: Several expressed increased interest in and excitement about the study when they realized that they could explain their arguments and opinions at length. The partisan activists—who had all been national convention delegates during the summer of the interviews—were particularly pleased about the openness of the format since they were frustrated with the sorts of limited and narrow questions they constantly fielded from journalists before and at the conventions. This group of forty-four informants was easy to interview since they were rather forthcoming and engaged, volunteering much information and examples from their work in politics.[73]

The next three chapters report on findings from the depth interviews and the larger survey project. When analyzing the interviews we will begin to see what lay theory about public opinion looks like, and how one's place in the social matrix is related to one's views of the democratic process. I was attentive to the sorts of arguments informants made, and in these chapters I try to wed their lay theories to our own academic theorizing about public opinion. The informants in this study had varying and indeed conflicting views of public opinion, and I will discuss these clashes in the context of democratic theory in the conclusion.

2 Policy Experts Think about Public Opinion, Media, and the Legislative Process

WE BUILD OUR causal models about the political world incrementally, weaving together our direct perceptions of local events, media reports of distant occurrences, the opinions of fellow citizens, and our past experience. While the definitions and "theories" we hold about political life are important, since these notions are most likely to determine the nature of our political activity (and inactivity), those who are directly involved in policy making must rely on their own theories for guidance in their day-to-day work. When the legislature is in session, staffers laboring in Springfield—as in most state capitals—are far too busy to develop new philosophies or approaches to policy work: They must fall back on the frameworks, tendencies, and rules of thumb in their repertoires. We should think of these staffers, who are vital to the design, revision, and success of legislative initiatives, as policy *managers* since they help orchestrate what political scientists call the "dance of legislation." In a state with a large, diverse population, a set of highly bureaucratized state agencies, and a myriad of complex regulations in all arenas, legislative committee work would be impossible without a highly skilled and sensitive staff. Members of the legislature wear many hats: They are ideological leaders, servants to their constituencies, and lawmakers. With these demands tugging members in multiple directions, their staff become technical experts who drive the legislative process along on its bumpy path. In addition, they are often thought to be—along with journalists—the repository of collective memory about policy matters. The latter function served by staffers is in fact crucial to understanding their role at the capitol, since they add a certain stability to a system that is constantly experiencing the departure of members and shifting ideological currents. This chapter reports on the sorts of theories or models twenty committee staffers in

Springfield use as they go about their work. It is important to note that these informants, as well as the ones discussed in subsequent chapters, tend not to believe that they *have* theories or abstract notions about public opinion. Yet when I asked them about democratic concepts and ideas, they were both forthcoming and engaged. At times they seemed surprised by their own statements, but they were pleased to articulate the connections between their "theories" and their work.

One of the most difficult tasks in the analysis of depth interview material is of course organizational. I have leaned very much in Robert Lane's direction, choosing to stay as close to the data as possible. One might develop a coding scheme and count the occurrence of particular words or phrases in interview transcripts, for example, but such an approach seemed entirely inappropriate for this analysis. It would distort—to a large degree—informants' statements, squeezing them into categories they may not truly occupy. So, in the spirit of Lane and of Barney Glaser and Anselm Strauss (see appendix A), my strategy is to scrutinize the transcripts as rigorously as possible, seeking to build grounded theory about lay models of politics. I did, like any researcher, approach my informants with ideas, questions, hypotheses, and theoretical possibilities, finding support for some and no evidence for others. And I was often surprised, discovering political notions and theories that I had not expected to find. In this chapter, and indeed in this book, I spend the bulk of my time discussing beliefs that will seem most problematic or even counter-intuitive to social scientists. In particular, many of the ways informants think about the meaning of public opinion and the relationships among public policy, public opinion, and media are at variance with our own scholarly theories about these matters. It is vital, as I argued earlier, to listen to those deeply enmeshed in policy work since they can provide us with insights into the process that are otherwise impossible for us to obtain. We must of course be skeptical of informants' views and opinions, so I tried to press them as best I could for specifics and elaboration. Let us begin this chapter by discussing definitions of public opinion, exploring how this group of twenty legislative policy managers thinks about public opinion in all its manifestations. After we get a sense of how they conceptualize public opinion, we can move on to a scrutiny of their simple causal models of politics, keeping in mind the relationships between occupational pressures and lay theories of politics—between thought and action.

A prefatory note about interview data: People rarely speak in grammatically correct formats, so those who have not participated in a given conversation invariably find a transcript of the conversation difficult to read. To make informants' statements reflect—as clearly as possible—their arguments and opinions I have "smoothed out" their remarks to the best of my ability. This does not involve substantive editorial intervention at all, but it does demand that I insert ellipses as well as explanatory articles and phrases in brackets.

What Public Opinion Is Not

A way to begin discerning staff theories about public opinion and its connections to media and policy is to figure out, from their perspective in the legislature, what public opinion *is not*. Public opinion is not, for the large majority of staffers, the result of opinion polls or sample surveys. In fact, only four mentioned polls and those informants viewed polls as useful only occasionally. I was most interested in issue polls, not pre-election polls, and upon close questioning those informants who mentioned polls as useful were normally referring to the typical horse-race surveys one sees during campaign season. One staffer told me that the House Democrats and Republicans "do polling virtually constantly." I asked for more explanation, since I had learned from previous interviewing that issue polls were rare, given the sheer number of issues and bills one finds each session. It became clear that he was speaking about pre-election polls conducted during primary season and before the general elections. Are issue polls used strategically in the policy process? Scholars find that polls have long been employed for strategic planning by presidents, but we still have very few empirical studies that demonstrate this instrumental use of polling in legislative settings.[1] In Springfield it seemed that issue polls—concerning pending legislation—are suspect because they are used so selectively by the parties for rhetorical purposes. Issue polls were not mentioned as central to planning legislative maneuvers. The following comment is one of the very few extended comments about polling I received, and it is very much about the strategic and rhetorical use of surveys. A staffer said:

> Polls, they're used by us when it's to our advantage and kind of discounted when they're not. For example, this spring we had a bill that went through the [other house] with a lot of fanfare. It got over here and our members weren't that crazy about it. . . . And they [party members in the originating body] had polling data that showed that the public according to their numbers, overwhelmingly supported a number of the concepts in the bill. And we were like, "No, that doesn't make any sense. We don't buy it." We fought them on that. . . . [Polling data can be used to] bolster your case. And I

don't think we have a problem with discounting it. If it's not going in the trash, we feel it should, at least as far as policy matters.

This particular staffer, and most with whom I talked, are able to critique polling quite easily—speaking to a range of problems, from the difficulty of wording a question to the time-bound nature of poll results. In fact, participants in the depth interview study across all three informant categories—policy managers, journalists, and political activists—could readily articulate their skepticism of polls. Their critiques of surveys are much like the ones we generate in our own methodological literature, minus the social science jargon. Those involved in politics know firsthand that survey design, implementation, and data analysis are a tricky business. For example, one of the staff members noted that the public polled is not necessarily the informed public: "The questions [on Illinois statewide polls] are not particularly specific. They don't ask specific hard line [questions]—'yes, no, do you know about this? Do you know how much?' I guess they're more [about] what you think, what you feel. So it's kind of fairly squishy."

Why are so few polls used in a large state legislature? There are several reasons. First, survey research is expensive, as many staffers pointed out to me. One quite powerful staffer noted that, while the governor has many resources, legislators do not, so polls are rare: "[A] poll has got to be done with political money. So, right there you're cutting into your actual campaign spending when you take a poll. It's the governmental funds against the political. And polls are expensive: A poll might be $25,000. . . . Polls are expensive, very expensive."

Newspapers in the state, particularly the larger ones, do on occasion publish issue polls, but staffers seemed rather uninterested in the statewide polls since they tend not to break the data down by district or region. Yet even if there were more monies available for polling, I got the sense that the data would not be particularly useful to those who help to initiate bills and work for their passage or defeat. The central problems in trying to integrate poll findings into legislative work are that details of bills are simply too complex to be collapsed into a few survey questions, and citizens are not informed enough to answer questions intelligently. One staffer pointed out how difficult it is to use polls for one of the most common and most controversial issues in state politics: the balance between property taxes and income taxes. This is a difficult problem that requires the self-interested citizen to analyze his own financial situation, and few have time to engage in such mathematical work, especially as multiple proposals and counterproposals swirl around:

[O]ne of the things that's interesting that I've noticed in my phone polling experience is that you'll ask people if they would like to see a reduction in property taxes, and everyone will say "yes." And the interest groups will all say that their members will support a property tax reduction. However, you ask them if they want property tax reduction with an offsetting income tax increase, then they don't want property tax reduction anymore. . . . [W]hat I'm saying is that many times public opinion doesn't really [help us]. . . . The poll's going to ask the general voter [about this issue] when what we're trying to find out is different.

A few of the informants who mentioned polls thought that perhaps the state polls and certainly the more abundant national polls we find in the mass media give us a very general sense of public feeling. For instance, one staffer noted that the public is very "anticriminal" right now and that much legislation, from sentencing guidelines to prison reform, is driven by this sentiment. He claimed that this vague public feeling against criminals, which he finds unjustifiable and counterproductive to good anticrime policy making, can be found in opinion poll data. Yet this staffer also argued that direct lobbying from victims and their families is far more persuasive and compelling to members and to their staffs than are poll data.

Staffers in Springfield find a chronic mismatch between the legislative process and the data available through opinion polling. There is the issue of content, as internal party or media issue polling could never "keep up" with the dynamic and complex debates on bills before the legislature. There is also a timing problem that makes it difficult to envision how polling might become a part of legislative activity at the capitol. The House and Senate are in session from January to May, and during that time work on legislation is so intense that members and staffers rarely have time to attend to what they believe are vague or dubious indicators of public opinion. This is not to say that they do not attend to public opinion while in session, because they are quite sensitive to the needs of constituents and interest groups. However, in their search for public feeling that will enable them to make policy under the various pressures imposed by a strict legislative cycle, staffers find polling of little value. On the whole, staffers read the occasional issue poll and more often, pre-election poll, but do not find them particularly useful. One staffer noted, for example, "I don't ever deal with poll data. I see it. I remember an article in the *State Journal Register* a couple of months ago. There was a statewide [pre-election] poll that determined that voting citizens were leaning toward Democrats more so than Republicans. So that article was of course copied and distributed throughout our offices and it was kind of like a rallying cry for Democrats. That's the kind of [use] those kind of public opinion polls have."

Occasionally, interest group leaders present members and staff with poll data regarding the feelings of their membership or the sentiments of the public at large toward a particular issue. One staffer gave the example of a poll of the general public conducted by a state police organization and presented to legislators as part of a lobbying strategy. The use of this poll did not have the intended persuasive impact and in fact angered many of the members and staffers working on the issue. The staff member explained that the use of polls by public servants—like police officers—seemed particularly inappropriate. I asked if it was unusual for the police to use a poll in a lobbying effort, and he explained:

> Yes, very unusual. [The poll] was not liked by a lot of legislators. . . . [The members didn't like the use of poll data] because they're [the lobby group] manipulating the process. Money is for arresting people, putting people in jail, not trying to manipulate the system so much where you can put in your two cents' worth regarding it [and] trying to generate your own news, I guess.

In this case, the poll was regarded as "dirty politics," as somehow lowly and manipulative. I got the sense, when talking to this staffer and others, that members and staffers can often take offense when presented with issue poll data: These policy professionals feel as though they have a complex and broad understanding of the public mood—what people want and the kinds of tradeoffs they are and are not willing to make for particular types of legislative maneuvers. In members' and staffers' eyes, poll data are simplistic and disconnected from the particulars of policy debate, so they have a rather elementary quality to them. Pre-election polls are a different story, of course, because they are in most cases fairly accurate predictors of real election outcomes. The content of specific policy outcomes, in contrast, is not discrete and certainly not always predictable via the use of surveys. Polls may demonstrate that citizens in a state share general ideological tendencies with their elected officials, but this vague matching is a far cry from predicting actual legislative activity.

Staffers' views of polling underscore the point made earlier, in chapter 1, about the relationship between technology for measuring public opinion and the nature of public opinion itself. The content of public opinion is quite directly shaped by our means of assessing it, and here—among the staffers—we see some resistance to polling as technology. Staffers focus not so much on the people or institutions that conduct polls but on the methodology itself. From their perspective, polling is a technique that comes out of the blue: It is a standard method, not fitted to the idiosyncrasies of Illinois legislative politics. This is an advantage of survey research in the eyes of social scientists, because surveying can provide data comparable across various political settings. But it is a disadvantage of polling as technology from the perspective of many staffers. This alleged "lack of fit" between polling and the particular culture of state policy debates reminds me of a chapter in the history of opinion polling—the resistance to the method in France from the 1940s through the 1960s. Although today France is among the leaders in published polls, and it witnesses heated public debates about the broadcasting of poll results before elections, French public officials and intellectuals resisted survey research for decades despite wide use of polling in the United States, Italy, Germany, and other democratic states. Newspapers did not commission surveys, and in politics, the notion of surveying seemed inappropriate since the elected Parliament and political parties were believed to be the most reliable representatives of public opinion. Interestingly, even French social scientists rejected polling as a sociological and political practice. Polling methods were deemed unable to capture the unique, textured, and complex nature of French public sentiment, leading one prominent sociologist of the postwar period, Georges Gurvith, to speak of polls as "les procédés dérisoires de Monsieur Gallup" ("the pathetic devices of Mr. Gallup").[2]

Staffers in this study were likely to mention two indicators of public opinion meaningful to them in their work—the activity of pressure groups and the content of the mass media. Let us begin with interest groups.

Public Opinion as Group Sentiment

Legislative staffers were quick to speak of interest group opinion as either synonymous with "public opinion" or one of the more reliable indicators of popular sentiment available to staff and legislators. This view was popular among legislative staffers, eight of whom mentioned interest and lobby groups—before I mentioned this topic—when I asked them a simple open-ended question about the meaning of public opinion. Other staffers eventually spoke about special interests in the context of discussing public opinion and were quite comfortable talking about interest groups as a "stand-in" for public opinion. Elections matter, as do letters and calls from constituents, though the latter are always looked on with skepticism because it is hard to get a sense of a constituent's level of knowledge about the issue or the intensity of his or her opinions. There is a feeling among staffers, however, that the nuances and intensity of public opinion are best captured in the various communications of interest groups. This argument—that interest group opinion is public opinion—took several forms in the statements of my informants. Staffers who made this argument mentioned four interrelated characteristics of interest groups that make them reliable indicators of public opinion: their communicative efficiency, their ability to crystallize nebulous public sentiment, their perceived honesty, and their capacity to communicate the intensity of opinion. Staffers tend to treat their interactions with lobbyists carefully, understanding full well that interest group leaders are intent on persuasion.

Lobbyists are efficient in their role as purveyors of public opinion because they are so well informed about their issues: They can get right to the point, keenly understanding who their opponents are. And the better interest group representatives are well attuned to the needs of legislators and the sorts of constituencies they must be accountable to. Staffers find that the public and public opinion are fairly amorphous entities, and some staffers exhibit a fair degree of impatience with knowledge levels among the general public, so lobbyists seem to them a reasonable and appropriate stand-in for the public. In response to my open-ended question about the meaning of public opinion, one staffer said:

> I immediately think of interest groups. That's how we gauge our public opinion. . . . I very rarely am clueless about where that constituency is because of the interest groups keeping me informed. . . . [V]ery rarely does personal public opinion matter to the General Assembly. . . . [Interest group communication is] just more indicative of what's really going on out there. Rarely will a group of people unorganized be able to, just normal constituents, be able to call up and change the way a vote is taken. I can only think of one issue in the General Assembly in the last year in my area where that actually mattered. I would have to say that from a public opinion standpoint, we don't really care what the average Joe thinks. I don't say that as if we're not representing them, but we're representing the people who represent them. It's one step removed from the general public.

Interest groups are more than simple surrogates for public opinion, in the eyes of this informant. They translate opinion, but during this translation process they also help to give public opinion a more solid and comprehensible form. Lobbyists are perceived to crystallize or clarify the content and intensity of vague public moods. On only a handful of the hundreds of bills before the legislature is the intensity of mass opinion apparent. One such case is the debate and legislative maneuvering over legalized gambling across the state, particularly land-based casinos in Chicago. The religious right, business leaders, and casino operators have all been extraordinarily vocal in this debate, and many citizens do have strong feelings about this issue. But this is quite rare: On most issues mass opinion is unformed or very difficult to discern, so lobbyists help staffers and members with this task. One staffer spoke directly to the issue of opinion intensity and how interest groups enable staff to get a sense of intensity (or lack thereof) on particular issues. In answer to an open-ended question about the meaning of public opinion, she immediately mentioned interest groups and said:

> If I only have one complaint about something [a bill], I'm not going to be too exercised over that. [This is a contrast to situations where] I have hundreds of complaints and I see hundreds of interest groups coming forward on a particular issue. . . . We're trying to [pass particular legislation but] we can't do it because the [name of interest group] is very aggressive in their opposition to promoting this. Now, *that's* public opinion, but that's also one particular group that is in opposition.

I asked this staffer if she would distinguish at all between interest group opinion and public opinion, and she said that she did not distinguish between the two. She cares very much what the "average person" has to say, but relies so often on interest group opinion as a form of public opinion measurement that she has internalized the positions and arguments of such lobbyists: "I take it all in [interest group opinion and opinions of the average person] and, obviously, I've become sensitized to what each interest group will be touting in their position on a particular issue. I can tell you which ones will be supportive of any issue." There is a sense among some staffers that if a segment of the public really cares about an issue, they will form a lobby around that issue:

> Obviously I think that the lobbyists and organized groups are much more effective [than average citizens] because they have an organized message. They have money and they're here. Whereas a lot of people, I think there's a lot of people in the state that just really don't care what goes on in Springfield. And that's one thing, you have a lot of people are always griping about [issues but] only people with money and . . . organizations have influence. Well, don't gripe about it, get involved, get a message, get organized, and raise money, and get in the game.

Staffers listen to lobbyists they perceive as honest, and most interest group leaders tend to be quite straightforward in their discussions with staff and members. Several staffers underscored a point well known by scholars—that a lobbyist's reputation is ruined if he or she lies (either point-blank or through omission of facts), so interest group representatives tend to be forthright about the facts while they try to persuade. One staffer, when asked about the meaning of public opinion, said that public opinion was both media content and the statements of interest groups, although she prefers the latter for their honesty:

> Listening to, especially the interest groups, as they come to us and talk to us about how maybe a particular constituency feels about a certain issue: That's probably the quickest, easiest way that we have to gauge public opinion. . . . I've had people [lobbyists] who have blatantly either misrepresented the truth or just lied to me. And I have a hard time dealing with them from that point on because I can't trust the information they're giving. And if I can't trust the information, then they really don't serve me that much of a purpose.

These views of staffers are consistent with the views of political science scholars of previous eras. Political theorists and researchers have long recognized the importance of party organizations, interest groups, and other social and political enclaves that hope to persuade legislators and the general public. Groups and social networks were of great concern to the sociologists of the Columbia School, like Bernard Berelson and Paul Lazarsfeld. More recently, Robert Huckfeldt and John Sprague have focused a massive research effort on groups—neighborhoods, churches, and local partisan organizations—in an attempt to understand how social context shapes public opinion and party identification. And in perhaps our most valuable empirical study of public opinion in the twentieth century, V. O. Key made it clear that studying groups and their activities is vital to understanding the formation and communication of public opinion. Key stated that interest groups may at times serve as a link between public opinion and government, but at other times they simply represent narrow interests not even shared by their own group members. Key and many political scientists who have come after him have made great contributions to our understanding of groups as mediators between the citizenry and government, yet few of these researchers went as far as Herbert Blumer.[3] Blumer, as a sociologist, was most sensitive to groups and their connection to public opinion. His work is unique in the public opinion literature because he does not, as Key did, argue that interest groups (or other sorts of organized enclaves) serve a mediating function. Instead, he argued that public opinion and group opinion were entirely *conflated*—that one could not even define public opinion without referring to group activity. These are two different views of public opinion: Key believed that an entity called "public opinion" (as discerned through surveys) existed apart from group action, and Blumer argued that the only interesting and important public opinion is the behavior and influence of organized groups.

Writing in 1948, Blumer echoed Arthur F. Bentley's remarks of forty years before. Bentley had written that "There is no public opinion that is not activity reflecting or representing the activity of a group or of a set of groups. There is no public opinion that is unanimous, none indicating the existence of any "social whole." Bentley further remarked that the abstraction "public opinion" can never be measured because it is a fiction. Groups, on the other hand, are real:

> There is no use attempting to handle public opinion except in terms of the groups that hold it and that it represents. Public opinion is an expression of, by, or for a group of people. It is primarily an expression of the group interest by the group itself, but where it has become a differentiated activity representing an underlying group we may say it is expressed by the opinion group for the underlying group. . . . When we examine this public opinion with its onward tendencies, we find that, besides being borne in a group, or given differentiated expression for a group, it always is directed against some activities of groups of men.[4]

Bentley's notions about public opinion are particularly interesting because they were formulated in the early years of the twentieth century, before the explosion of pressure groups we have witnessed in the last few decades. He seems, in *The Process of Government*, to foreshadow much of the interest group literature and our current concerns with the power of the so-called special interests. Blumer, writing in mid-century, extends Bentley's argument about groups as the basis of public opinion but attempts to broaden and elaborate this view.

As a starting point in his discussion of public opinion, Blumer began with oppositional rhetoric—a critique of opinion polling: Surveying treats society as an aggregation of atomized individuals when it is in fact composed of groups. He scolds sociologists of his day for forgetting this "fact" in their growing fascination with newly developed polling techniques. Blumer was concerned that groups and their leaders, who drive social and political activity in a democracy, were ignored by sampling techniques, which tend not to recognize social structure and organization—neighborhoods, local parties, interest groups, and the like. Recent work in political science, such as the studies of Huckfeldt and Sprague, have tried to correct this problem by incorporating some network variables into their surveys of citizens during election campaigns. Yet if Blumer were alive today, he would not be entirely satisfied with this work since it still assumes public opinion to be the results of surveys, even if people are queried in these surveys about their social and organizational connections. Why was Blumer so insistent on defining public opinion as the functional analysis of group action? The central reason is that his approach—which must entail at least some textured case study work—*recognizes power differentials* in society. Survey research paints over the complex and important inequities in a democracy, he argued, where some people and some organizations have enormous resources and others struggle. Blumer could not fathom how opinion surveys, which imply that all voices might be weighted equally, could explain policy outcomes or social change more generally.

Surveys—or any method that assumes opinions to be of equal weight—are a naive approach to the analysis of political dynamics, from Blumer's standpoint, and it is the case that polling cannot always help us predict major political occurrences. As noted earlier, there is some narrow correspondence between opinion poll data and selected policy outcomes at the state and national levels, but there are still many incongruities between the two. Sometimes we are unable to predict interesting and important political movements. One example was the emergence of Ross Perot as such a strong third-party candidate in the 1992 presidential election. Of course it would be difficult to foresee the appearance of this particular idiosyncratic politician, but those of us who study public opinion should have been able to see—in advance of the campaign—the possibilities for such a large mobilization of voters. In the realm of policy, it is possible in retrospect to link tendencies noticed in surveys to certain legislative outcomes. But we are quite far from predicting all of the important forms of political behavior (individual or group) from polls. Sophisticated survey researchers, political consultants, candidates, and journalists understand very well these limitations of aggregate measures of public opinion. And V. O. Key's work reflects these problematics also: On one hand, he defined public opinion as the sentiments government finds it necessary to heed, while on the other, he often used survey research, which assumes all opinions to be equal. This struggle, to study the very real presence of power in a political system and at the same time develop rigorous methods for assessing public opinion, is still very much with us.

An oddity of recent academic history is that scholars who study interest groups and those who study public opinion are not engaged in any sort of sustained dialogue. Although Bentley, Key, and Blumer engaged in wide-ranging analyses, contemporary fields devoted to the study of mass opinion and the study of group opinion (e.g., "issue publics" or interest groups) are fairly distinct. This has much to do with the forces of Weberian rationalization in academic fields, but it is also related to real events and trends. There has been a steady rise in the number of interest groups to study, so evaluating such groups is far more difficult and time-consuming than it was in previous decades. And, in the arena of opinion research, survey methodology has become more challenging: New techniques are always being developed and tested, while city, state, and national populations have become more diverse and more reluctant to talk to pollsters.[5]

On one level, staffers' references to interest groups are perfectly appropriate, since legislative staff have constant and rather productive interaction with lobbyists representing small and also quite large segments of the citizenry. On another level, their willingness to name interest groups not simply as indicators of public opinion, but as *synonymous* with the notion of public opinion is quite strange, since in both academic and popular rhetorics, interest groups are usually seen as "at odds" with public sentiment and the public interest. In one recent scholarly collection, Mark P. Petracca writes in the introductory essay that the role of interest groups in governance represents a "triple tension": Interest groups are inevitable, indispensable, and dangerous.[6] The complaints about pressure groups are well known, and most are rooted in the question of fair representation. There are concerns (very prominent in Illinois at this writing) that wealthier groups are able to buy greater access to legislators and therefore have a greater chance of seeing their favored bills passed. Others worry that large groups of citizens fail to organize effective interest group representation at legislatures, and that these groups—the poor, unemployed, minorities, immigrants—are unable to break into a fairly closed system of influence peddling.[7]

This book does not address whether current configurations of interest groups are or are not truly representing large and diverse populations, but I should mention that defenses of interest group politics are as loud as complaints about them. For instance, Robert Salisbury has argued that the increasing number of interest groups in Washington has meant that individual groups have less access and influence than they did in previous decades. Legislators are lobbied by more interests, so each interest group must struggle harder to get its voice heard. In addition, the composition of interest groups has shifted, Salisbury argues, with a large growth in the number of "citizen lobbies." Some of these groups are organized around a specific policy decision or issue (e.g., abortion rights), but others are much broader in their goals (e.g., the AARP or Common Cause).[8] Regardless of narrowness of focus, the growth in interest groups is found not only in the more traditional areas of manufacturing, business, or professional societies. Others who study pressure groups and their tactics argue that the conventional business lobbies often conflict with each other, and that this conflict can dampen their influence. Furthermore, the underprivileged are now often represented by social welfare agency lobbies or other such groups. Perhaps we should think of interest group influence as it relates to the fine points of policy, as Kay Lehman Schlozman and John Tierney argue. They conclude that, "while the broad outlines of policy are rarely dictated by organized interest preferences alone, the power to influence details—whether of congressional legislation, agency regulations, or judicial findings—is not a negligible form of influence, for it is the particulars that govern the nature and extent of the impact, if any at all, a given policy will have."[9] Finally, some have argued that the benefits of access to information provided by interest groups should outweigh concerns about undue influence, since interest groups are useful in providing data to legislators and their staffs that can be used in ways often contrary to lobbyists' wishes. Such lobbies provide important information and argumentation, which enables more effective and more efficient policy making. Jane Mansbridge has gone even further with this argument, noting that interest groups can even provide a forum for deliberation, a crucial component in democratic theory.[10]

Much of the important literature about interest groups concerns their influence on Congress, for obvious reasons. There is an established bias toward studying national politics, and interest group resources are generally focused on lobbying in Washington. It is in Washington that lobbyists can efficiently visit and attempt to persuade large numbers of policymakers and also maintain close contact with federal agencies, other allied interest groups, and journalists. Yet state legislatures were the forums for domestic policy making in the nineteenth century, and as I argued in the last chapter, they are regaining much of that importance as more responsibility for domestic policy shifts from the national to the state level. One study of state lobbying was conducted by Alan Rosenthal, who has tried to document the increasing professionalization of state legislatures and the particularities of interest group activity within them. It is as difficult to determine the influence of lobbyists in state legislatures as it is in Congress, and Rosenthal argues that interest groups at this level tend to be viewed as influential on the basis of reputation more than on actual services rendered to their clients. The *perception* that a lobbyist is honest, organized, and persuasive is as critical at the state level as it is at the federal level, and lobbyists' impacts are greatest on lower-visibility or narrowly focused bills. At the state level, as at the national level, lobbyists are crucial in creating the compromise positions represented by so much legislation: Interest groups are in the debate from beginning to end and, through sheer tenacity as well as great effort and expenditure, are often able to influence critical details in major bills. The concerns about representation noted above—that common citizens, especially poor ones, go unrepresented by lobbies—are present in state politics. Yet when researchers question legislators closely, they find that legislators are hard-pressed to agree on who exactly (which demographic groups) were underrepresented. This lack of consensus may indicate that our concerns about lobbying groups and their agendas are inflated, or more likely, it may be a call for more and better research on power differentials among lobbyists—power differentials that may in fact be extraordinarily dangerous.[11] Again, however, this book cannot shed light on questions of power and interest groups (e.g., whether or not specific lobbies representing our wealthiest citizens always have the most influence in a legislature).

Two staffers denied the link between interest groups and public opinion; they preferred to define public opinion as something other than interest group opinion. And their views have precedent. Political scientists, journalists, legislators themselves, and citizens have long worried about arguing that interest group opinion is synonymous with public opinion (the strong version of the argument) or an effective conduit for public opinion (the weaker form of the argument). Perhaps the comments of George Gallup and Saul Rae, in their 1940 tract *The Pulse of Democracy*, are instructive on this issue. They argued that it is impossible to tell whether an interest group argument represents the interests of more than just a few individuals, no matter how many people or letters interest group can produce through mobilization. For Gallup and Rae, survey research is the only way to get at the truth about public opinion: Lobbyists are self-serving, potentially dishonest, and narrow in focus. As the authors put the query, in citing an early 1930s lobbying effort for pensions: "How was the legislator to know whether or not this movement really represented a dominant current in American opinion, or merely the exuberance of a few apostles of utopia?"[12]

The two staffers in this study who did not believe public opinion and lobbying to be synonymous still did see important connections between the two. When I asked one of these informants whether he had separate mental categories for lobbyists and "the public," he said that he did, mostly because he feels as though the common man is underrepresented in his area of legislative expertise. I leave off his initial comments, which might reveal his identity, but he moved to more abstract discussion after speaking to his own committee work. "I probably do tend to put [lobbyists] in a different category as opposed to public opinion. I suppose if a lobbyists can generate grassroots efforts, then I think they kind of move over into the public opinion, citizen participation area." In this case, the staffer focuses on effects of lobbying: If the interest group can mobilize large numbers (through letter-writing or phone campaigns) they become public opinion conveyors, but if they are holding meetings with individual legislators and engaging in a lot of private consultation, they are not. This is an odd view of interest groups, since we know that their representation of public opinion must in fact take both public and private forms. Yet this very experienced staffer thinks that there are legislative "moments" when interest group discourse and action may be treated as public opinion, and other moments where such communication should not be described as public opinion.

The readiness of this group of highly engaged legislative managers to name interest groups as valuable conveyors of public feeling does not surprise those who study legislatures and who maintain a benign view of lobbying influence. Interest groups come to state capitols and to Congress with the express purpose of representing some narrow or broad segment of the population. Yet the willingness of these committee staffers to think of interest groups as "stand-ins" for public opinion is a somewhat different matter. Scholars and practitioners who spend their time measuring public opinion typically do not focus on the activities of interest groups; they leave the study of such lobbies to legislative specialists. This is unfortunate, since so much early twentieth-century work in public opinion theory—writings by Bentley, Truman, Blumer, and Key, to some extent—emphasize the importance of groups and opinion enclaves where beliefs are held with high intensity and are articulated in clear and unbending ways. There is an elegance to thinking about public opinion as coherent and often highly ideological group opinion, even if these groups are small and not particularly concerned with canvassing average citizens on a regular basis. Staffers treat interest groups with skepticism but find their ability to crystallize vague public sentiment to be enormously useful. And interest groups have advantages over other forms of public opinion measurement in the eyes of staffers, who normally have little access to poll data and who would place little value in it if they did.

Most interesting to students of public opinion is that staffers remind us of the group-oriented meanings of public opinion that were so pervasive in the nineteenth and early twentieth centuries. Tocqueville, Bryce, and many other political commentators understood the vital nature of groups, though we have been distracted from these conceptual schemes in the late twentieth century, perhaps because we prefer opinion measurement that values equality of opinion, like surveys. Important is the fact that staffers' meanings of public opinion are *arguments* about public opinion. Very rarely did someone answer my queries about the entity of public opinion without a definition plus a strategic assessment and a normative judgment, in addition to anecdotes and shards of evidence gleaned from the legislative context.[13] To offer a definition about public opinion is to offer a fragment of one's own version (or critique) of democratic theory as well. It is through questioning informants about basic democratic concepts, in fact, that we start to get some sense of their elaborate or fairly simplistic models of the abstract "public sphere." The public sphere is known to scholars, those who work in the tradition of Habermas and those who do not, as a constellation of institutions and social forces outside of private life. To legislative workers, the public sphere looms large as they try to design appropriate bills, negotiate with members, and work toward passage. And their theories about the public sphere are very much shaped by experience in the day-to-day workings of the assembly, a process most of us only read about on occasion. That public opinion is, to them, *group* opinion matters because it guides their expectations for and commitment to public policy. If public opinion is a *constraint* on what staffers feel the assembly can and cannot do, the nature of this constraint is of vital importance. Staffers are not in thrall to interest groups, and neither are members. Yet when they must consider public opinion, either before legislative debate ensues or as it comes to a close, they draw information about the nature of mass opinion in large part from the arguments of engaged and active interest groups.

Before we move on, it is vital that we evaluate the pressure-groups-as-public opinion view in light of some of our best studies of political practice and the widely used notion of "issue publics." In chapter 5 I will elaborate on these connections, but it is worth mentioning them here. Throughout my discussions with legislative staffers I thought about the well-known concentric circles Richard Fenno describes in his book on congressmen in their districts, *Home Style*.[14] Fenno argues that a "constituency" is in fact a mental construction on the part of the congressmen—a "theory" in the language of this book, about whom he or she represents. Fenno believes that congressmen imagine (based on both casual and more rigorous assessments of the empirical evidence) several broad and then more narrow constituencies. A member must keep in mind these groups—his geographic constituency, his supporters, his strongest supporters, and his intimates. Such mental divisions that congressmen hold in their heads are instructive to us here, since staffers also have multiple constituencies in mind—although they are in a very different political role than congressmen. Interest groups are one sort of constituency, one sort of public opinion. There may be multiple publics out there, though in most cases staffers feel as though interest groups represent the most vocal ones. Also relevant here is the literature on "issue publics." These are groups of citizens who have particularly strong feelings about particular policy areas and so tend to act on these strong attitudes. Again, our staffers resonate with this work in the scholarly literature, because they are often thinking of narrow segments of the public—issue publics—who step forward on issues that matter to them.[15]

And we cannot leave this discussion of groups as publics without a mention of E. E. Schattschneider's contribution to the practical study of politics.[16] Schattschneider, working very much in the tradition of sociological conflict theory, emphasized the role of divisiveness in political culture. All political strategy, in all political environments, is keyed to what he calls the "scope of conflict." How many parties are involved in a conflict, and how do they make their concerns known? How large and influential are these groups? All of these questions are critical if one is to analyze practical politics and what people derive from it. It is very useful to think in general terms about Schattschneider's work, in relation to the staffer interviews here. First, and while this was not a focus of my interviews, it did seem as though the scope of conflict was related to staffers' ideas about public opinion. When the scope of conflict is small—where the proposed bill is largely technical—interest groups are crucial as representatives of a nebulous public opinion. But when the issue is broader, and the scope of conflict wider and more inclusive, staffers are also likely to bring in media content (discussed below) as evidence and indicator of public opinion. This seems quite sensible: When the scope of conflict is narrow, the public at large is not particularly knowledgeable. But when it is broad, it is broad because the issues are both important to average citizens and comprehensible to them. The media often serve as citizens' direct conduit (or so the staffers often believe, as we shall see). A last insight from Schattschneider concerns his well-known statement that conflict among interest groups is broader than it appears on the surface:

> In the nature of things a *political conflict among special interests is never restricted to the groups most immediately interested.* Instead, it is an appeal (initiated by relatively small numbers of people) for the support of vast numbers of people who are sufficiently remote to have a somewhat different perspective on the controversy.

He then argues that, "The distinction between public and special interests is an indispensable tool for the study of politics. To abolish the distinction is to make a shambles of political science by treating things that are different as if they were alike."[17] Schattschneider would find the staffers' equating of public opinion with special interest opinion problematic since it does not take seriously the possibilities for *discord* between interest group opinion and the opinions of the public at large. But let us take up this contrast—between informants' views of politics and those from scholars—in the concluding chapter.

Public Opinion as Media Content

Perhaps more surprising than the readiness of staffers to think of public opinion and interest group opinion as nearly interchangeable is the belief held by many of these informants (twelve mentioned it directly) that mass media content *is* public opinion. Media scholars from a variety of empirical traditions have argued that exposure to the news and public opinion formation are linked: Some researchers posit that media most often "set agendas" for citizens and policymakers, while other researchers go much further, arguing that media content can change the basic nature of our beliefs and values.[18] These sorts of arguments propose that public opinion and media content are two distinct and measurable entities, a dichotomy with which social scientists have long been comfortable.[19] It seems that few of us are willing to take seriously Lippmann's more extreme position, that public opinion is in fact journalistic opinion. For all the citation of Lippmann on issues of stereotyping and elite behavior, very little of his theorizing about the conflation of media and public opinion has been acknowledged or explored. What explains our lack of attention to Lippmann's notions about the conflation of media and public opinion? One reason is the decidedly undemocratic nature of this conception: If public opinion is simply a "phantom" projected by an elite corps of journalists and policymakers, what does this mean for democratic theory? Where is the vox populi if we only have media representation of the vox populi? The second reason we tend to ignore Lippmann's views on the conflation of media and public opinion is that they present a plethora of measurement problems. Media content is most often found in narrative form (news stories, investigative reporting, cartoons, dramas, etc.), and it is a challenge to think of political cognition or public attitudes as structured in narrative fashion. Media content is, in other words, *creative* and imaginative, while we have long thought of public opinion as expressed in linear or (on occasion) in simple dialogic formats: Academics or pollsters design queries—experimental or survey-based—and citizens answer (or fail to answer) such queries. In rare instances researchers probe respondents beyond a simple categorical query, but they typically accept answers quickly and move on to new questions. In any event, respondents or experimental subjects are not generally asked to put their ideas in narrative form.

Maybe, the conflation—or extreme interconnectivity—of media content and public opinion is the reason why media effects on the popular mood have been so difficult to detect. Interest in media effects on public opinion began with the Payne Foundation studies in the 1920s and the Columbia School's focus on the impact of radio in the 1940s, yet we still debate the fundamental existence and extent of these effects. Mass communication researchers have long puzzled over the nature of media impacts and have focused on the ways that selective exposure to media and the power of interpersonal communication can dampen the effects of mass media on public opinion. Scholars interested in public opinion produce tracts with revealing titles, like James Lemert's *Does Mass Communication Change Public Opinion After All?* and Benjamin Page, Robert Shapiro, and Glenn Dempsey's, "What Moves Public Opinion?"[20] And there is a continuing debate over the effects of political campaigns and television news. At some moments we can detect what we believe are clear media effects. But very often the causal order of these relationships can be rather murky since the *initial* content of journalism does reflect the views and concerns of readers and audiences: In fact, if media content did not appeal to attitudinal currents already flowing through the social world, we would not find such texts attractive or relevant to our lives. It seems that nonsystematic evidence supporting the conflation of media opinion and public opinion is everywhere, and perhaps it is incumbent upon scholars to create a theoretical framework for acknowledging this possibility—very much in the tradition of Lippmann. This is not to say that we must abandon the notion of media effects, although scholars from cultural studies have encouraged us to do so. Yet the possibility of public opinion/media conflation does present to us a tremendous challenge that can only help us understand the unique nature of contemporary American politics. Let us turn back to our legislative staffers on the question of media/public opinion conflation.

Upon hearing my open-ended question about the meaning of public opinion, twelve of the staffers answered "the media." Some of these men and women mentioned interest groups as well, but all believed that newspaper, television, or radio content was not simply a conduit for public opinion expression: In their view, it is the very essence of public opinion and can support or destroy legislative initiatives. One staffer said that, when he thinks of public opinion, he conjures up "the major newspapers putting the spin of the moment on different issues." Another said that he thinks of public opinion as

> The editorial page and certain commentary-type people, people like Thomas Hardy [of
> the *Chicago Tribune*]. Things like the "Inc." column [also in the *Tribune*] where you get
> little snippets. That's what I think of when I think of public opinion. We don't do a lot
> of polling. At least if we do I don't know anything about it. I know they do some
> [polling] in the campaign side of things, but I don't deal with that [as legislative staffer].
> And we only do that [have poll data] once every year or so. Mostly it's listening to
> people and the senators themselves have a pretty good instinct for what's important to
> them and what their constituents want. We follow people like Thomas Hardy and
> Kup's column [in the *Chicago Sun-Times*], and people like Bill O'Connell [a long-time
> journalist, recently retired, who was based] in Peoria.

Again, we see in this comment from an experienced staffer that quantitative opinion data in the form of survey research is hard to come by in the legislature. Polls are used frequently in campaign season, of course, but policy workers must do without such indicators. And, as noted above, policy polling is looked at skeptically even when available because it does not measure intensity of feeling (e.g., what polled respondents would or would not be willing to do or pay to achieve particular policies). This staffer cites the influential *Tribune,* the *Chicago Sun-Times,* the Springfield newspaper, and the few others that cover legislative events carefully as places to look for evidence of public opinion. Why is the content of both news and editorial media useful to legislative staffers interested in public opinion? For one thing, newspapers are efficient ways of knowing public opinion in just the same ways as interest groups that selectively present public viewpoints. Staffers note that journalists can create public opinion themselves but also are conduits publishing the opinions of "regular folks." Media content indicating the nature of public opinion is available on a fairly regular basis for the more important issues in areas like education and crime. The staffers consider an often mind-boggling number of bills while the assembly is in session, so they use any informational efficiencies available.

Evidence about public opinion is used symbolically by staffers and members in the assembly as elsewhere, and media representations of public opinion are very helpful in this regard. One staffer mentioned a specific case where he had to write up a report on an amendment to a bill, and he cited media accounts to represent public sentiment. Another said that, in one case, media were used in conjunction with other forms of opinion data:

> [W]e were arguing against the position of the House and a lot of the media coverage
> seemed to focus on concerns about the legislation. We would use newspaper articles.

> We would use radio stories and that type of thing in our negotiations with the House and say, "Look. This doesn't have a lot of support statewide. We need to change this. . . . We used the media articles. We used letters from people. We used phone calls. Some of the groups that we're concerned about generated a lot of phone calls on this issue. So, we used all of those things.

Note how this staffer easily arrays media alongside other more traditional legislative means of knowing public opinion (constituent mail and phone calls): Media are thought to occupy a place in the category of opinion measurement techniques. Were media used strategically, as ammunition in the specific case this staffer described? Yes, they were: "We were kind of inclined to not to favor [the bill] anyway. And so when the articles came out that had the coverage of negative comments about it, it just served to bolster what our members' initial thoughts were anyway." Another staffer explained, in answer to my open-ended query about evaluating public opinion:

> I read about five or six articles over a week period, and then I'll sit back and think about it, and we'll have discussions on staff, informal discussions, just talking about the issue or politics, and we try to get one step beyond it and try to think, "What did the voters, how did the voters, see this. Did the voters care about this? . . . Just reading, it's amazing. Reading newspapers in the morning is most important because that's how the editorials in the newspapers will give us some insights on how people out there are thinking about government. You really have to be careful because most of those editorials in the newspapers are from the policy staffs here in Springfield. Or how they want you to spin it. We have so many spinmasters.

In this comment and others informants are going a step further than using media as conduits of public opinion. If they were simply treating media content as one indicator of mass sentiment, this would be worth noting, but indications from this small study are that media portrayals of issues and narrative descriptions of policy debates in the news are themselves public opinion data to legislative staffers. If media were simple conduits for public opinion data, staffers would have named specific bits of media content—published polls or letters to the editor—viewing newspapers as channels through which these data are disseminated. But such specific items or formats within media are rarely mentioned. Instead, it is the *totality* of media attention, the general slant or tendency of coverage (discussed below) that is synonymous with public opinion here. This is unsatisfying to the public opinion analyst, of course, looking for cues as to the specific media content of most interest to legislative policy workers. Perhaps even more problematic is the reminder from reception theorists of media: that people view and use media content selectively, and treat the text with seemingly boundless creativity. If this is the case, and numerous examples populate the mass communication literature at present, it is difficult for the analyst of media as public opinion to speculate on the uses of media content by professionals without talking to those users: Perceptions of content by readers (in this case, legislative staffers) are vital, as they try to glean meaning about public opinion on specific bills from newspapers, radio, and television. Finally, if media and public opinion are seen as conflated by policy managers, we scholars might reassess our own models for understanding the relationship between these two phenomena. This is one topic—how lay theory about public opinion might be used to alter our own scholarly theory building—to be taken up in chapter 5.

Media Bias

If media are for many staffers either synonymous with, or central conduits of, public opinion, then we must explore how these legislative managers think about the characteristics of mass media more generally. Since this is not a study in the fine points of audience reception, I have not exposed informants to any particular newspaper articles or television broadcasts, looking for their interpretations. This might be an interesting exercise, but I thought it more appropriate to query informants about the role of media in the legislative process more broadly in order to get beyond the short-term effects of specific and idiosyncratic media texts. These staff informants, as well as the journalists and activists I discuss in the next two chapters, are great consumers of information. Most read the Springfield and Chicago papers and attend to a variety of broadcast media. All staffers also keep abreast of particular media reports in their own areas of committee work, via the internal clipping service within the legislature. These clips are very important because the staffers are not able to read all local dailies in Illinois, and they do need to get a sense of media coverage of issues across the state. Members often bring articles from media in their districts to the legislative staff in Springfield in order to illustrate the needs of their constituents.

Even though many staffers believe that media content does represent public opinion, and that news reports are (along with interest groups) a crucial source of data in the policy-making process, they also see various biases in media coverage. They know that media are biased in particular ways, but despite these slants, they still rely heavily on constructions of reality brought to them through print and broadcast channels. The staffers were split on the issue of bias, with some claiming to detect ideological or partisan bias in media content and others preferring to speak about misinformation or ignorance of journalists covering legislative affairs. Three staffers did not believe bias to be a significant problem, though particular brands of journalistic antigovernment sentiment were mentioned by two informants. Let us first explore the minority claim of antigovernment media feeling then move to the more common claims about bias.

The notion that journalists who cover the assembly for Illinois media (including the St. Louis major daily newspaper, which covers the legislature for reasons of proximity) are cynical about government is interesting because it resonates with recent debates inside the field of journalism itself.[21] Leading journalists and journalism educators now recognize that the American press is inordinately skeptical about the possibilities for honest, constructive government. Only one staffer brought up cynicism in response to my specific questions about detectable media bias, but other staffers brought it up when they spoke about their interactions with reporters related to specific bills. One experienced staffer who has served on a particularly powerful committee denied any consistent or serious ideological bias in the media coverage of the legislature and instead spoke about cynicism. Unlike most of the other staffers I spoke with, this one had extensive interaction with journalists and did not rely on a communication director to serve as "go-between." After the staffer explained that media bias is probably not ideologically based, we had this exchange:

> STAFFER: It's more of a deal, in my opinion, where [journalists] are biased against anyone who is in state government, federal government, or any government. The assumption being that they're [government officials] doing something wrong; they're not working hard enough; it's all politically based. The presumption seems to be—right off the bat—that we're not on the "up and up."
>
> SH: [For journalists] there's no such thing as a public servant? The old model of public servant [who is] well-meaning?
>
> STAFFER: Some of these people [members] really are [public servants]. They come from a safe district. They don't ever have to play around [with] politics or their campaign is enough and they don't even have an opponent. They have the luxury of being just a good person. And yet everything [they do is viewed by journalists] through this lens of "Are you hiding something? Why are you doing this? Are you doing this for . . . money?"

Another staffer who also had significant experience with reporters said that journalists' initial instinct is cynicism: "Their first assumption is that somebody is trying to screw somebody, and they can't get over that."

One way the first staff member gets past journalistic cynicism about the various bills under consideration by the legislature is to develop friendships with the more influential reporters, using "off the record/on the record" switching techniques to persuade them of his own viewpoint on the issues. Another staffer will, for example, go out for drinks with a reporter (both putting on their metaphorical "hard hats") and talk about a particular bill. Yet at a certain point this staffer will say to a journalist (he used the name of one in particular to make his point) that he'd like to talk off the record, expressing himself more bluntly and more forcefully than he might when speaking in his official capacity. Legislative aides like this one may have techniques for circumventing cynicism, but most aides usually leave interaction with journalists up to communication directors (who are discussed at the end of this chapter).

Six of the staffers believed the press to have some fairly obvious ideological or partisan bias, and these slants in the news troubled them to differing degrees. As with most claims of ideological bias, the staffers who believed they could detect these tendencies at times pointed to reporters and at other times to publishers as sources of news slant. One staffer was particularly concerned with the biases of the Springfield *State Journal-Register*, since it is one of the newspapers that covers the capitol most extensively. Of the owner, this legislative aide said, "He's a proclaimed Republican . . . and he takes what appears to be his conservative, 'don't spend the money [attitude],' [and fears about government waste] into his editorials." While the staffers understand well the journalistic separation between editorial and news content, they at times pointed to the permeable nature of this boundary. In fact this particular staffer, in discussing the conservative nature of the *Register,* argued that in a mayoral campaign the news reporters for the paper simply ignored one of the candidates because of the partisan preferences of the publisher. More often though, claims of partisan bias were pinned on the news outlet more generally instead of directly on the publisher. The following section of one interview was quite revealing because it drew together staffers' concerns about partisan bias of journalists, their views of press cynicism, and their ideas about the comforts of established reporter/source relationships. Speaking about reporters' (and therefore the public's) understanding of budget matters, this legislative manager explained:

> If I say, "This year I'm going to allow welfare spending in Illinois to go up 3 percent"
> but the Governor may have asked for 5 percent, or someone else's program might
> have had 7 percent, suddenly I'm "cutting welfare spending." That's not true. I
> mean, what we are talking about is being able to deal with a rate of growth, not a re-

duction of service of any kind. . . . That's frustrating to me because that's not valid, and I see it all the time, all the time, all the time. And it's all perception based. I mean, you and I can argue. We can say that my trend shows that for the next four years welfare spending is going to go up 8 percent, but you have an equally decent model and it shows it's only going up 5 percent, and I'm saying you're cutting it 3 percent when you're not.

SH: [Referring back to staffer's comment about liberal press] Why do you think there is a liberal slant? Do journalists tend to be liberal?

STAFFER: That's a hard question and my gut feeling on that only is that I think that most journalists tend to be—I'm not going to say liberal—I think a lot of them are libertarians. They are very cynical, but on the whole, [when] I look at the media corps down here [in Springfield], they tend to be more comfortable with (1) people that they've known; and (2) people that tend to have a little more liberal slant to their politics. They try to be as unbiased as they can. . . . [I]f someone is going to tell me that they *can't* see a liberal bias to the stories that come out [in the press], then I'm going to wonder what they are really reading.

Beyond trying to influence the journalists' attitudes about a piece of legislation, and therefore their reporting on that bill, staffers try to put news articles in proper ideological context for themselves and for the members. Since all staffers have access to a clipping service they can compare articles from different newspapers and get a sense of whether partisan bias does or does not influence coverage. As one staff member put it, "You try to [sift information] because there is always your truth, my truth, and the true truth. I view the media that way too."

Troubling to many of the staffers, with seven of them actually calling it a form of media bias, is journalists' frequent simplification or even misunderstanding of issues before the legislature. Staffers recognize, as do members, that the press is looking for interesting leads and so may ignore much of the complexity of bills as a result. One staffer noted that on one piece of legislation, the reporter, "got the bill wrong. We amended that portion [discussed in the news article] out of the bill, and there it was. Absolutely 100 percent incorrect." With journalists, another staff member noted, a long conversation is often boiled down to a few points—many of which don't reflect the interview: "[T]hey take the words at face value and they don't necessarily look at the whole meaning of how everything was put together. So, sometimes I find that to be very frustrating because something I might say, or that a member might say, is just totally misrepresented." In an example from one staffer, Senator Pate Phillips (Senate president) gave reporters a ten-minute lecture on a complex piece of legislation but none of the reporters were taking notes. They asked, "Pate, give us a quote." He made a sarcastic one-line remark, about a leading figure in the controversy at hand, and that remark made all the papers: "They waited and waited and baited him into saying something off the cuff, and that was the story."

Those within academe and without, in Springfield and throughout the country, commonly observe that media distort and simplify. What is interesting to us, as we try to discern the "lay theories" or arguments staffers make about the public sphere, is that *many who see media as synonymous with public opinion also believe that media are biased.* Since they are so knowledgeable about state issues, these staffers believe they can "see through" media bias and still glean some useful data about public opinion. They are, in fact, reading the papers (among the media, newspapers cover the legislature most thoroughly) much the way nineteenth and early twentieth-century political leaders read the partisan papers of their eras—with great interest and great skepticism. Staffers are stuck, in a way: They rely on media and on interest group communication because polls are rare and not particularly useful in their eyes. And other indicators of the public sentiment, such as letters or calls from constituents or small demonstrations at the capitol, are also quite infrequent and difficult to interpret. When a citizen writes or sends a postcard to his legislator, it is rarely clear whether or not that person holds the expressed opinion with great intensity. What might the citizen do if the legislator does not act in the way this citizen would like him to act? Demonstrate? Vote against the member in the next election? The consequences of "going against one's mail" are hardly predictable, and with the ability of interest groups—on all sides of an issue—to instigate mass mailings, letters from constituents are far less useful than they were during previous periods in American politics.[22] In the end, then, many staffers believe that interest groups and media can communicate *intensity* of feeling about an issue quite well, despite the recognized problematics associated with both indicators. Both reporters and lobbyists can write, talk, and argue with a sort of focused and sustained attention one does not find in the citizenry. After all, attention to the legislature is what both journalists and lobbyists are paid for, and so their interest in doggedly pursuing issues is great. Interest group communication and media reports have multiple characteristics that make them excellent sources for information on public opinion: Their communications are perpetual, articulate, and readily available.

Making Arguments about the Public Sphere

Definitions that staffers—or nonacademics more generally—provide about the meaning of public opinion do not stand alone: They are connected to arguments that these individuals make about public affairs more generally. Granted, the staff informants in this study work in just one political environment—the state legislature. Yet the ways that their definitions of public opinion are connected to their broader perspectives of media and public policy making are provocative to students of politics. In this section, I describe some of the "lay theories" and arguments these men and women make about public affairs. I did ask informants directly about the generalized connections among media, public opinion, and policy, but this sort of questioning tends not to be as instructive as the more indirect approach: discerning their causal models by asking them to describe and analyze recent legislative events. By asking informants to tell me about a recent, important policy debate in their domains, I was able to understand how their definitions of public opinion and their narratives about politics fit together. I realized early on that the most effective way to probe staffers (and journalists, discussed in the next chapter) about their models of the public sphere was to work *with* the very textured nature of their professional experience instead of trying to force them to do significant abstraction from this experience. Asking about the meaning of particular terms like "public opinion" or "ideology" was somewhat unnatural to them, but it was still productive. It would certainly be possible to ask them to lay out components of the policy process (e.g., interest group input, pressures on the members, media, etc.), and to specify causal links among them, since informants in social science research tend to be willing and cooperative once they agree to participate in a study of this sort. But it would be difficult. Even the most sophisticated political workers and journalists tend not to think in such abstract ways about their experience. In fact, they tend to scoff good-naturedly at our scholarly tendency to generalize about political processes the way we do. As one staffer said,

> [Policy making is] an art; it's not a science. It should be a political art if you are going to work out here in the trenches where I work. With all due respect to the academic world . . . it's just not ever like it says in the [political science] textbook. . . . It's a messy business. . . . It's not really sexy. Federal government stuff—Congress does a lot of big neat stuff. You're debating whether to send troops in somewhere or debating these broad issues. [Yet] state government does 90 percent of the work—what affects people every day—and it's not pretty stuff. It's technical, and it deals with basically how your money is spent.

Perhaps legislative work is not easily described in systematic terms, but staffers' definitions of public opinion and their models of the policy process are quite consistent, as revealed in this small set of interviews.

Most staff members did define "public opinion" as media content and/or the expression of interest groups. How do these definitions become arguments about legislative work and the nature of the public sphere more generally? It is clear in analyzing these conversations that the "public" as conventionally defined (e.g., those common citizens expressing themselves through action, letters to lawmakers, and even responses to opinion polls), does not appear in staffers' theories about the way things work at the capitol and in politics more generally. Their mental models of political process are somewhat varied, since staffers differ in terms of their tenure at the legislature and the types of committees they work on. For example, those staffers who deal with education, health, and aging issues are more likely to have contact with ordinary citizens who visit the legislature or engage in demonstrations there. On the other hand, the staff who work on legal matters with the judiciary committees or with budgets and appropriations are less likely to have this sort of contact. I asked staffers to tell me about a recent, important initiative or debate they were involved in, trying to see if—in the spirit of building grounded theory (see appendix A)—I might connect their definitions of public opinion with their broader arguments about policy making. If one defines "public opinion" as media content or interest group sentiment, what are the causal connections between these phenomena and the actual design and implementation of policy?

The staffers were all sensitive to what they believed to be the public good, and their comments reflect a very real commitment to certain professional norms. Many of the staffers serve the public directly at times, keeping in close touch with citizen groups and taking trips to different parts of the state when the legislature is not in session. And staff believe they serve the public indirectly as well, by guiding the members who compose the committees in both the House and Senate. In most cases, staffers know more about the issues in question than the members, who are concerned with policy but always face enormous electoral pressure, which is in part manifested in constituent work. Members also need to put great energy into their (good or bad) relations with colleagues and with party leadership in the assembly. That staffers are normally the "experts" on legislation is useful, and this reflects the general trend toward increasing professionalization and indeed Weberian rationalization of state legislatures across the nation. This point is crucial: Since staff know the issues they can often conceptualize public pressure and public opinion in ways that matter greatly to the formulation of policy. In most cases staff write formalized assessments of bills with analyses of public opinion embedded in them. But much of their evaluation of public opinion is communicated in person to members throughout the course of debate about a policy. Their beliefs about what legislation can and cannot do—the constraints and possibilities of public opinion—are vital. Yet, the definitions of public opinion staffers provide and the mental models staffers hold are strangely dismissive of popular sentiment. This is not rooted in elitism, which I found very little trace of in all my interviews. Paying only lip service to conventional notions of public opinion (polls, letters from constituents, rallies of ordinary citizens, and even election returns), staffers are likely to leave public opinion out of their "theories" of public policy making altogether. The public for them is large and potentially powerful, but rather sleepy and inattentive. Staffers see that media content and interest groups are excellent crystallizers of a nebulous public opinion. The public is vague in its feelings and easily manipulated, staff members tend to believe, so it is most efficient to look to the sources of persuasion—interest groups and media—if one is to understand the nature of public opinion.

But let us look closely at some of the very simple causal reasoning patterns developed by staffers when they speak about particularly important recent policy initiatives. There were a few staff members who did not name media or interest group opinion in their definitions of public opinion, and interestingly these were the informants who produced the vaguest narratives of the policy process. This lack of clarity about the relationships among media, public opinion, and policy may simply be a function of the particular individuals in this small, purposive sample: Perhaps it is simply coincidence that those with the fuzziest notions of public opinion did not make particularly strong arguments about larger political processes. This is possible, but my interpretation of these few conversations leads me to believe that when staffers provide ill-formed or vague definitions of public opinion, they are revealing even *less* attentiveness to public opinion than staff who see public opinion as interest group opinion or media content. Take this one excerpt from a conversation with a very experienced staffer, who had defined public opinion early on as what he hears when he is "just sitting in a café or listening to people talk." He explained, "I find out a lot more about what they're worried about than I would if I polled them." When I questioned him about a particular policy debate, I asked him about public opinion—how his "coffeehouse" (or "discursive," in scholarly terminology) notion of public opinion helped him understand popular sentiment in the case of this legislative activity. But he could not elaborate, and instead agreed quickly that "people were aware and talking about it." Then he moved back to the specific policy issue and the ways his party leadership moved strategically to persuade the media of their partisan perspective. The same inability to articulate a simple causal model of the policy process—with regard to media coverage and the representation of public opinion—was evident in an interview with one other staffer who also had a vague notion of public opinion (e.g., what "the regular Joe off the street" thinks). Neither of these two staffers is unintelligent or inexperienced. Yet neither had given much thought to the connection between public opinion assessment and their work, even though they assess and talk about public opinion (employing varied terminology) constantly—particularly while the legislature is in session and bills are introduced and debated.

The majority of staffers were articulate on the subject of public opinion and its causal relationship to the two other components of interest in this study—media and policy making. With a small, purposive sample of professionals, one cannot map out causal models in the ways that political psychologists have recently done with citizen survey respondents: "Elite interviewing," as it is often called, resembles a conversation between equals more than the typical survey situation where the interviewer has a fairly rigid agenda and largely controls the course of the conversation. As a result, analysts of such conversations must tease causal models out of some rather nonlinear discussions. In the case of legislative interviews, then, my goal was to discern causal models within the stories staffers told me about important bills. I would begin by asking them to tell me about a recent and significant legislative matter they had worked on, and then I would probe them about how media, public opinion, and policy making (e.g., research, design, debate, and voting on legislation) were connected. The staffers sometimes offered up causal linkages very clearly, but at other times I had to probe about causality, asking about the ordering of components—media coverage, the expression of strong public sentiment, legislative maneuvering, etc. The simple, dominant causal chain discerned in the staffers' legislative narratives is difficult to represent graphically, but it most resembles figure 1.

In this model, "climate of opinion" is sociologist Robert Merton's terminology, here customized to describe the very general environment that gives life to a bill. I use this shorthand because staffers believe that the opinion processes that produce legislative action are complex and difficult to summarize: A bill might be the brainchild of a member, the result of long negotiation with industry officials, or the reaction to a short-lived but intense citizen outcry. And interest groups undoubtedly play a role in the establishment of the climate of opinion. Yet many staffers in this study were more concerned about interest

FIGURE 1   DOMINANT STAFFER MODEL

Legislative action ------▶ Public opinion ------▶ Further or "corrective"
(driven by climate   communication   legislative action
of opinion)   (interest group and/
                                          or media reaction)

group activity in *reaction* to bills; reactions that can be both interesting and worrisome since they can take even the most experienced staffers and members by surprise.

This model is perhaps most interesting in contrast to other possible lay theories staffers might have articulated, and for the elements omitted. For one, public opinion—even in the forms of interest group or media content—is in fact reactive. The public, narrowly defined for almost all staffers as interest groups and media, is "woken up" by legislative activity and is forced into action. If there is "grassroots" public participation in the process, as denoted by the conventional public opinion indicators of constituent mail, demonstrations, public hearings and the like, it comes *after* public opinion communication as denoted in this model. When interest groups feel as though conventional public opinion might be useful to put pressure on legislators, they "trigger the trip wires" as one particularly well-placed staffer put it, and members get scores or even hundreds of calls. The interest groups have an infrastructure in place to convey what they conceptualize as "old fashioned, grassroots" public opinion expression, if they feel this expression is necessary. In the case of several of the legislative matters described by staffers, the staffers said the initial legislative action was "sneaky" or included a "minor" provision that was "found out" by interest groups or by journalists—a discovery that set into motion public debate. In general, despite the fact that members and staffers have a sense of what the public will or will not accept, they are often surprised by the sorts of reactions even the most seemingly harmless bill can elicit. The model in figure 1 fits squarely with the dominant definition of public opinion one finds among the staffers and is in fact an argument about the mechanics of communication in the policy process and causal links among components. Missing then, are the conventional forms of public opinion expression scholars look for—constituent mail and telephone calls, opinion polls, election returns, and the like. This sort of model also has no place for major ground swells of public opinion that are possible in a democratic state. Members tend to preempt this by gaining and maintaining a thorough understanding of constituent needs and working with staffers on legislation before much of an ideal-typical grassroots campaign can emerge.

From the perspective of macro-level theorizing about public opinion we find *multiple* scholarly conceptions of public opinion embedded in the model. This is interesting, since students of public opinion tend to choose their own favored definition and assumptions about the phenomena and then organize empirical inquiry around that *singular* connotation of public opinion. Here, though, among political practitioners we see several conceptions of public opinion at work simultaneously, and hence we find more evidence that the notion of public opinion is an extraordinarily malleable sociolinguistic construction. Many different social indicators and many cultural artifacts seem to "count" as public opinion, but these cannot simply be dismissed as multiple measures of the same entity. We have both different *meanings* of public opinion and different *measures* of public opinion at once. There is, for example, Merton's notion of "climate of opinion" embedded in the model. He and others have argued that public opinion is not feeling directed at a particular policy at a particular time, but it is instead synonymous with political culture itself. These general feelings among citizens—norms, values, hopes for the future, and the like—are antecedent to initial legislative action in this model. Members and staffers believe they have a good sense of what citizens need and want in certain policy areas, so they always work within the constraints of that climate of opinion. Measuring such a nebulous phenomenon like the "climate of opinion" is, of course, extraordinarily difficult for researchers and nearly impossible for busy members and their staffs. Assessment of the climate is an incremental process, and all good politicians have some skills in this area—talking with all sorts of constituents, reading the media in their districts, attending events and meetings, consulting with other members, and the like. In the staffer model of opinion processes, we also have Bentley's and Blumer's models of public opinion as the opinions of groups—interests and lobbyists, in the case of the legislature. We have Lippmann's conception of public opinion as a phantom created by the media. That staffers can hold multiple—and very different—notions of what constitutes public opinion simultaneously indicates that the meaning of the vox populi is dynamic and fundamentally contingent or context-dependent. This cognitive flexibility about the nature of public opinion clears the way for rhetoric and argument: If public opinion can be many things, it can be strategically constructed and reconstructed to suit one's immediate purposes. For staffers, there is no *real* or concrete public opinion in districts across the state: The public is far too re-

Policy Experts Think about Public Opinion

FIGURE 2   TWO ALTERNATIVE STAFFER MODELS

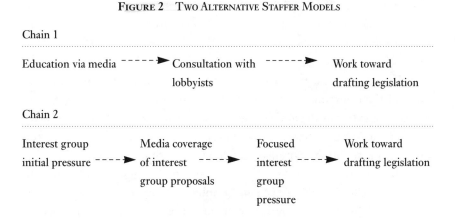

Chain 1

Education via media `----▶` Consultation with `-----▶` Work toward
lobbyists drafting legislation

Chain 2

Interest group   Media coverage   Focused   Work toward
initial pressure `---▶` of interest `---▶` interest `---▶` drafting legislation
group proposals   group
pressure

moved from the policy process and is most often stimulated by those two vital actors in the opinion communication equation—interest groups and media.

Although figure 1 depicts the model inherent in most staffer narratives of
recent legislative initiatives they knew well, there were other views that also
omitted more conventional public opinion indicators (constituent pressure,
polls, election results). Figure 2 lays out two such models. In the first causal
chain, which outlines the path one staffer indicated to describe the way public
opinion and media contribute to the policy process, media serve as inspiration.
This staffer, like so many others, defined media and lobbyist communications as
public opinion. In direct response to my question about the relationships among
public opinion, media content, and policy (which precedes which), he explained:

> Well, the only way we are fed ideas, for the most part, is through the [media]. If there's
> an article out there on [names an issue], after I read that, then I say, "Okay, there may be
> a problem in this area or that area." At that point in time, then, I will talk to maybe the
> lobbyist [expert in this policy area] and perhaps state agencies that might be
> involved. . . . Or a senator may do the very same thing [react to media articles]. . . .
> Then we begin the discussions. If there's an agreement that there is a problem,
> legislation is drafted. . . . And then we start the public discussions, committee hearings
> and things like that, with the lobbyist. And the media, at that point in time, is really in a
> pansy role, by their own choice, unless they want to pick up on it and run with it. . . . If
> [the media] truly do their job—and I think their job is to cover everything as much as
> they can—then they can have a definite influence. Of course, now it's up to the staff
> person and the legislators to pick up on this.

Interesting in this comment is how easily the staffer accepts the notion that journalists are responsible for surveillance of the environment. The media, as he notes in another part of the interview, display some partisan bias but are still one important source of inspiration on matters of policy. The second model included in figure 2 is also from a staffer who defines public opinion as media content and the communication of interest groups. In this chain of events, an interest group begins the initial surge toward legislative action, inspires media coverage, and stays on the scene until final passage (or defeat) of the bill. In this model, again, traditional notions of public opinion are absent.

What we have here are not fully fleshed-out models—the sort one might be able to discern through sustained ethnographic and interview work with staffers at the capitol. Instead, we have only fragments of such models, but enough fragments to begin to build theory about political thinking and action. Public opinion as conventionally defined in politics (e.g., polls, referenda results, election results, letters to officials, demonstrations, etc.) is absent in these models. This is not because the public does not matter to staffers, but because the definitions of public opinion as media content and/or interest group communication are so compelling to these policy managers. Are the connotations of public opinion among staff members "correct" with regard to our scholarly literature? This a matter of one's research paradigm; while a Blumer or Lippmann might believe these policymakers to be realistic and empirical, others might find staffers' meanings of public opinion difficult to swallow. In the end, if we are trying to understand how important actors in a system see that system, our normative judgment of their public opinion connotations may not be particularly relevant.

I have noted repeatedly that the staffers' definitions of public opinion are context dependent, although models across informants—who are involved in very different issue areas—do have many of the same components and omissions. The meaning of public opinion is often murky in the realm of complex policy matters and is contingent on so many factors—interest groups, media, activity levels among citizens, interest level among the members, staff expertise and advocacy, and of course, strategic value of the issue at hand. The contingent nature of definitions of public opinion was obvious throughout the interviews, but perhaps an excerpt from one conversation with a staffer will illustrate the relationship between contextual variables and informants' conceptualizations of public opinion. The case this staffer described involved a very sensitive issue in the area of health and human welfare that affects millions throughout the state. In this case, public opinion was very difficult to discern and the policy choices were not easily linked to partisan interests. That is, there was no official Democratic or Republican position that the party leadership conveyed to members and staff. There was mass confusion among members about this complicated but important issue and strong feeling among those in the electorate who were affected by the legislation. The legislation had passed rather quietly, but it was soon recognized as problematic by affected citizens (see the chain depicted in figure 1). In this case as in most, the staffers see their roles, in part, as communicating public opinion to the members. The members receive other communications as well, but they value highly staffers' notions of public opinion because they are specific to bills and therefore key to casting votes. On this particular issue, where public opinion was mixed, the staffer told members on her committee and members of the entire assembly that all she could do was describe the policy options:

> And a member would say, "Well, I can't believe we're doing this. Why are we doing this?" [referring to the provision already passed by the assembly]. And I would say, "Do you have five minutes so I can [explain it to you]? I really want you to understand because I can't tell you what to do [how to vote] on this. There is no Republican or majority stance on this: You're on your own.

This is an extreme case, where the staffer felt—given her expertise on the issue and concern for the members—public opinion was nearly impossible to assess. Interest groups with similar constituencies were split on the issue, and the media were not taking a position. Polls would have been entirely inappropriate because of the complex nature of the legislation, and this also probably accounts for the lack of mention in this staffer's comments of constituent mail and calls. In the end, as the staffer predicted, members were on their own without any sort of guidance from public opinion and simply used their best judgment. This staffer felt confident in the interview that public opinion should be defined as media content and lobbyists' communications, but in this particular case, neither were helpful.

Communication Directors: The Bridge to the Media

There are four communication directors or press secretaries (the two have slightly different responsibilities and staff sizes) who serve—with others at the capitol—as formal intermediaries between staffers and journalists. A few of the staffers I spoke with did have direct and sustained contact with leading journalists in the state, mostly because they served crucial, "high profile" committees that were dealing with issues of great media interest. Yet most staffers do rely on the communication directors to answer media queries about legislation. The communication directors are interesting to us because they are highly partisan—working closely with leadership and committee chairs—but are very sympathetic to journalists' and reporters' needs to tell balanced stories about legislative activity. Like most people in their positions, all three communication directors I spoke with had been journalists before they came to the assembly and so were entirely comfortable with reporters and with the demands journalists must juggle (particularly when the legislature is in session): deadlines, difficulty getting information from particular sources, conflicts with editors, and the like. When journalists have questions about particular legislative matters they often turn first to communication directors, who are likely to provide explanation (what the bill entails), interpretation (its underlying goals and relation to other policy areas), and of course, partisan spin. All communication directors answer to the party leadership. Since there are only four such communication directors, and I could interview only three (the fourth was too busy), we should treat these interviews simply as provocative in helping us contextualize the journalistic perspectives on the legislature and on public opinion—the subject of the next chapter.

As far as the meaning and evaluation of public opinion, communication directors do not consider interest groups or media as reliable conveyors of public opinion. There are several reasons why. For one, communication directors like to think that journalists are very malleable—that they can be "spun" by the opposing party leadership and communication director. If journalists can be manipulated, and indeed persuaded to accept the leadership's interpretation of public opinion, then those interpretations will not necessarily reflect citizens' attitudes. A second reason for communication directors' failure to equate the media with public opinion is their general distrust of reporters and their skeptical treatment of journalists' interpretations of the world. Communication directors see themselves as cynics, although with strong party affiliation, and they believe that journalists share a similar cynical sensibility. One director told me:

> [Journalists are] cynical, and it helps that I'm a former journalist, so I'm cynical too. . . . There've been many times where maybe I've said an off-color remark or talk in a bar, make a joke . . . like anybody does, and make some smart-aleck remark about my boss or something like that. You kind of help foster that cynicism together. If they reported that, I'd be fired, and they know that, and I know that. So it's kind of like, "OK, that's off record . . . ha, ha, ha."

Communication directors do not feel as though the cynicism about public affairs that they share with journalists is also shared by voters. So the notion that journalists can somehow "represent" voters and their sentiments does not make much sense to them. In direct contrast to committee staffers, one of the communication directors said that "[Public opinion is] what the average person on the street feels about an issue. Often, I think the term "public opinion" gets a bit misinterpreted to reflect what the media think or the captains of industry think." These communication directors generally note the nature of public opinion through multiple sources. They do pay very close attention to the press, despite their skepticism of the generalized journalistic approach to the legislature, they talk to members about perceived attitudes in their districts, they examine voting patterns, and they also look at the polls. They are savvy about survey research and point to the usual advantages and problems—high cost, question wording and the like. These informants use polls strategically, clipping poll results and articles that are "supportive to what we're [the party] is talking about."

The most interesting aspect of communications work in the legislature, and perhaps in politics more generally, is the nature of the relationship between communication directors and journalists. Press officers spend almost all of their time getting the party's message out and making sure that journalists understand their positions on various policy matters. Journalists need the communication directors so that they can discern the issues at stake and the intensity of feeling among leading members of the party. Reporters listen carefully to communication directors, trying to separate the "truth" from the "spin." Both parties—communication directors and journalists—understand that much of the communication that passes between them is false, but they must both put up with non-instrumental dialogue in order to do their respective jobs. One of the communication directors said that he engages in both direct and indirect forms of spinning:

> [Y]ou go down to [the pressroom] and kind of drop little tidbits. Say [to the journalists], "You might want to check this out. You might want to talk to so-and-so. Be on the lookout for this—it's coming today or tomorrow." That kind of thing. Or, if I'm going down there to directly spin them on something: "Senator [names a leading senator] said, 'ABC,' and that's a lie. The truth is 'XYZ.'" That's a direct spin, and they understand that, and oftentimes they'll need to get a[n opposition party] rebuttal anyway, so they'll use a spin [in their copy]. But it's a delicate process because you don't want to make the reporter feel like he or she is being used as a tool, but that's exactly what's going on . . . and I think they [reporters] know that. But you can't make 'em

feel like that. You have to be very sensitive to their level of professionalism and respectability—and vice versa. So it's kind of an interesting little waltz that you have to do.

Communication directors do, of course, have reporters that they reward with scoops, and they cultivate strategic relationships with journalists they believe they can depend on to give them positive coverage. As one communication director said, you establish close relations with a journalist you can "count on to see things as a story when you say [it's] a story." Communication directors have many conflicts with journalists also, and the directors tend to seek out reporters who they believe have covered the legislative maneuvering of their party unfairly. This is tricky business, of course, because communication directors are trying to scold the journalist and at the same time, avoid offending them. As one director put it, "you can kinda go down [to the press room] and say, 'Wait, come on, you screwed us on that thing. Come on man, what is that all about?' And you . . . have a good laugh about it, but [you communicate to the journalist that] 'Next time you better make sure that you cover it this way."

I used this small group of interviews with the communication directors simply to get a feel for the nature of journalistic work at the legislature, and it was extraordinarily helpful in focusing subsequent interviews with reporters. It is very useful, for example, to understand the kinds of persuasive pressure communication directors employ if we are to get a sense of how journalists navigate among all their sources, communication directors included. Communication directors also underscore, both directly and indirectly, many of the fundamental problems of journalistic work in the late twentieth century: cynicism, a tendency toward self-reflexivity, the low knowledge levels of media audiences, and the difficulties associated with understanding public opinion. From a practical standpoint, in deciding which journalists to interview, communication directors were also helpful. They emphasized the importance of the print journalists as opinion leaders among the press corps, so I made concerted efforts to speak with newspaper reporters. Print media are more important than other media in understanding journalistic coverage of the legislature for two reasons. First, newspaper articles tend to have a longer life span: They can be clipped and circulated by communication directors, by staffers, and by members themselves. One of the directors said, "I know that newspaper report is going to have a little more shelf life [than a broadcast report] even if it's just for that one day. That newspaper's there from 3:00 that morning until 3:00 the next morning, so that's a whole lot of time for somebody to pick it up and read it and clip it and use it [in a mailing]." The other reason why print media tend to be more important is that they cover the legislature more closely than do broadcast media—particularly in the large Illinois markets like Chicago and surrounding communities. About the differences in media, one communication director explained:

> You'll find that print media still is a bit tradition-bound in the capitol . . . where they have [one or two people to cover state government and cover politics in Springfield] . . . so they have more time to work on it [than broadcast media journalists]. Even the Springfield television stations, right now at least, have people assigned to cover the capitol but that may not be what they're doing full-time. So, I think that their [broadcast journalists'] time is much more limited. And before you ever get to the question [of whether to cover a story] . . . you need one that has some visuals to it to work for television.

And in connection with the state of television coverage of legislative events, another communication director noted that, while downstate television reporters do give some attention to activities of the state assembly, there is little coverage in the largest media market in the state: "The coverage from the Chicago TV markets is nothing short of pathetic. It really is a shame." Newspaper journalists do give the legislature far more extensive and analytical coverage, so print reporters are the focus of the next chapter.

On Defining Public Opinion

Scholars have their preferences for measuring public opinion, of course, depending on their theoretical conceptions of the term and the methodologies such conceptions dictate. Yet the legislative managers interviewed here have their own notions of what constitutes public opinion and how it might be discerned in the context of various policy scenarios. These definitions and theories are, perhaps, less complex and well articulated than we would like, but they are theories nonetheless: They specify variables and the causal relations among them. Here we see that staffers resist aggregation-oriented views of public opinion that surveys or even elections provide, since neither of these give the sorts of precise information about public opinion one needs when engaged in research and strategic planning on particular bills. This resistance to aggregation is not simply a rationalization because opinion polling is expensive: Even when legislative managers have poll data, they are skeptical of it.

Some may find the definitions and theories about public opinion held by people in key state policy positions somewhat disturbing. To think about interest groups and the content of mass media as synonymous with, or useful indicators of, public opinion does ignore the many issues of sampling and representation that scholars in political science have struggled with quite directly since midcentury. Recent scholarship on interest groups demonstrates that they are somewhat less worrisome than more popular conceptions of their role would have us believe, but this is certainly not evidence that lobbies are entirely representative of mass opinion. And such respresentativeness is rather difficult to measure, as we know, because the raison d'être of interest groups is to crystallize and communicate nebulous public moods. Mass media serve much the same role: Journalists conduct constant informal and formal surveillance of public moods, with an eye toward crystallizing issue debates, creating stories, educating us, and entertaining us. Unlike interest group communication, which is directed and strategic, news reports about policy issues and debates are written for readers and audiences, so the two sources (news and interest group communication) taken together are thought to be quite valuable for many of the staffers I interviewed. Strategic communication from interest group representatives results in the display of clear issue positions, and it does usually tend to clarify where constituencies within the mass public might fall. In some cases, it is easy for staffers and the members they advise to discern just how many citizens are represented by particular interest group communications, but in the case of most legislative initiatives, this quantitative work is nearly impossible to do. Much the same problem exists with media, but despite this problem and the biases staffers recognize in media content, news reports are still enormously valuable as public opinion artifacts. Journalists can create compelling narratives about a policy debate, weaving together quotes from members, from interest group representatives, and—most importantly—from "regular folks." These stories, which can be made even more vivid with the use of photography, have their own inherent persuasive power when the content is well constructed.

Regarding the use of media as artifact of public opinion, we should also keep in mind what technological theorists of mass communication tell us about the impact of media: Much of its power lies in the sheer fact that we know thousands of readers are reading the same material.[23] So whether staffers are themselves affected by content or not is important, but also vital are their perceptions that this content does affect the mass audience. This is sometimes called the "third person effect": Regardless of whether a staffer, a member, or an average reader of a newspaper finds an article or editorial persuasive, he or she may believe that thousands *are* in fact persuaded by that article. This belief ("I'm not persuaded,

Quotes

but I know everyone else will be") does affect behavior of individuals, as several researchers have demonstrated.[24]

It is always difficult to make direct connections between generalized political cognitions of policymakers (or in this case, policy managers) and their actual behavior in legislative strategizing and debate. This linkage is particularly problematic in the case of lay theories about the public sphere, which tend to be somewhat vague and highly contextualized. What was clear to me in my interviews with staffers, however, was that since public opinion for them is typically defined as media content or interest group communication, *uninformed* or passive citizen opinions are not part of their universe. This is not to say that staffers do not think of the common citizen and what he or she might feel about important policy issues debated in Springfield. In fact, several staffers went out of their way to mention particularly compelling citizen testimony at hearings or demonstrations. Yet most often, in their world, democracy runs quite smoothly without attention to surveys, direct constituent contact, or other forms of conventional public opinion measurement. In an interesting way, the legislative enclave studied here is very much—to borrow words from Robert Entman—a "democracy without citizens": Citizens are certainly the ultimate *object* of policy, but they are not conceptualized as anything but peripheral to the policy-making process.[25] Although we shall discuss empirical and normative implications of staffers', journalists', and partisan activists' lay theories in the concluding chapter, I should note that models of the public sphere that treat public opinion as interest group communication and/or media content might be viewed as highly problematic from the standpoint of democratic theory. The staffers conceptualize public opinion very much as Herbert Blumer did, believing (perhaps realistically) that the opinions most intensely articulated are the ones that matter. Blumer did not applaud this possibility and in fact was very much concerned with the oppressiveness of power inequities in mass societies. Unlike Blumer, though, the staffers do not struggle with this chronic moral and practical problem in representation: For these highly trained professionals, it is imperative to think about—and indeed "theorize" about—public opinion, media, and policy in the most instrumental ways possible. They have important work to do, particularly when the legislature is in session, and they must serve members and the public as best they can in the intensely complex and politicized world of the state capitol.[26]

Again, the narratives we have from these staffers are gathered from a small sample. As a group, the informants are key policy managers in a very large and important American state. Yet, since this is a small sample, we must treat the models and theories we find among these men and women with caution. The goal of this book is to build grounded theory about conceptions of public opinion. Theory testing may perhaps be done most effectively and systematically in a lab or through a survey, but building theory about the empirical world of policy and media demands immersion in that world and queries to the important people who populate it. In Springfield, as in Washington, however, there are multiple perspectives on the policy process. One important and heretofore unstudied group is the legislative press corps, a fascinating and diverse assemblage of reporters who are assigned to the state capitol by major regional newspapers or wire services. Their conceptions and theories of the public sphere are quite different from those of policy managers. In the end, the important correspondents' views of the policy process and significant legislation dictate the content of our daily newspapers, so their views matter very much. Journalists' conceptions of public opinion and their perspectives on the linkages among public sentiments, media, and policy are the subject of the next chapter.

3 Journalistic Views of Public Opinion

WHILE THE PRESS has always been a vital and dynamic force in American politics, we still have much to learn about the norms, practices, and socialization of journalists. There is a small and growing body of knowledge about the sorts of procedures reporters use in their attempts to construct meaningful narratives about the day's political events, and in this chapter I draw on some of these studies to put my own informants' comments in proper context.[1] Yet there is very little research on the ways that political journalists conceptualize and measure public opinion—particularly when they do not have access to polling or put much faith in polling (a common sentiment among newspeople). This chapter again focuses on the Illinois state assembly, a large and highly professionalized legislative body that has serious ideological fissures and politically sophisticated members, staffers, and lobbyists. A legislature provides a good environment for the study of journalistic notions about public opinion because popular sentiment is normally a topic of high and sustained interest there. Politicians, staffers, and journalists readily use phrases like "the public interest" and "the public good" because there is great sensitivity to the material needs and ideological biases of the citizenry, regardless of whether these needs and biases are heeded. Another advantage of studying legislative journalism is that the system is fairly small and bounded, so one can easily conduct a comprehensive study of journalistic culture and norms. In the case of the Illinois assembly, there are many actors and much change with each new session, but there is much stability as well. There is, in fact, a large core of members, staffers, press secretaries, journalists, and lobbyists who know each other well. I was told by many informants that Springfield is, like so many state capitols, a "company town," where most people are somehow connected with the opera-

89

tions of government. Staffers, lobbyists, and journalists frequent the same restaurants, send their children to school together, and run into each other at sporting events and other recreational venues.

There are no comprehensive studies of legislative journalism at the state level, but there are a few analyses of congressional reporting, and these works do illuminate some of the unique aspects of legislative reporting across levels of government. In one study of congressional journalism, Timothy E. Cook evaluates the ways journalists on Capitol Hill approach their work and the manner in which they interact with members and press secretaries.[2] There are several points of similarity between journalistic work at the level of Congress—as described by Cook—and reportage in Springfield. First, there is a mutual dependency of members and journalists. Members need journalists if they are to communicate their issue positions and their chosen "frames" for legislative initiatives. And journalists need members and staffers if they are to produce interesting coverage of the legislature. The journalists in this study noted that gaining access to members, and indeed to the leadership of the House and Senate, was easy: One can locate and accost members coming out of meetings and in their offices at the capitol to seek comments and reactions to bills. This is not to say that relations between members and journalists are always friendly, as many reporters conveyed stories of conflicts with assemblymen or senators over the way they covered an issue or campaign. But the symbiotic relationship between members and reporters described by Cook can also be found in Springfield. Staffers and communication directors on staff are also vital to this network, as staffers often have the technical information and ideological "spin" necessary for constructing a proper journalistic account of legislative activity. This interactivity among staff, communication directors, and journalists is crucial, in fact, for understanding how news about the legislature is made—the sorts of stories that receive coverage and the elements of particular bills that are emphasized. On occasion, public interest in legislative action takes journalists, policymakers, and staffers by surprise, but on the whole, these parties share similar ideas of which issues and policy debates might be important to the public at large.[3]

In addition to sharing similar relationships with lawmakers and staff, journalists at the state capitol and at Congress also share a similar *function*. The press corps in Springfield, as in Washington, is very useful to members in their bids for reelection. Members and communication directors cultivate journalists in order to receive coverage of their favored initiatives and their positions on issues. Press secretaries and communication directors at the state capitol carry out many of the same tasks outlined in Cook's study of congressional press officials, namely responding to all press inquires, seeking out reporters in order to provide them with the leadership and party "spin" on issues, designing press releases, organizing public meetings, and the like. As we shall see in this chapter, journalists are not quite *dependent* on the press secretaries because—with some effort—they can circumvent them if they need to. But on the whole journalists find these intermediaries useful and collegial. The press corps in Springfield, as on Capitol Hill, is also (to use Cook's language) quite "permeable": Members and others who need access to journalists find it easy to penetrate the corps, and those covering the legislature do not reflect the closed or elite mentality one finds in other pools of reporters.[4] Finally, in terms of similarities between the congressional press corps and the journalistic circle in Springfield, both sets of reporters have a very strong sense of professionalism and fairness toward the people and subjects they cover. They are sophisticated enough to know that objectivity—complete lack of bias in reporting—is impossible to attain, but they are careful to cover *what they believe* are all the relevant and important angles of a story. Most of the informants in this study spoke about the challenges of presenting news in an evenhanded fashion, and how critical it is to use sources across the ideological spectrum. Whether they are successful in collecting such diverse opinions and whether the news reflects their good intentions is another story, of course, for another study. What is important here is the journalists' mindset about their work, and how this conception of work fits with their theories about media effects, public opinion, and policy.[5]

Similarities between the congressional press corps and the culture of the reporter pool in Springfield abound, but so do contrasts, which are keyed to size differentials between the legislative bodies. Since the Washington corps is much larger, there is more stability, with many "old-timers." In Springfield there are a few men who have represented their newspapers, radio stations, or news services for more than a decade, but many of the reporters are quite young and new to legislative journalism. And while the Springfield press corps is quite competitive, the intensity of competition among its reporters is probably less notable than it is among Washington journalists. Finally, because national attention is focused on Congress, journalists covering this body are undoubtedly under greater pressure to cover public opinion more often and to use the larger number of polls one finds at the national level. Journalists working in Washington do share many of the same skeptical attitudes toward polling found among state reporters, but nonetheless, congressional reporters must contend with survey data far more often than reporters at the state legislature. In addition, the structure of the news industry creates a myriad of other differences between journalistic work in the two bodies. At the federal level, there is greater diversity among reporters and greater variance in the demands placed on them, depending on whether they work for an elite newspaper with large circulation or a smaller regional or even local paper. And television coverage of Congress is much greater than television coverage of state legislative activity, so the influence of broadcast media (the reporters and their coverage) is pervasive in Washington and quite small in Springfield.

In this chapter, and indeed in this book, I am not interested in the day-to-day routines of journalists, which are described quite extensively and vividly in the academic literature. Instead I focus on the conceptions and theories journalists hold about public opinion and its relationship to media and policy making. While I will hold comparisons across informant groups until the concluding chapter, it is important to point out that journalists at the state legislature know far less about policy than do staffers, and they therefore cannot reflect as well upon the effects media coverage can have on policy. Journalists know much more about policy making in the legislature than do academics or citizens, but staffers are better placed to understand the intricacies of policy development and the pressures members face from their varied constituencies. On the other hand, journalists have a type of extensive and particularized knowledge of public opinion that eludes most staffers. Just as members have reelection pressures that hover over them session after session, journalists have to please readers and viewers. The news business is highly competitive across the country, and Illinois is no different, so journalists must struggle to find ways to appeal to the public, to engage them in the content of the newspaper or broadcast news report. This is an especially difficult challenge when it comes to state political affairs, since the public knows and cares much less about these matters than they should. Staffers and journalists alike in this study were baffled by the low levels of public attention to crucial state issues, since they believe that legislative outcomes in Springfield—from education and crime to taxation and regulation—have a much greater effect on the lives of ordinary citizens than does congressional action.[6]

Despite their frustration in trying to interest the public in state affairs, journalists do their best to educate readers and viewers while also utilizing the well-known journalistic techniques to pique citizen interest—focusing on conflict, flashy legislative personalities, scandal, and the like. This desire to generate reader attention and sustain that attention demands a sophisticated knowledge of what the public cares about. The more experienced journalists believe that they have a very strong intuitive sense of how public interest in certain issue areas expands and contracts, but even the younger reporters in Springfield learn about the needs of readers fairly quickly from their colleagues, their editors, and their sources. Journalists' professional and financial interest in keeping subscribers and audiences makes them key informants about public opinion. Again, as in the previous and subsequent chapters, the question is not whether journalists' evaluations of the nature of public opinion rise to academic standards. Some scholars may believe that surveys are the most effective way to know public opinion, and others may prefer election statistics or other methods, but all researchers must realize that working professionals in the "trenches" of legislative activity do have a uniquely important view of the topic. Their perspectives are inherently interesting and provocative, but it is most crucial to appreciate that staff and journalistic notions of public opinion affect the way they do their work in designing legislation or reporting on it. Because policy development and passage is such a long and complex process, with involvement of so many individuals and institutions, we may never be able to map whether a particular article or news frame was responsible for the defeat or passage of legislation. Yet we can learn much about the cultural and cognitive forces that drive various actors to do what they do.

Before addressing the central topic of this chapter—the manner in which journalists "theorize" about public opinion—we need to put the state press corps members in proper institutional context. I did not engage in ethnographic work at the pressroom but instead relied on journalists' reflections about this milieu. Their reports matched each other very well, so I feel as though we can weave together an accurate report of journalistic culture—at least the way it is perceived by leading journalists.[7] So in the first part of this chapter I will describe the informants, their working conditions, and the various pressures they face while the legislature is in session. The remainder of the chapter is devoted to their views of public opinion.

Reporting on the Legislature

The press corps in Springfield is a professional group, most of whom had academic training in journalism or experience reporting in other venues before landing in the state capital. The two major Chicago newspapers, as well as the important news services and downstate media, have established bureaus at the capitol that operate when the legislature is in session and in recess. Before journalists formed the Illinois Legislative Correspondents Association in 1946—a professional organization of journalists for all media covering the legislature—reporters did not have much status at the capitol and in fact "wrote their copy, elbow to elbow, in anterooms and under stairs," according to one history.[8] Journalists held low status but improved their lot over the years by working with state officials to set up a modern pressroom. Today reporters have their own space in the statehouse building, which accommodates print and broadcast media.

Like the legislature itself, the press corps has become increasingly professionalized over time. As state governments become more important in the American policy-making process, coverage of bills and their implications becomes more prominent as well. One journalist I spoke with, while describing the culture of the press corps in Springfield, thought it best to contrast the dominant journalistic mentality with the *outgoing* culture, and this person's comments do highlight certain aspects of the contemporary scene quite well. This reporter argued that there were a few "pre-Watergate" journalists working at the capitol, but on the whole, the corps was very modern and professional in its outlook. Speaking about an older reporter, and the fact that he was like a lobbyist for his region, this journalist said:

> He [a journalist of the "pre-Watergate" generation] was very proud [of his "lobbying"] and it was the old way of doing things. . . . Although, of course, most of us would never think [to act as he did since] that's the antithesis of what we [journalists] should be. . . . He understood [the lawmakers] very well. And he had a knack for reporting what they said and did in a way that was not only accurate and cognizant of their agenda, but also presenting it the way *they* would, probably. . . .
>
> SH: He wouldn't try to analyze [lawmaker's agendas] too much?
>
> JOURNALIST: Right. Like, he's the kind of reporter who would never have gone up to [Senate majority leader] Pate Philip, heard Pate Philip call Chicago "a black hole," and then reported it. Because to [this older journalist], that's tangential. That is not interesting. What's interesting to him is how many road projects his district is going to get out of Pate Phillips, right?

These comments and others from journalists in state press corps are interesting on a variety of levels. First, there has been a distinct change—particularly since the 1970s—in the nature of the relationship between journalist and lawmaker. In the past, members relied on reporters to print or broadcast their views in an uncritical or at least respectful manner. However, journalists are no longer seen by lawmakers as public servants who communicate events at the capitol in a straightforward and largely nonanalytic style. This comment is very much like comments from other journalist informants, who see the events in Springfield from the vantage point of battling interests and will report on legislative activity in just that way. Personal or ad hominem attacks are now believed to be "news," and indeed journalists have been known to goad lawmakers into providing these sorts of racy quotes when they are not found naturally in the course of legislative activity.

My sample of informants was purposive in nature. While the twenty committee staffers I spoke with were chosen at random from the committee listings, I sought the more important journalists working for news organizations—those with either a wide audience or a prestigious place in the journalism hierarchy. All the premier newspapers that cover the Illinois legislature are represented by this group of twelve informants, and there are a few others as well who are influential in the newsroom but work for less prestigious news outlets (see chapter 1, table 2). There were a few news service reporters I was unable to interview because they were too busy, but from what I gathered from other journalists, many of the news service reporters have such large territories to cover that they do not necessarily concentrate on the legislature. In fact, one wire service correspondent I was able to interview told me that his "beat" covered most of the state, so he was constantly torn between covering politics and covering other stories. He said, "My primary purpose here is political, but . . . if there's a plane crash and everybody dies in Pontiac [Illinois], it's my turf and it'll be my story that goes national." The sample of journalists in this study is small—twelve in all—but so is the press corps. There are only forty-eight journalists portrayed in the *Illinois Blue Book*'s section on journalism at the legislature, and this number includes wire service reporters, television reporters who do only a few stories on the legislature each session (usually a "wrap up" at the end of session), and photographers. I am confident that this sample includes most of the influential and active journalists who were covering the capitol at the time of this research in 1996.

Day-to-day work covering the legislature varies, depending on whether or not the assembly is in session. When the legislature is out of session, journalists work on investigative reports or compile databases for later use (on prison records or campaign spending, for example), but their days are slow and a bit dull (one informant said summer is "almost a desperate time" in terms of finding material). During the session, on the other hand, journalists are extraordinarily busy going to hearings and talking with members, staff, party operatives, the governor's office, communication directors for the leadership, and press secretaries for state agencies. Many journalists depend somewhat on the Associated Press agenda for the day, which is available on-line early in the morning. This bulletin alerts journalists to the day's events in the legislature. The better, more experienced reporters do not need to check this AP "digest" and in fact take it as a point of pride *not* to depend on the digest or anyone else for guidance on how to spend their day. Most reporters do glance at it, though, just to make sure they are not missing any meetings or debates of importance.

A journalist's bread and butter at the state capitol or anywhere else in the world is, of course, his or her network of sources. The newer reporters in Springfield have less extensive networks than do the old-timers, who seem to know most of the important actors at the legislature. All the journalists have sustained contact with communication directors and press secretaries, who visit the pressroom often in hopes of "spinning" the news in their favor. And even though journalists have excellent access to members, they often seek out communication directors, who are a vital link with party leadership. Communication directors provide the coherent "party line" on legislation and so are a very efficient source of information for journalists working under the constraints of a tight deadline. As was mentioned in the last chapter, the party leadership asks staffers not to speak directly with reporters, but there is some communication between these two parties anyway. Because Springfield is a small town, in the sense that most people are connected to government, staffers and journalists often have personal relationships outside of the legislature and so feel comfortable talking about work despite the rule against these conversations. As one journalist explained to me, staffers are vital sources because they are the keepers of institutional memory at the capitol:

> We've had a tremendous turnover in the General Assembly in the last six years as well as just the turnover of power from Democrat to Republican as a result of the 1990 [remapping of districts]. And there's a very strong political role, too, that they [staffers] play. . . . [There is the fact that staffers] have more expertise on these substantive issues . . . than the legislators who are actually, you know, voting bills up or down. And one essential role of the committee staff is to make sure that nobody sticks their foot in it, and causes a vote or causes anything embarrassing that is going to show up in a campaign brochure against them. So there's definitely a strong political role [that staffers play]. I mean, they work for the legislative leaders and their role is to advance the leadership agenda.

One difficulty with staffers and communication directors as sources is that they must couch their appeals and arguments to journalists in the language of the public interest. Although it is obvious that the party leadership, on both sides of the aisle, have their own interests, they must make it clear that what they want is ultimately what citizens need. Journalists find lobbyists to be good complementary sources because lobbyists are not typically burdened by the language of the broad public interest. One journalist said that lobbyists are more useful than press secretaries because they make no "bones about the fact that they've been hired by somebody and that they have a particular point of view." The lobbyists, several journalists noted, often are engaged in high-level discussion with leadership so they have early information on upcoming bills and issue debates. One journalist said:

> Some [lobbyists] don't really like to deal with the media, but a lot of them do, and they're very useful. . . . If there's some major bill that's being discussed in back rooms someplace, the lobbyists are always the first ones to find out about the details. And in many cases . . . they'll either tell you what's going on, or at least you can get some sense from them of other people you can ask about it [the bill at hand]. . . . [Because of] the nature of their work, they spend a lot of time schmoozing with people. They're in constant communication with lawmakers and even if they don't necessarily want to talk about something they're working on, they hear things about what other people are working on. Sometimes they'll tell you about it.

His colleague concurs: "I find that a lot of times lobbyists are the best [sources] for telling you what's going on behind the scenes and filling you in." But lobbyists as sources must be handled with care, one journalist pointed out. They can be very "rabid" and dislike it when "[you] show even the slightest indication that you might not agree with them." So this reporter lets them speak, listens carefully, and "bites his lip" when they "start talking garbage." Journalists spend their time during the session navigating among their best sources—members, lobbyists, communication directors, staffers, agency officials, and each other—to weave together meaningful reports on legislative debates. The work is complex, but it is made easier by journalists' tendency to share information (as long as it is not too novel or valuable) and by the relatively closed environment at the capitol. As with covering most legislatures, there is no travel involved, so it is easy to locate key players, documents, and meetings.[9]

The culture of the Springfield press corps is both cordial and competitive, and most of the journalists stationed permanently at the legislature make efforts to be friendly to each other. There was, in my interviewing, the occasional disparaging remark made by one journalist about another, but on the whole the regular reporters speak of each other with a fair amount of respectfulness.

Journalists watch each other closely and tend to know when colleagues have a scoop or a lead (they will close their doors and generally avoid communication in the pressroom), so this always injects an element of mystery and anxiety into the environment. Some reporters are known for breaking stories, while others seem content just to make sure they have not missed any story that might be important to their editor and their readers. This reporter's comments about the relationships among journalists provides a good summary of what others told me about the balance between collegiality and competition:

> [When I worked in a large city-government pressroom] there were some reporters there who will go out of their way, trying all the sneaking around, making all their phone calls from pay phones down the hall, and going out of their way to play the cloak and dagger routine. And we don't do that as much here [in the state capitol pressroom]. . . . And there [are] maybe a half dozen [reporters] around here that I will openly share everything I've got with, and I can pretty much count on the other guys to do the same. . . . There are other reporters I wouldn't share with. I'm not going to give anything I've got to the [news organization I'm in direct competition with].

Before the recent professionalization of legislatures, journalism at state capitols was seen as a sort of "backwater"—a place for young reporters just beginning their careers or for those who were not particularly ambitious. Times have changed, however, and now the legislatures in the more populous states are interesting places to work. With more responsibility for social and economic issues falling to state government, journalists find reporting in this environment to be challenging and important. A few of the reporters I spoke to asked to be moved from large city news operations to Springfield and most were happy to spend the foreseeable future working at the capitol. All the news organizations represented by this sample of correspondents do experience personnel changes, so the composition of the press corps in Springfield will undoubtedly look somewhat different in three or four years. Young reporters are often moved around by editors who "try them out" in various locales. Yet there were several journalists in the sample who will most probably spend their entire careers in Springfield, since they have created extensive source networks, know their way around the capitol, and like the pace of this "company town."

Journalists and Polling at the Capitol

Even before the diffusion of the sample survey in the 1940s, American journalists had a great interest in polling. They recognized that counting public preferences might provide a "check" on their instincts about the nature of popular sentiment, so they enthusiastically conducted straw polls beginning in the mid-nineteenth century.[10] Journalism and opinion polling are so closely linked in contemporary political culture, in fact, that we rarely elaborate why such data are so useful to media professionals. On the most fundamental level, poll data represent a reality journalists try very diligently to describe: Public preferences are the backdrop against which policy debate occurs. So reporting poll data helps journalists "set the stage" in their narratives about particular political issues or controversies. But polling has always had other functions for journalists. Predicting election outcomes is a key goal of political reporting and there is no doubt that pre-election polling enables the most accurate types of forecasts. Another reason that journalism and opinion polling make such good bedfellows is that the reading (or viewing) public likes to read about itself. In the jargon of contemporary psychology, polling enables social comparison on a mass scale: Newspaper readers get to see themselves and their opinions in the poll data they read, and they can find out what their neighbors think as well. Journalists understand this process and so they seek ways to provide portraits of the public to the public. During election campaigns we see the largest number of polls in our mass media, but there is an abundance of issue polling and even lighthearted entertainment surveys in print and broadcast outlets between elections as well.[11]

Like the legislative staffers discussed in the previous chapter, journalists who work in Springfield covering the assembly are very wary of issue polling (pre-election polls are thought to be very useful, on the other hand). They struggle with polls at times, trying to figure out how they can make productive use of such figures. Their difficulties with survey research as a tool for knowing public opinion are familiar: Polling is too expensive to do very often, and even when poll data are available, journalists do not seem to find them rich or interesting enough to work stories around unless the poll was conducted or funded by their news outlet. Interestingly, despite their own acknowledged cynicism about the political process and their willingness to admit how uninformed citizens are about politics, reporters are careful not to speak in a patronizing fashion about their readers and/or audiences. We do not find, in this small sample of correspondents, much talk from journalists about the ignorance of readers and their inability to answer polling questions. Polls have a variety of problems, journalists point out, but these difficulties are keyed to the polling method or to misuse of polls by cynical politicians or interest groups and not to low levels of citizen knowledge. As one experienced journalist noted, "If we're going to write about polls, we're going to do our own story, based on our own research. . . . [I]f you don't have any control over what questions were asked, if you don't know how the questions were asked, the information is suspect or tainted and I don't like to get involved in it." The sense I got from journalists is that polls are a minor fragment of evidence about public opinion, but like any source on any issue, these data need to be viewed skeptically: Reporters feel they cannot take the data on face value but must question their origin and put them in context with ongoing legislative debate. Here one journalist discusses dubious lobbyists' polls on the gambling issue, which is continually debated as part of the state search for revenue:

> [The interest groups on both sides of the gambling issue] are both fibbing a little bit, but you can get some idea when you talk to them about where you think their support is. How strong they think their support is. I called . . . the lobbyist for the antigambling folks and said, "What do you think about this Chicago dock gambling business?" He'll say, "Oh well, we have this poll that shows us that umpteen percent of the American public thinks this is a rotten idea and there is no way they should do this." The other side will have their own polls. You can't rely on numbers like that from these lobbyists, obviously. But, you can get a general feel for things.

The problem with use of nonelection polls by journalists, excepting the rare poll conducted by the journalist's own news organization, is that it is too difficult and time-consuming to distinguish between well-executed and poorly executed surveys. Academics and professional survey researchers do not find it difficult to separate good polls from bad polls, but we are accustomed to the critical analysis of data in ways that journalists are not. Philip Meyer and other advocates of "precision journalism"—the use of social science methodology in reporting—hope that, with proper training, reporters might gain sophistication in handling poll data.[12] But journalism has not taken up his approach, as is evidenced by the press corps in Springfield. These journalists, in moving from job to job, have not acquired the skills to analyze survey data and it is unclear that such an investment of time would result in much benefit to them in reporting on the legislature or other environments.

Many journalists, including those covering the legislature, approach polling from a completely utilitarian standpoint, using them if they are available and might enhance a story. Pre-election polls are very valuable, of course, but the issue polls are less useful and less common. One journalist explained that issue polling is very general and gives journalists only the vaguest notions of public opinion: They can get much better information on popular views of legislation through other means, as we will see shortly. This reporter noted:

> I'm more interested in who's [which candidate's] leading the race than what people think of welfare reform and stuff. That's a terrible thing to say, but I kind of know everybody wants welfare reform. And I think I scan [issue poll data] to make sure that I'm not way off. . . . There are little surveys that, like our state representatives and senators send out, and I actually enjoy [them] very much, even if it's not scientific. . . . [Such polls can tell you for instance that] 90 percent of the people like this law to allow the neighborhood to know if there's a convicted sex offender in [that] neighborhood. It just gives you an idea that even in a nonscientific, self-selected poll, you have an overwhelming feeling for something.

This is a very interesting remark because it reveals an ambivalence I gather from many journalists: They understand, in a general way, why unscientific polls (those conducted without random sampling techniques) have response biases, but they find them useful anyway. From an epistemological standpoint, this ability to both accept and discount unscientific poll data is odd. But journalists are accustomed to the notion that all sources are flawed and it is up to them to discern the "grain of truth" in the various communications they received on a daily basis.

One of the most interesting remarks about polling came from one journalist who has covered the legislature for several years, a journalist whose news organization kept him extraordinarily busy, whether the assembly was in session or not. He had little patience with polls, "downplaying" them in stories when he did have survey data. Instead of making the familiar, simple argument that respondents in polls do not have enough information to give informed opinions, this reporter argued that there is an intervening variable—ideology. Poll data are corrupt because highly ideological citizens, or at least those with very strong opinions, are unable to process the facts about legislative issues that he puts into his stories: "It's just a sense that somehow people who actually get polled might be a little . . . too wrapped up in an issue and [the poll] might not reflect [good judgment]. . . . I don't want to use the word 'clueless' [to describe respondents], but . . . I try to keep in mind constantly that not everyone reads every damn work I write and that they might not know every single detail about every single issue." This is a rather complex way to look at polls, and an interesting one, because it underscores a point made by staffers and described in the previous chapter: One of the central difficulties with polling is the problem of intensity. This reporter is arguing that intensity of feeling and emotion makes citizens irrational. They fail to read his stories in the *way he had intended them to* and instead view the problem in an overly ideological and imbalanced manner. The fact that high emotions are often reflected in survey data is not particularly bothersome to social scientists, who believe that attitudes combine beliefs and emotion. The problem with this viewpoint, from the perspective of this very experienced journalist, however, is that emotion actually contaminates beliefs: Because emotion prevents thoughtful attention to media, it also prevents the formation of informed opinion.

Public Opinion as Conversation

Polls are of limited value for journalists covering this large state legislature. Even when they are available, journalists—much like staffers—find it difficult to use these simple statistics when reporting on fast moving, complex legislative activities. Instead of using polls to discern public opinion, they turn to the more traditional journalistic tools for assessing the public mood: talking with members and staffers, attending public hearings about legislation, talking with lobbyists and party operatives, discussing public affairs with friends and neighbors, and the like. In many ways, despite the diffusion of survey research over the past few decades, covering public opinion about state affairs parallels general reporting on public opinion in the earlier part of the twentieth century.[13] There have been major changes in communication technology that make the gathering and transmission of information much quicker, of course, with the AP wire about legislative events being a good example. And transformations in the structure and nature of partisanship have also had an impact on reporting, since party bosses (of a sort we no longer have) were an excellent source of local—even street-by-street—data on the public sentiment. Most evident from my interviews with journalists here were two meanings of public opinion, both very traditional from the perspective of journalistic history, although scholars have not focused on them in any elaborate way: public opinion as imagined by journalists themselves and public opinion as the content of interpersonal conversation. It is important to note, and I will explicate this point further below, that journalists are not simply thinking of their own opinions or conversations as *indicators* of public opinion. They are, in fact, arguing that public opinion is *synonymous* with these two entities, in much the same way that staffers believe the essence of public opinion to be group communications (interest group opinion) or media content.

Before analyzing each journalistic definition of public opinion, though, I must say a word about plurality of publics. While most of the journalists inter-viewed worked for one news organization, three were affiliated with news ser-vices that have many clients—newspapers and radio stations in particular. When journalists think of "the public" they do tend to refer to the audience for their writing, but in the case of wire service reporting this simple equivalence becomes difficult to support. Two of the three news service journalists did seem to make the usual connection between an entity called "the public" and their own audiences (heterogeneous though they may be). Yet one reporter insisted that while we can speak about an entity called "public opinion," there are mult-iple and overlapping publics. In fact, he unknowingly falls on one side of the scholarly, theoretical debate over how to discuss publics: Is it reasonable to speak of a mass public in this day and age of media diversity and the politics of iden-tity?[14] This debate rages in the literature, but journalists have quite practical concerns when it comes to the question of multiple publics. With regard to my queries about defining public opinion, this wire service reporter said:

> One of our clients is [an ethnic minority newspaper]. . . . There [are] times when I'm trying to figure, "How can I put a minority spin on this story, to try to appease them and get something they would be interested in." Or sometimes I'm writing for a station like [names a small radio station] . . . very rural, nothing really around there, yet I'm trying to keep in mind . . . what issues could be of interest [to their listeners]. . . . And [then there are] bigger stories that then go out on a wire nationally, coast to coast. For that fact, there are clients around the world. I've had stories that might turn up in papers in Hong Kong and I've got to try to find something they would be interested in too.

This is an interesting statement from the perspective of public opinion theory since the journalist so readily equates the public with the audience for media. A natural line of thought for a media professional, perhaps, but not for all: Political leaders tend to think of the public as voters, for example, or even citizens—whether they vote or not. The media-centric view of the public—as a group of geographically dispersed individuals brought together through their attention to a particular medium—is really quite sensible and efficient from the journalis-tic perspective. People get information about policy from media, and media pro-fessionals are sensors who can gauge public reaction and report this information on public reaction back to readers/viewers, lawmakers, interest group leaders, and the like. Despite this segmented view of his public as enclaves of readers of different newspapers, this journalist still believed in a larger mass society entity called "public opinion" that moves and acts in certain ways.

In answer to the simple question—what comes to mind when they hear the phrase "public opinion"—four of the informants in this group spoke about conversation. They listen to interpersonal dialogue—sometimes prompting it themselves, other times coming upon it unintentionally—in order to discern the nature of public opinion. Again, this use of citizens' conversation as data about public opinion should not be seen as simply a methodology. It is far more than that because it reveals an underlying argument about public opinion as an entity embedded within, and having meaning within, the strictures of face-to-face communication. Journalists have always talked to common citizens about politics and they probably always will, but through these conversations they are retrieving much more than snippets about the public sentiment: They believe they are getting a feel for opinion on an issue and frames people use to talk about that issue, and also a more general sense of what "riles people up" and why. Journalists in this study, and political reporters more generally, do pride themselves on having a cumulative knowledge about what moves public opinion and why. This knowledge is based on all sorts of data—election outcomes, polls, policy debates, letters to their news organizations, and other methods of discerning public opinion. However, it is still important, many journalists argue, to talk to people in order to get a larger framework for understanding the texture of public opinion and for predicting how it will play out in various policy debates. When asked how he gets a sense of public opinion one journalist said:

> A lot of it is just off-the-job, trying to pay attention to what people around me are saying, what they are thinking. Sometimes I feel the people [who live in] my apartment complex are my biggest sense of what the hell people—pardon my language—are thinking. That talk around the laundry room or whatnot. If I see a woman actually getting worked up over a story, a particular issue I've been covering, I keep that in mind. If I see that nobody has ever heard of a story that I'm putting [time into], . . . then it makes you wonder, "What am I wasting my time for?"

Another veteran Springfield reporter notes that, "in homespun colloquialism, public opinion is what the folks talk about down at the local grain elevator or the local coffee shop, and how they perceive what they think is really going on." Yet another long-time correspondent said that it is interpersonal dialogue that gives him a broad sense of public opinion and also serves as a corrective to the problematic opinion poll:

> A lot of times I just have to go with my gut, and I think I get a fair impression just from all the conversations I have with people close to and not so close to the [political]

process, about who thinks what is good. I really enjoy just talking to people about politics or other things and hearing their opinions. Because you pick up clues, and [evaluating public opinion is not] an exact science in any way—other than polling. I enjoy looking at polling data because it tells you some things. It gives you a framework from which to start. I think a lot of that ends up being inaccurate, so [getting a sense of public opinion involves] the combination of things you hear, studies you hear of, and just what people on the street are saying.

Here we see a very bold contrast between journalists and staffers. While legislative staffers undoubtedly have a large number of conversations with average citizens—those in their social networks and those they meet in their professional lives—staffers do not see these communications as public opinion. Journalists do, however, make mental notes about the opinions citizens express, the intensity with which they articulate their positions, and their perceptions of issue debates. The notion that interpersonal dialogue is the basis for opinion formation, and that conversation is in fact synonymous with public opinion, has a long pedigree in political theory. Perhaps this connection between interpersonal dialogue and the idea of a "public opinion" dates back to the eighteenth century, when French finance minister Jacques Necker is said to have coined the phrase "public opinion" to describe the elite discussions in the drawing rooms of the *ancien régime* (the *salons*). It is, in fact, instructive to briefly draw some parallels between the literature on public opinion as conversation and the remarks of journalists in this small study. [15]

Two of the most eloquent arguments in favor of defining public opinion as interpersonal dialogue come from European theorists writing before or just after the turn of the century. Ferdinand Tönnies, the German sociologist well known for his distinction between *gemeinschaft* and *gesellschaft*, organizational categories for analyzing social life, argued that there are three forms of public opinion that we can observe: discussions or debates; public behavior (e.g., rallies or demonstrations); and newspaper content. [16] This tripartite division is actually quite useful, since it underscores the fact that public opinion is manifest in interpersonal and mass communication. Yet the distinction among these three forms is very much based on a nonreactive or unobtrusive view of public opinion: For Tönnies, writing in the days before opinion research formally began, there was no thought of actively measuring public opinion. Instead, leaders must depend on conversation or social action *already in motion* for cues about political attitudes. This same sort of reliance—on public opinion that is manifest around the keen observer—was one focus of French sociologist Gabriel

Tarde, who in the 1890s wrote extensively about dialogue and its relation to opinion formation.[17] For Tarde, unlike Tönnies, the mass media (newspaper, in his day) serve as a springboard for interpersonal dialogue. It is in discussion about public affairs that people begin to develop considered opinions—opinions that are informed and thoughtful. After a while, if the issue is an important one, those opinions are picked up by the press and serve as the basis for action and policy. As Elihu Katz puts it, "Tarde implies that everybody talks politics," and so this model serves us more as a theoretical ideal type than a description of empirical reality in the nineteenth or twentieth centuries. However, Tarde recognizes the multiple roles that the press can play in both initiating conversation among citizens and serving as a "weathervane," sensing the shifting directions of public opinion.[18]

Tönnies and Tarde both help us understand the journalists' views about the usefulness of conversation, since our journalists treat the relationship between media and conversation in much the same way these early twentieth-century thinkers did. First, the journalists are quite aware of their ability to "get people talking," to provide the raw material for political discussion and also the frameworks for conversing about political issues. Second, journalists know it is their task (and perhaps even their civic responsibility) to listen and observe conversation and social action already in motion. Unlike Tönnies, they also see the importance of intentionally seeking out and measuring public opinion but, as noted above, polling (one premier method of active, strategic assessment) is not very useful to them in reporting on public feeling about legislative action. Finally, journalists understand—in ways that early theorists did—that public opinion does have a dual nature: It is about the opinion formation and expression process that occurs interpersonally, but it is also about the media that drive conversation, shape it, and report on it. Interestingly, at least one twentieth-century scholar takes the opposing view to that of Tarde and Tönnies, arguing that media (with their ideological biases) can actually shut conversation down or at least make it one-sided. Elisabeth Noelle-Neumann has attempted to prove that those who feel that they hold a minority opinion—after they read an ideological press—tend to avoid expressing that opinion in conversation.[19]

Why is it that conversation, as source for public opinion "data," is so functional for journalists? There are several reasons. In the perpetual search for measures of opinion intensity, conversation serves journalists well. Though conversation is not a rigorous measure of intensity in any social scientific way, reporters can get a sense of which issues or issue positions engage people most and why. It is through participating or simply listening to dialogue among citizens that correspondents working on legislative issues get a vivid sense of how citizens' interests clash, for instance. With polemical letters to the editor, citizen demonstrations (rare at state capitols, given the large number of bills debated), or other nonreciprocal communications, there is no manifest conflict. Conversation, however, has the potential for direct clash of argumentation, and journalists find this extraordinarily useful in trying to piece together narratives about policy debate. One journalist who mentioned his reliance on, and great interest in, talk radio was drawn to it because it helped him get a clearer picture of public opinion. I would argue that it is the conflictual nature of political talk radio (even if this conflict occurs when a highly ideological host squashes objections from callers) that makes it interesting for many political journalists covering different levels of government.

But beyond the usefulness of conversation in clarifying public opinion is its significance in connection with the notion of political lay theories. To think of public opinion as conversation is to make an argument about the popular sentiment and how one might go about measuring shifts in public moods. The argument assumes that, contrary to the views of Lippmann and other elite theorists, at least some citizens are engaged in policy debate and are able to express somewhat informed opinions. So average voters, in this lay theoretical construction, are endowed with a potential capacity for very real, participatory citizenship. Journalists who view public opinion in this discursive sense are also assuming that talk matters: Regardless of whether or not the citizens they hear conversing actually engage in the conventional forms of political action (e.g., voting, writing letters to public officials, demonstrating, etc.), their opinions are worth noting. Perhaps more than staffers, and even more than members of the legislature, journalists view rhetoric as a valuable commodity because they themselves see words as currency. Journalists have a distinct and long held belief that communication of messages and patterns of information exchange are at the heart of political life, so it is not surprising that conversation holds a place of honor in their repertoires for knowing and understanding public opinion. In a way, journalists concur with J. L. Austin, who argued that we perform social action through speech acts.[20] And this assumption or theory that words matter is also very much in the spirit of Habermas, who posits that talk helps to sustain the public sphere itself. For him, conversation and rhetoric compose the lifeblood of civic space, since it is only through communication that we can articulate our critiques of the institutions that surround us. The observation that journalists place great value on conversation as a way of knowing public opinion does not imply that this is the only way journalists assess the public mood or the majority of conversations they initiate or observe are productive. There are many instances where journalists are appalled at how little their readers know about policy issues that correspondents have so dutifully explained in print. Yet what is important here is the more general lay theory about the potential uses and value of conversation. Talk among citizens has a rich texture, which is quotable and sensible in the eyes of reporters, so it has clear instrumental uses in constructing news narrative.

It is important to note that journalists in this study did not systematically seek out specific persons or groups of people for conversation about current affairs. They seem always open to conversation and willing to initiate it themselves, but they did not name particular conversational partners who were regularly consulted. None of the reporters said that a certain group of workers who gathered everyday at the local diner or the group of parents who attended their child's evening soccer games were regular discussants. The journalists' conversations were far more haphazard, and their "informants" seem to appear and disappear as casual opinion givers instead of sources for sustained dialogue. It is likely that many journalists have such sources, but when asked about their conversations as indicators of public opinion, journalists described no bounded groups of citizen conversants. Sometimes the opinion givers were family members or friends, sometimes they were neighbors using the apartment laundry room, sometimes they were shoppers or coffee shop patrons. Often the public is composed of people journalists run across as they go about their own business, and if they are actively working on a story, they may work hard to get people talking. But what sort of a "construction" of the public is this? It is a view of the public as an aggregation, not of anonymous individuals, but of people embedded in their routines: These people can produce opinions in conversation but do so very much in the context of discussion and perhaps even deliberation, which occurs here and there. These journalists are conscious of citizens' routines but also of their experiences: how their opinions—as manifested in conversation—tend to be a reflection of their lives in progress. Listening to journalists reflect on interpersonal dialogue as component of public opinion reminded me very much of the views of Tarde and Tönnies, but also of remarks by Clyde Lyndon King, an early twentieth-century political scientist who defined public opinion this way in a 1916 lecture:

> Public opinion is not the mob howling in the street; it is not merely a people indignant; it is not a facile, shallow, popular impression of the moment; it is something more than a

preponderant opinion, or a general opinion or a public judgment; it is a mature, social judgment reached after experiences have been recounted, hopes and fears expressed and results weighed.[21]

Perhaps King envisioned a public that took a great deal of time to deliberate. Americans seem not to have that kind of time, however. So journalists are more likely to see public deliberation and assess public opinion itself "on the run," as it is discovered in the cycle of daily life. King's notion that public opinion might emerge from the mix of "experiences" as well as "hopes and fears" fits quite nicely with the highly contextualized nature of public opinion that these journalists attempted to articulate as they brooded over the meaning of public opinion in this study.

Publics, Real and Imagined

Four of the journalists in the group I interviewed argued quite clearly that understanding and "measuring" public opinion were at times largely a matter of imagined audiences: Good reporters have a keen sense of who their "average reader" is, and we might think of this reader as a composite of public values and interests. This fictional creature serves as an internal guide to busy reporters, who are in the business of appealing to readers and empathizing with their concerns. A few of the reporters had blended definitions of public opinion, which mentioned conversation (the discursive view of public opinion) and also equated public opinion to the ideological tendencies of the fictional reader. When they are constructing a story, some reporters like to think of a personal contact and direct their stories toward that particular representative of the public. A long-time journalist said, "When I do a story I kind of think of my mother who has no interest in politics." One of the more experienced journalists illustrates this notion—that public opinion for journalists is often related to the fictional construction of a citizen—by describing the techniques of a well-respected colleague. His comments are worth quoting at length because he also addresses other challenges facing the legislative correspondent:

> [T]here's a good colleague of mine who just retired and he'd been doing this [covering the state legislature] for forty-one years. And one thing he created are these fictional characters called Grace and Elmer. And every time he got caught up in the bureaucratic nonsense he always tried to remember that he's writing for Grace and Elmer. And I tend to think of my folks as Grace and Elmer, and trying to prioritize what I'm doing. . . . [W]hat is going on down here [in the state capital] and what do they care

about it? The issue of public opinion in covering the legislature, in covering government, is a real struggle, especially when you're—you know—hundreds of miles away from the [news] outlet that you're writing for. But it's a real struggle because these places tend to be company towns. And everybody is working for the government or working for a government vendor, or something of that nature. . . . [Y]ou have to remind yourself that there is a "mini-beltway" kind of thing, and you have to remind yourself that you're not writing for the beltway. [A]s far as quantitative assessment of what the public thinks, I try to keep those things in mind, but there's no way, really, that I can necessarily gauge [public opinion]. I mean, every day I'm just trying to come up with a story that I think is something that the people ought to know about, ought to be interested in, and ought to keep in mind: that this is what the legislature is doing *to* you and *for* you.

Here we are solidly in the territory of conventional American journalism. Editors have long encouraged their reporters to imagine an ideal reader and then write for that person as best they can.[22] This technique is, of course, very valuable, as it gives the correspondent—writing alone and trying to navigate among an enormous range of possible story frames—a "rule of thumb" when he or she is facing both a submission deadline and confusion about the appropriate tone and level of complexity. Listening to conversations, reading other media, attending public hearings, perusing poll data, and using other opinion evaluation techniques—taken together—enable journalists to create and maintain their image of the imagined audience. In a very interesting way, journalists are envisioning what reception theorists call the "ideal reader"—the reader who will appreciate and understand the text (in this case, news narrative).[23] However, the interviews reported on here demand that we try to reconceptualize this rule of thumb about imagining readers, going beyond its sheer efficiency for reporters, and thinking about it as a guideline for the evaluation (and persuasion) of public opinion. Journalists may think of one real or imaginary person (or a "composite") as they write, but as they do, reporters are highlighting particular kinds of information and omitting other sorts as they direct their reportage to this imagined audience. Stories are, in fact, *tailored* to audiences, so the nature of the audience imagined obviously dictates content of reporting.

The imagined reader as guide and "rule of thumb" is indeed efficient, and in theory, systematic as well: If journalists always keep the same portrait of the public in mind, they develop a consistency of approach that might serve them well in appealing to readers and sharpening their own techniques for covering stories. But can the journalist in actuality maintain a constant imagined reader in his or her head? It seems as though this task would be very challenging, since the public interest and political environment can vary so much during different issue debates. If a bill on property taxes is proposed, it might be fairly easy for journalists to imagine public response since issues of taxation are chronic and there is replication of past debates and expressed interests. But with other issues—those that tackle a new or unique social problem—imagining public response must be far more difficult. And unless the journalist can check his or her own imaginative construction of public opinion against some type of empirical evidence—qualitative or quantitative—speculating on public opinion about an unusual issue seems downright dangerous.

The conceptions of public opinion provided by journalists—that public opinion is embedded in conversation and that publics can be effectively "imagined"—are interesting and came naturally to informants in this study. We should not be naive about these statements (or those of our staffers in the previous chapter, for that matter), and we must realize that journalists often must do their jobs in highly conflictual settings under much pressure. Even if they want to report on public opinion using information and emotional content of conversations they have had, this may not always be possible. The more established journalists in this study, for example, often act quite independently, but all reporters must ultimately answer to editors and management. And it is possible that their statements about public opinion were made for my benefit somehow, though this seems unlikely. Journalists provided examples, spoke quite naturally and without hesitation, and seemed entirely uninterested in whether they were impressing me or not. None of the reporters spoke as though they were trying to "look good" in the interview: On the contrary, in comparison with their powerful sources (members of the legislature, the governor, important interest group leaders), speaking with an academic was more like a conversation with an unthreatening acquaintance. That their comments would be recorded and eventually published was of little interest to them, since the reporters were intent on speaking their minds and seemed to care very little about my cautious reactions to their statements.

Although staffers interviewed in the previous chapter did not speak about "ideal citizens" in answer to my questions about public opinion, it is possible that they hold such conceptions. Threaded through the interviews with staffers were their comments about typical citizens of various regions around the state. Yet journalists are more comfortable with, and more articulate about, imagined audiences because journalists and writers are so often encouraged to write with an imaginary conception of the public in mind. The imagined public, as discussed directly by the journalists and referred to more indirectly by staffers, is problematic from the standpoint of public opinion communication and democratic theory. But let us save these concerns until the concluding chapter of the book and instead explore journalists' own views of media bias—a chronic concern inside and outside of the reporting profession. The committee staffers saw incompetence in the press covering the legislature and also worried about ideological biases. We would expect that asking journalists about media bias would yield little beyond defensive statements about their own attempts at objectivity. Yet many of the journalists covering this state legislature were more candid than I expected about the challenges of neutrality, so let us briefly examine these views before trying to sort out their causal arguments about public opinion.

Media Bias and Legislative Reporting

In this study I chose not to analyze the content of specific stories produced by journalist informants, since I was more interested in their approaches to work and their general theories about reporting, public opinion, and policy making. Additionally, linking their reporting to their comments might reveal their identities, and I promised confidentiality and anonymity to all informants in this study. Querying journalists about media bias was rather productive, since it enabled informants to discuss and defend their specific approaches to legislative reporting. Journalists who report on the state assembly do face many of the same sorts of deadlines, financial constraints, and editorial pressures from above that other types of reporters face, and much literature on the sociology of journalism nicely describes reporting at the legislature.[24] Yet by asking specifically about media bias, and their perspectives on it, I was able to simultaneously learn about their approaches to work *and* get a better sense of how they see their audiences and how they view their position in the political process in relation to policymakers and the public. My initial question to them was quite simple: How do they think about media bias? In order to prevent informants from focusing simply on left/right partisan biases, I mentioned that some scholars argue for structural biases and others for ideological biases in the American media. And the broad nature of this question did enable us to get past—as the conversation progressed—simplistic notions of liberal or conservative "slant" in the news.

All of the journalists in this sample realize that neutrality or objectivity is a myth, and they argued that they try their best to be evenhanded, although they are not always successful. Some bias is inevitable, they believe, but they have their own techniques for checking themselves. One reporter noted that many of her sources for one story came from the Republican side of the House, and even though she did not know their counterparts on the other side of the aisle personally, she made a concerted effort to speak with them and get their viewpoints. This is typical: Balancing one's sources is the most straightforward way of avoiding overt partisan biases. Journalists understand well how the cultivation of particular sources makes for slanted news, and so balance among sources is usually the first thing they think about when trying to put together an even-handed narrative. When speaking about source balancing, one journalist said that avoiding obvious bias was a matter of pride among reporters in the tight-knit Springfield press corps:

> [W]ith most reporters I know it's really a point of personal pride not to let [your own partisan] bias enter into your reporting. And personal pride plays a big role because a lot of these people [journalists] are smart enough to make a lot more money doing something else. So I really feel like the professional standards drive a lot of people. They at least don't want to appear biased. But the biases you can't get around [are related to the fact that] you have sources in particular quarters. . . . I might have great sources among Republican staff members. And so when I get a story going it's natural that I'm going to start putting out calls to all the people I know who know something about it. And I don't adopt their bias, but I get the facts that they happen to know and their facts tend to support their point of view, right? So I think all reporters are biased by the people that they talk to even though they try really hard not to be. . . . So I think the best thing you can do, as a reporter, is try to be aware of that. Try to be aware. . . . .
> [Y]ou really have to over-report things a lot to try and overcome your perspective bias.

This is an interesting response because it acknowledges the efforts of reporters to balance sources and the notion that "facts" provided by sources are necessarily selective. One other reporter mentioned the low pay of journalists and the idea that enjoyment and pride in the profession keeps them in it. Worth underscoring is the notion that "over-reporting"—often going into great (and unnecessary) detail on legislative debate—keeps one honest. This is more likely a technique of younger, less experienced reporters than veterans with more confidence in their ability to be evenhanded.

So, journalists mention source balancing and are well aware of how the constraints they work under can lead to biases in the content of their stories. They would like to be more thorough, one reporter notes, but they rarely have time (during session) to research a story as much as they like. Journalists were most dismissive of their own partisan biases, stating that they find liberals and conservatives among the ranks in their own group. One journalist told me that one "top government official" informed him that he had looked up that reporter's voting record in primary elections and found he had been voting Democratic. He responded to that official: "[I]f that's the only way you can tell that I voted Democratic—by looking up my voting record—then I must be doing something right in my reporting."

One bias mentioned by a few staffers was a combination of an antiauthority attitude among journalists paired with a cynicism about the legislators. Suspicion about the motives and the activities of the powerful does have a long history in American journalism, even before the Progressive era. And deeply embedded in the culture of journalism, of course, is Watergate—often thought to be journalism's proudest moment: Many reporters look to the work of *Washington Post* investigative journalists as the premier example of what good reporters can and should be doing for the public.[25] Throughout my interviews most of the journalists displayed subtle or obvious tendencies toward skepticism and even cynicism as they discussed the legislative process.[26] When I asked one reporter about media bias, we had this exchange:

> JOURNALIST: I've not found most reporters to be overly liberal or conservative. . . . It's a bias against power. If somebody's in power you tend to be more inclined as a reporter, I think, to assume that these people are doing something wrong or are capable of doing something wrong. I don't think you give a lot of thought as to whether they're Democrats or Republicans. In fact, I've had the opportunity, since I've been here [covering the legislature] to see a shift in power [from the Democrats to the Republicans]. . . . I've not seen any change in the level of [journalistic] cynicism or suspicion [about] the leadership. The Republican leadership is kind of viewed in much the same way as the Democratic leadership was when they were in charge. I think the bias that exists is a general bias against authority and political figures.
>
> SH: . . . [A] lot of the committee staffers complained about this. They didn't quite call it antiauthority bias . . . this bias against the members particularly.
>
> JOURNALIST: Frankly, a lot of it is justified. Maybe that's my bias talking, but these guys. . . . A certain type of person gets into the business of politics and [they've] got some unsavory characteristics.

Generally speaking, legislative journalists in Illinois I spoke with worried about sticking with professional norms of ideological evenhandedness, but they admitted other more structural biases exist due to time and resource constraints. Journalists rarely, during session, have the luxury of reporting on a debate in all its complexity, but they do the best they can given the wealth of their news outlets. Some news organizations have multiple reporters covering the legislature and so are able to do a more thorough job than others that have only one journalist covering the assembly.

While I found mostly consensus among the journalists with regard to the biases they are accused of and the ones they believe to be truly problematic, I did stumble upon a rather direct disagreement between two reporters about their approaches. This conflict is worth mentioning, because it highlights the struggle among legislative journalists about "straight" reporting of assembly debates and more analytical reporting. One of the more experienced journalists was vehement about what makes good news and the pedagogical role of the reporter:

> I don't think an objective news article necessarily tells anybody anything. I mean, I think that part of our job is to show what's going on here [at the legislature], explain more deeply the motivations of why things go on here, and that way, the people can make up their own minds. But I think that also comes, too, with experience and some institutional knowledge, and some knowledge of the players involved, as to why things happen the way they do. But . . . I don't know that you can necessarily do that in writing an objective piece, because an objective story on a bill passing would be: "The legislature passed this bill today. Period. So-and-so said it was good. So-and-so said it was bad. The bill now moves to the Governor." That's the end of your story, and I don't think that [approach to reporting] really serves any purpose, [if the reporter doesn't delve] into the motivations of why people do things.

This journalist is not saying that he abandons evenhandedness norms or attempts to be fair in balancing of sources. He is emphasizing that background information and insights into strategic operations of key players in a policy debate are important, if we are to understand action in the legislature. Another journalist I spoke with argued directly against this reporter's approach, positing that the more analysis you do, the more potential for bias:

> I think that every journalist that I know—especially people who work in the statehouse I know—are very responsible journalists, and I think that they try really hard to keep out the bias. Now there are some reporters who [informant here asks for confidentiality and names the previously quoted journalist's news organization] . . . don't really write straight news stories, which just give the story and the sides of the story. [The other

news outlet's reporters] often try to analyze the issues, and they do this in almost every story. They try to analyze an issue, and so when you do that in a news story it comes across looking a little more biased than if you just gave the straight story. . . . [Informant notes this is a recent development]. They think that is what readers want now. . . . I think the [other news outlet's] stories are really sometimes more interesting to read, but sometimes they go to an extreme and maybe exaggerate a little [due in part to ideological bias].

I find this conflict instructive on a variety of levels. There is undoubtedly a note of competitive spirit in these two views, but there is also a fundamental difference in how they view their role as legislative liaison to the mass public. Even though staffers and journalists alike worry about the low levels of information among the general public about state policy, they have differing views on how to address this lack of knowledge. The first reporter thinks that he can engage the public in legislative matters by giving as much of the "inside story" as he can obtain. His colleague at the other news outlet understands that this approach is more engaging for the reader, but he seems to think it too risky from the perspective of journalists' professional norms of evenhandedness. This second reporter went on to give an example of how, through selective citation of background "facts," one could allow bias to enter into an account of a contemporary policy debate. It seems clear to the second journalist that more straightforward reporting without analysis is indeed truer to the prized doctrine of objectivity and therefore superior to the more textured approach of the first reporter. The second reporter seems to think that the *strategic* information about behind-the-scenes legislative activity is not particularly relevant to the mass public even if it is helpful to journalists trying to understand the policy debate in motion. This matter—whether and how to integrate analysis into news reporting—is, of course, hotly debated in the field of journalism. Some newspapers label stories as "News Analysis," but most observers know that this designation does not necessarily indicate an absence of analysis in stories without this label.

More troubling than this disagreement over the role of news analysis, however, is the rising cynicism in reporting discussed above. This is an aspect of American journalism that has received much comment in the scholarly literature and in more popular forums, and it is present to a great extent in the Springfield press corps. In the context of my concerns here—particularly, journalistic conceptions of public opinion—the antiauthority biases are very much in keeping with the definitions of public opinion reporters provided. Recall that two oft-mentioned definitions were (1) that public opinion was either the conversation one hears or initiates and/or (2) that public opinion is a projection of what an imaginary reader/citizen might think about a public problem. It seems that the first notion—public opinion as conversation—does cohere well with the antiauthority bias journalists are accused of and tend to admit to. Conversation with citizens who are somehow less jaded and less ideological than public officials does offer relief from the cynical, rough-and-tumble world of the state assembly. For journalists, citizens/readers are not without flaws but they have a sincerity and even a naïveté about politics that journalists can contrast with the attitudes of the self-interested politician, communication director, or staffer. And the second notion of public opinion mentioned by the journalists—that public opinion for them is what they believe the average or ideal reader might think—also fits well with the antiauthority bias. Again, the imaginary citizen is someone with integrity, someone they can feel good about in contrast to legislators, who are normally trying to subvert or circumvent the public good. In many ways, this imaginary reader—who is not particularly knowledgeable about public affairs but knows good policy from bad—keeps the journalist going: It is difficult to work in the cynical world of politics without both highly codified professional norms (evenhandedness and balance, for reporters) and an attractive vision of the democratic citizen.

Journalists' Causal Arguments

We saw in the previous chapter that public opinion in the sense of a scientific or unscientific aggregation of individual citizens' opinions was largely absent in staffers' models of the policy process. I asked the journalists in this study to think about a recent legislative debate they covered that they believed was of great salience, in order to discern their causal "models" about the relationships among legislative action, public opinion and media coverage. Extracting these models from my interviews with journalists was very difficult since, like many sophisticated informants, they have a lot of information to impart and tend not to relay this information in a linear fashion. I have tried to analyze the interviews with causality in mind, attempting to weave together their comments to produce a schematic journalistic argument. Several of the journalists were unable to speak at length about a recent policy debate they covered because they do more general reporting and cannot spend considerable time on any one issue. The journalists who do have this luxury, however, seem to recall recent legislative controversies in a similar manner. I did encourage journalists to speak about a legislative battle they viewed as significant—one that could potentially have moved or been motivated by public opinion. This is not difficult, of course, because legislative reporters seek these stories out and either ignore or give little press to minor, technical, or uncontroversial legislative debates. The issues brought up by journalists concerned taxation, funding for education in the state, or the controversy over a bill—introduced by a Republican legislator—to institute chain gangs for convicted felons in Illinois. Each of these issues was conceivably of great interest to the general public: The first two concerned their pocketbooks and their children, while the latter resonated with current worries about crime and punishment. The chain gang proposal, which was withdrawn after negative reaction from a variety of assemblymen, also had an interesting racial component: The legislators who were vocal in opposition to the proposal thought it an offensive reminder of southern racism of earlier decades.

The model outlined in figure 3 summarizes how legislative journalists tend to think about the coverage of activity in the statehouse. This chain of events or phenomena is, I must emphasize, a condensation of multiple informants' rather nonlinear narratives of recent controversies they had covered. As with the models presented in chapter 2, my attempt here is to build grounded theory about lay arguments. The causal chain in figure 3 begins with something journalists have often called (although not in this study) "news sense": their assumptions about what the public is interested in and wants to hear about. All good journalists have (or believe they have) a sense of what their readers need to understand about their legislature and particularly policy areas. One correspondent explained:

> I think good reporters have an innate feeling for what is interesting to people. What is interesting to me is probably interesting to other people, with only a few exceptions, probably. And I just know that when I go to parties and when I talk to my friends about things, and I mention some of the things I've reported lately, they always want to go off on [complain about] prisoners. They always want to go off on the Department of Corrections. So I think [to myself], "Yeah, you're reading that [public feeling] right."

FIGURE 3   JOURNALISTS' CAUSAL MODEL FOR LEGISLATIVE REPORTING

Development --▶ Legislative --▶ Discussion --▶ Initial reporting --▶ Editor or
of "news sense"   action   with sources   client
                                                                              reaction

                                                                         Public
                                                                         reaction

Journalistic news sense, gained through experience and contact with other reporters and one's own editors, determines what correspondents consider salient. They are drawn to more controversial legislative activity, they engage in ongoing discussion with colleagues, communication directors, interest group representatives, and lawmakers, and they then begin reporting. Their editors and their clients (in the case of wire service reporters) react to coverage in a variety of ways, wanting more, or less, or different coverage. Of most interest to us is public reaction and its place in this causal model. For journalists in this small group, public reaction was normally quite weak due to the variety of factors mentioned earlier—lack of interest or knowledge about public affairs generally, and about state politics in particular.

In the discussions of public opinion with journalists it became clear that rigorous exploration of public attitudes was lacking. We saw that issue polls play little role in their conceptions of public opinion, and that journalists tend to rely on conversation as indicator of public moods or on their image of what readers want to know ("news sense"). The public appears at the front end and the back end of this causal model: News sense is an ongoing "feel" for public opinion, and journalists (and their editors) do pay attention to reader reaction. Unfortunately, reader reaction is normally absent or weak. And while journalists are generally glad not to have complaints aimed at them from angry readers, they are also frustrated by what they perceive to be a very sleepy public. To illustrate this point, we can take one recent event in state politics that several journalists mentioned: allegations made during the 1996 Republican primary by senatorial candidate Al Salvi against opponent (and lieutenant governor) Bob Kustra and Governor Jim Edgar's administration. A few days before the election, Salvi accused the Edgar administration of having a secret plan to propose a tax increase for education right after the election. Edgar denied the allegation but then turned around and proposed just such a hike after the election. One journalist explained how the press corps felt about this incident and also expressed his frustration about the lack of public outrage. His narrative on this series of events is worth quoting at length, because it gives us some feel for the often contentious relations between the press and the press secretaries, the difficulty of engaging readers in political battles, and other matters:

> I was covering the [Republican] primary at the time and it was kind of a dilemma for us. It looked like a cheap shot [from Salvi]. Here we had forty-eight hours to go [until election day] and suddenly Salvi is unveiling this explosive allegation and not really having much to back it up, but claiming to. We ended up reporting [it]. Most people

did. The Edgar administration was furious, and then sure enough, two days after the election, [Edgar] unveiled a proposed tax increase. When you call a press guy [the governor's press secretary], who two days earlier had been calling you every name in the book, you [want to say], "You slimebag! How can you fall into this?"

He continued a bit later:

Maybe we didn't do a good enough job of reporting [investigating the allegation] ahead of time. I did notice quite a bit of restraint on our part and on other [journalists'] part because we assumed it was a cheap tactic on Salvi's part.

SH: What evidence did [Salvi] say he had?

JOURNALIST: People inside the [Edgar] administration leaking it to him or something, but he wouldn't elaborate and I think one of the television stations in Chicago had made a similar allegation right around the same time. But again, with no real proof. But, of course it turns out to be true. It really kind of made me wonder not just about our work [as journalists] but about the attention span of the public because it was almost as if, in that four-day space between the time [the allegations were made and the time the governor unveiled the proposal], the public had almost completely forgotten [the governor's initial denials]. The way the stories were written [by the press], we were almost compelled to remind them [readers] that, "Hey—this is the same proposal that they were denying they were going to [make] just a few days ago." Not much [public] reaction. I was really surprised by the lack of reaction.

SH: Now, during this four-day period, how did you assess public opinion? Or was it not really there to assess?

JOURNALIST: It wasn't really there to assess. Usually you can tell—you'll get letters to the editors. Or you can hear [public reaction] on the call-in talk shows on the radio. . . . The Democrats slammed [the administration] for their hypocrisy, but at the same time, they didn't slam them very hard because [the Democrats] were in favor of the tax increase. So, you have a kind of muting of the whole thing. I was a little disappointed in the public reaction. . . . We got a real lesson as to just how "out of touch" we are with the public, because unlike the public reaction, we [journalists] were astounded. Everybody was just dumbfounded by this thing. I remember being in the room when the press conference [occurred]. It was actually piped in from Chicago if I remember right. We were down the hall at the radio station [listening]. We kind of looked at each other like, "Oh my God. He's really proposing this."

In this anecdote, the public is described as sleepy and forgetful, even in the realm of important pocketbook issues.

The general causal model depicted in figure 3 fits well with the meanings of public opinion journalists provided in the interviews. The "public" in their definitions is mute and uninformed, and the same conceptualization appears in this model. The absence of a very active public in this model has a clear empirical basis since journalists—perhaps more than any other party—do have a good sense of what kinds of information levels about state politics and policy exist among the citizenry. And these levels are low. Journalists, despite their cynicism and low expectations for citizen participation in politics, are still often surprised at just how uninterested and uninformed their readers can be. So, reporters feel justified in ignoring the particulars of public opinion but are still confident about their news sense—their feel for what the imaginary reader wants and needs to know. Just as the legislative staffers in the previous chapter felt they kept the public interest and public opinion in mind by paying heed to interest groups and media content, journalists have their own techniques and rules of thumb that seem to make the development of a rigorous system for assessing public opinion unnecessary.

This parallel between staffers and journalists is very interesting, since the two groups of professionals are engaged in such very different sorts of work at the legislature. Staffers work hard to develop a textured knowledge of their policy areas, sometimes starting with no background in these fields at all. There were some exceptions—the judiciary staffers tended to be attorneys by training—but on the whole, part of becoming a skilled committee staff member is gaining expertise in agriculture, education, commerce, or other areas represented by the committee structure. Staffers work to gain expertise and at the same time work closely and privately with the leadership and committee members, helping them map out legislative strategy. Journalists, on the other hand, try to develop expertise when the legislature is out of session, but they mostly move from one issue to another as members introduce and debate a huge and diverse number of bills each session. And these journalists are often forced to cover the various state agencies and the governor's office as well, so they are generally spread thin in terms of their intellectual focus. Many political issues distract them from policy. For example, there are continual and heated battles between the mayor of Chicago and the governor, and these clashes tend to make the sort of news that journalists for the Chicago papers or the wire services must cover. And there are many other differences between work as a staffer and as a journalist. The staffers are, despite their interest in technical matters and public service, party operatives. Journalists, on the other hand, are constantly trying to remain evenhanded and nonpartisan, whether they are successful at it or not.

Yet despite these and other differences between what staffers do and what journalists do each day, they are both beholden to and oddly removed from public opinion. Both will use a mediating entity to judge public opinion *for them*, in lieu of investigating public attitudes themselves. This is not to say that journalists or staffers pay no attention to polls when they are available. And both parties attend numerous public hearings where they hear from interested citizens on a variety of policy matters. However, both staffers and journalists are content with letting interest groups, news outlets, random conversations, and imagined publics ("news sense") mediate between the mass of citizens and themselves. I am not arguing here that there is a true or best way to discern public opinion and that staffers and journalists are not taking advantage of polling or some other method that might let them ascertain public opinion correctly. Instead, I am positing that staffers' and journalists' arguments or "lay theories" about public opinion are very unlike our own scholarly frameworks for thinking about and measuring public opinion. We are likely, in academic research, to rely on polling data, voting patterns, or even (as of late) focus groups as indicators of the public mood on particular policy matters. Yet staffers and journalists find that their own indicators, which are clearly biased toward the more vocal and articulate constituencies among the public, serve them perfectly well.

These findings about journalists and the way they approach their work should be interpreted in light of general trends in news gathering. I focused my interviews specifically on the ways state correspondents think about public opinion, and I did not ask reporters to talk about issues of newspaper ownership or how changes in news corporations affected their work. Beyond deadlines, idiosyncratic pressures from editors, and the desire to appeal to readers, today's journalists also face pressure (direct and indirect) from the corporate executives and marketing directors who are highly influential in the news business. Whether these sorts of financial pressures have diminished the "news hole" devoted to reports on state politics and state legislatures is not clear, although this is certainly a researchable question. Regardless, we should keep in mind that journalists work under financial constraints that have produced—in the 1980s and 1990s—more entertaining and perhaps less informative news products. It is difficult to link such corporate marketing pressures to the work of individual journalists, but we need to understand the challenges working journalists face.[27]

Although I leave to the concluding chapter discussion of how lay theories of public opinion match up with democratic theory more generally, it is useful to point out that journalists' perspectives on legislative process both cohere with and depart from ideals of participatory democracy. On one hand, the notion that several journalists value conversation—conversation they incite, conversation they stumble upon, and the electronic conversation of talk radio—is rather inspiring. Many theorists interested in deliberative democracy emphasize how important it is for citizens to converse, and for highly placed political actors—journalists, policymakers, interest group leaders, and the like—to *recognize* that conversation.[28] And it is very clear why conversation matters so greatly: It is through dialogue that citizens educate themselves, try to persuade others, and move from the arena of private consideration of an issue to public consideration. When people act on their political beliefs, by participating in demonstrations, donating money to a cause, or even devoting sustained energy to a social movement, they are inspired to do so by interpersonal communication with others. In fact, even the smallest, most limited political action campaign begins with the excitement generated through dialogue. So, journalists are attuned to conversation for good reason, in their attempt to get a feel for what public opinion is on any particular issue and what it might become over the course of time.

On the other hand, however, the idealized reader that journalists write to—their internal manifestation of public opinion—does not fit as comfortably with normative, participatory democratic theory. When journalists believe they need not talk to citizens at length—preferring to use their own news sense to predict public interest or lack of interest in issues—they clash with democratic ideas in a very fundamental way. Citizens are thus creatures of the journalistic imagination instead of the very real and complex people who inhabit the state and read their newspapers. It is difficult to fault very busy, overworked, and underpaid legislative journalists for not covering public opinion in a more sustained and systematic way than they do. Reporters have very limited resources and limited time to spend on particular policy debates. Additionally, the public is badly informed about the particulars of both national and state public policy, as so many political scientists have pointed out. Yet this absence of the flesh and blood public in journalistic mental models of the political process should be disturbing to us as well, just as it is in the case of staffers. Public opinion may be constructed differently by different parties for different purposes. But these constructions matter very much, as they become embedded in journalistic or legislative work habits and work patterns. If one sees public opinion as the communication of interest groups, as media content, or as the hypothetical opinions of imagined readers, querying average citizens—by use of any technique or method—may seem less and less vital with the passage of time.

4 Conceptions of Public Opinion and Representation among Partisan Activists

WHILE LEGISLATIVE STAFFERS and journalists play critical roles in Congress and the state assemblies, there are other groups of knowledgeable individuals who are of great interest to us in the study of lay political theories. This chapter focuses on politics outside the confines of the legislature, exploring how political activists think about public opinion, representation, and the media. In previous chapters I focused on professionals who are paid to both understand public affairs and communicate their specialized perspectives to policymakers and citizens. But here we shift our gaze away from professionals and toward the unpaid political minions. How do these citizens, who are very knowledgeable about politics and devote much of their time to political activity, think about issues related to public opinion and democracy itself? This is an important question. First, this query enables us to elaborate the mindset of the partisan activist. We have studies of such citizens in the literature, but none explore the linkages of interest here, between political activity and views of public opinion processes. Second, we can use activists in this study as representatives of the most informed segment of the mass public—those ideal-typical citizens of democratic theory who really do pay attention.

In this chapter we shift away from experts but also away from Illinois and state government as a locus for research. This may feel abrupt, and it certainly would have been possible to maintain focus on the state legislature, interviewing citizen activists there, and even lobbyists, members, state agency heads and their communications staff, and staff connected directly to members rather than to committees. Yet I very much felt the need to expand the focus of this study by trying to get some views of public opinion from outside the fascinating but somewhat closed world of the legislature. The activists studied here are far from that world, and indeed they are the closest people in this book to the average citizen. They do not get paid for political work, and most of their time is spent on their careers, families, and communities. In the past I had interviewed a few non-activist citizens as exploratory groundwork for this study, and while that is an interesting exercise, I decided here to choose a happy medium between political professionals and average voters. Activists are more informed about politics than most citizens yet are part of the citizenry in so many compelling ways. They give us something we miss in the interviews with staff and journalists: a sense of what the political world looks like when you have little power to shape public opinion and you mainly watch the currents of popular sentiment swirl around you.

The activists queried here—via survey methods and depth interviews—are all deeply engaged in Democratic or Republican politics and committed to the party system. All participated in their party's conventions in 1996, and many had at one time or other held elective office, typically at the local level. The activists of this chapter are not as knowledgeable or as involved in politics—day to day—as the professionals studied in earlier chapters. Yet they are far more engaged in public affairs than the typical American, and it is this engagement that makes them ideal for the study of lay theories. In many ways, our partisan activists are the ideal citizens who appear in normative democratic theory: They are informed and active, and they sincerely believe in the efficacy of their work in the public sphere. Whether this belief in their effectiveness is well founded or not, the partisans of this study maintain an optimism about party politics that seems alternately naive and sophisticated to those of us outside their circle. And perhaps it is their generalized confidence in "the system" that shapes their views of public opinion, media, and representation. In this chapter we shall see that activists—unlike our political professionals at the legislature—believe public opinion to be the aggregation of individual opinions. Some are skeptical of polls but do articulate a "one person–one vote" perspective when asked about the nature of public opinion. Unlike legislative staffers and journalists, partisan activists worry very much about biases they detect in media and interest group communication and so believe these sources to be unreliable means for evaluating their fellow citizens' opinions. Yet in addition to having a cautious optimism about polling and its ability to assess the vox populi, the activists in this sample believe that public opinion also has an important interpersonal component: Polling is useful in detecting public opinion, but the conversation people make within their social network provides the real color and texture of the popular will. In many ways, the partisan activists hold meanings of public opinion de-

rived from classical, participatory theories of democracy. Our staffers and journalists, on the other hand, have strayed a bit from these models of participation
and representation.

In the previous chapters I focused on political professionals' views of the
connections among public opinion, media, and policy, but these sorts of links
are difficult for partisan activists to make since they are farther away from the actual policy process. Instead I focus on their views about public opinion and their
"theories" of representation. Because issues of representation were explored
through a survey, I have not been able to probe respondents in the manner of
depth interviews. But the lack of depth is perhaps compensated in part by the
larger sample, which has obvious benefits. One interesting finding about representation is that partisan activists note many cases where they believe public officials should ignore public opinion. In this chapter I explore the circumstances
under which these active and engaged citizens cede control of the policy agenda
to their leaders.[1]

What We Know about Party Activists

There is a long tradition of studying party activists in America, particularly with
respect to their ideological positions in relation to nonactivist citizens.[2] And
their belief systems are vital given that activists—as the rank and file loyalists of
a party—do influence both policymakers and their own less active friends,
neighbors, and family members. Party activists are the glue binding leaders and
the mass public: They form the organizational structure for mobilizing citizens,
raising funds, and performing other vital tasks related to party survival. It is loyalty among activists, often developed during their formative years within politicized families, that keeps the parties alive through failed presidential races and
troubled presidencies. Perhaps activists are most obvious during political campaigns, when our attention is captured by the horse races among candidates. But
even between state and national election campaigns party activists are working
away, raising money, persuading others to take up their cause, and trying to
shape their local communities according to their beliefs about government.
Party activists tend to be forward-looking, focusing always on the next battle instead of brooding over past defeats. This future orientation is critical if they are
to derive the full benefit of participation in the political realm, since much of the
spirit of activism is associated with *development* of the parties. This development
comes in several forms, including expansion of the party membership itself, resource management, and building the communication and organizational infra-

structure necessary for future election campaigns. Party activists are everywhere in America because the two-party system has been in place for so long. But there is one moment every four years when party activists are most prominent: during the two national nominating conventions. In this chapter I use these conventions as a source of activist respondents, capitalizing on these meetings as magnets that draw true believers in the Democratic and Republican parties.

There is a real confusion in the academic literature about where to place party activists: Are they "elites" in much the same way that office holders are? They are certainly very knowledgeable about politics and believe in their own efficacy. And many party activists have held local political office and have even served in state legislatures. As it turns out in this sample of party activists, there were no statistically significant attitudinal differences between those who had held political office (typically at the local level) and those who had not. So I am not plagued by difficulties associated with the alleged heterogeneous nature of delegates to party conventions. Here I am on solid ground, since it turns out that other researchers have also found that convention delegates—whether they have held office or not—are similar to each other in important ways.[3]

Much of the research on political "elites" focuses on whether or not their belief systems indicate more ideological "constraint" (in Philip Converse's words) than those of "nonelite citizens." Also of great concern has been whether or not citizens—elite and nonelite—understand ideological labels in the same way academics do: What does "conservative" or "liberal" mean to activists in comparison to the mass public? Some of the samples used to explore these varying degrees of constraint are office holders, and other samples are political activists or well-informed citizens who have not held office. Regardless, the debate centers on just how organization and consistency among political attitudes can vary with engagement in politics. Most of the research demonstrates that "elites" (and again, there is some variation in the definition of this term) are more ideological: There is greater consistency across their beliefs and greater stability over time. And in fact much of the recent work in this area reaffirms Robert Putnam's influential studies of attitude stability among Italian elites, which found them to hold beliefs quite consistently over time. Elites do change their attitudes, Putnam found, but these changes are genuine and are not evidence of instability of beliefs.[4] I should note that some analysts of survey data have taken exception to this general conclusion.[5] And Robert Lane finds much complexity and consistency of beliefs in his study of working-class men, which does not disprove hypotheses about elite/nonelite comparisons but does present some theoretical and methodological challenges to the literature.[6] In this chapter I am not interested in the nature of constraint in belief systems among individuals since this has been handled ably elsewhere in the literature.

But who are party delegates exactly and what are some of their general ideological tendencies? Political scientists began studying these groups in the days when conventions mattered a bit more than they do today. In previous eras, the national party conventions were imbued with tension and excitement because a "dark horse" could emerge and take the party by storm. But in the current period delegates arrive at the conventions already committed to candidates and so there is little chance of surprise. Presidential nominations are typically decided on the first ballot at both party conventions. Yet conventions and the delegates who compose them are still important phenomena. The conventions are crucial from a symbolic standpoint as they anoint the party candidate and signal to the larger public what each party believes the election is about. Parties attempt to demonstrate a degree of unity and a sincere excitement about their candidate and what he or she represents in order to prepare the mass public for the campaign. The conventions can set the ideological and semantic agenda for the fall presidential campaign, and it is important to try and transmit information to the mass public directly and forcefully.[7] Conventions are important as a signaling device—which can communicate ideological content as well as information about candidate personalities—and they also allow convention delegates to have a say in the construction of the party platforms. So the makeup of the delegations and the discourse that occurs before and during the campaign do have an effect on the official policy document produced at the convention. In 1996, for example, there was significant debate among Republican party convention delegates about the parts of the platform devoted to abortion. Dissension within the ranks of delegates and among leaders of the party resulted in a platform with an addendum on the subject.

Aside from signaling effects and party platforms, these large meetings have long provided social scientists with an efficient means of finding an excellent sample of highly involved and knowledgeable partisans. In the literature we have longitudinal studies of changing delegate composition as well as projects focused on particular conventions.[8] Much of the research on delegates in recent years has been conducted by Richard Herrera. He finds that delegates (whom he labels "political elites") do have a firm sense of what it is to be liberal or conservative, and that they view this ideological continuum as a valuable frame for understanding American politics. Regardless of academic debates about the usefulness of such a continuum or challenges to the continuum by minority parties in the United States, convention delegates are comfortable with this structure. In one study Herrera draws on surveys of delegates in the 1980s and argues that party delegates are ideological and drawn together for better or worse:

> The two parties in 1980 and 1988 look like what one might expect if traditional classifications were the key referent. In other words, we might always expect the Democrats to be more liberal than the Republicans. This is the case. In all the years examined, the two parties were at their respective ideological positions with the degree of difference between them becoming more pronounced from 1980 to 1988. The cohesiveness levels of the two party organizations are both similar and stable. Low levels of unity are common to both parties. . . . Though the forecast for elite-mass communication may be gloomy, there is reason for optimism. The cohesiveness of a party organization is, after all, only one factor affecting the ability of parties to communicate successfully with the mass electorate. It appears that some, more basic, political beliefs, such as general ideology, are communicated and shared. Indeed, there is evidence that party elites may be quite able carriers of political information.[9]

Regardless of their own cohesiveness, a party's delegates sense that they share more with fellow party members than with the opposing party, and that is enough to keep them on board. And it is vital to think about delegates as representatives of the party membership at large. Research has demonstrated that delegates to the national conventions are more extreme in their policy views than the rank and file members of the party spread throughout the country. Yet of great import is whether they *realize* this extremity and still try to act rationally to appeal to the entire electorate. Do delegates have a good sense of where their party membership is, ideologically, and do they realize that moderation will help their party win in the general election? A recent paper by Steven Greene demonstrates just that. He finds that 1992 convention delegates, when asked to evaluate the "ideological mood of the electorate," do fairly well. There are other biases and distortions in delegates' views, but they seem to (either consciously or unconsciously) realize that their own views are more extreme than those of most party members.[10]

Studying the 1996 Convention Delegates

Delegates to the 1996 convention were, as in previous years, highly engaged and active in their respective parties. Surveys of the delegates conducted by the *New*

York Times/CBS News polling group found them to be more extreme ideologically than all Democratic and Republican voters and also found them to be better educated and wealthier than party members not attending the conventions. And the ratio of men to women was higher at the conventions than it is in the party membership at large. It is on specific policy issues that one sees the large gap between delegates' positions and the positions of the mass public. A few examples are particularly glaring in this regard. On whether the "government should do more to regulate the environment and safety practices of businesses," for example, 37 percent of all GOP voters agreed with this statement, while only 4 percent of Republican party delegates agreed with the sentiment. On abortion, which was hotly debated before and during the Republican convention, only 11 percent of delegates agreed that "abortion should be permitted in all cases," while double that number of Republicans at large agreed with the statement. On the Democratic side, one also finds real differences between delegates and other party members. While 59 percent of Democratic voters agree with the statement, "Affirmative action programs should be continued," 81 percent of their party's delegates agreed. And while 66 percent of the Democratic voters at large believe that "organized prayer should be permitted in public schools," only 20 percent of their delegates take this position. Claims by convention organizers that delegates match party membership at large should be disregarded, since demographically and ideologically there are enormous differences between delegates and nondelegates. These differences did not stop Haley Barbour, Republican party chairman, from claiming that the 1996 convention in San Diego was a diverse gathering of "real people living real lives in the real world." Technically the statement is true, but his attempt to argue for representation of actual Republican voters rings false in light of the *Times* poll.[11] The ideological extremity of the activists was to be expected, given the pattern in previous campaigns' conventions. And the delegations' failure to represent the public in terms of income or education is also to be expected, given that party activists do have the time and money to devote to party activities at the local, state, and national levels. Also, as one delegate in my own study reminded me, delegates are fed at the conventions but they must cover their plane fare and take time off from their jobs. Yet as scholars have demonstrated, delegates and party leaders try to—despite their own beliefs—keep in mind the more moderate views of the general electorate and the kind of rhetoric and candidates that might be successful in the fall campaign.

For this study my collaborator Robert Eisinger and I obtained lists of convention delegates from both parties' state organizations and divided the delegate lists into five regions (Northeast, South, Midwest, Southwest, and West), then randomly selected states within each region. The total number of state delegations studied—from both parties—was 19. In the end, 528 delegates returned our questionnaire, giving us a response rate of approximately 28 percent for each party. This response rate is a bit lower than one might like, but in general the response rates for surveys of this type range from 28 percent to 56 percent.[12] Response rates would have undoubtedly been higher had our lists been more accurate (the state party lists were riddled with errors). Also, my informants in a companion depth interview study told me that they were bombarded with so many surveys and journalists' inquiries that they were exhausted by the attention and were turning down interviews constantly.[13]

The delegates in this sample were a diverse group, although they were still better educated and much more likely to be professionals than the average American citizen. The individuals in this sample ranged in age from eighteen to eighty-four, and most were in their forties and fifties. They represented twenty states (nineteen plus the Illinois delegation used in my depth interview study).[14] Most were of European descent, although 7 percent described themselves as African American and 3 percent claimed Hispanic origins. Men outnumbered women by a margin of 10 percent, and most delegates had completed their education with either a baccalaureate degree (31 percent) or a graduate or professional degree (43 percent). Forty-five percent of the delegates in the sample had at one time held public office, mostly at the local level and when, asked about their occupation, many respondents (29 percent) wrote that they held legal or legislative-type positions. The majority of respondents in the sample were Democrats (62 percent), reflecting the fact that the state delegations at the Democratic convention are much larger than the same delegations at the Republican meeting. Since the questionnaire contained several open-ended questions, it was clear how thoughtful and well educated the sample delegates are: They often wrote long reasoned arguments in response to questions, using sophisticated language and ideological terminology. These responses, in addition to what we know about delegates more generally, indicate that this is a good purposive sample of the politically engaged. The survey questionnaire was mailed to respondents shortly after the party nominating conventions. It was three pages long and was accompanied by a cover letter from the researchers asking for delegates' help with the study. In the letter, we promised respondents confidentiality and wrote, "Your answers to this survey will help us understand the role of convention delegates in American politics, and will enable us to share this knowledge with our students and colleagues." (The survey form can be found in appendix C.)

In addition to analyzing the survey responses from 528 Republican and Democratic delegates, I conducted depth interviews of ten members of the Illinois delegation—five Democrats and five Republicans randomly selected from their state's delegate list. These telephone interviews, which lasted on average about forty-five minutes, enabled me to probe more deeply activists' notions about public opinion and media. These were structured interviews with open-ended questions (see appendix B). I began the interviews by asking the informants how they got involved in politics and how they became convention delegates in 1996. I also asked about their occupation, educational background, media use, and other demographic characteristics in order to get them comfortable with the interview situation. I then asked them to define public opinion for me and tell me how, if they wanted to find out about public opinion, they might do so. I mentioned specific means for assessing public opinion (the same ones from the mail questionnaire) and also asked them about media biases. Among the informants were a retired social services worker, three self-employed businessmen, two housewives, two teachers, an insurance salesman, and a communications consultant. Most of these delegates were in their late forties to mid-fifties, although one was forty and another seventy-one. All were longtime political activists with a great commitment to local, nonpartisan public affairs as well as partisan politics. Some had attended previous conventions. These men (six) and women (four) had all "paid their dues" to their respective parties and so were chosen as delegates as a reward for great loyalty to their parties. I found all of the informants to be thoughtful and knowledgeable about politics, although their sophistication about the political process varied somewhat. One of the informants was running for high public office at the time of the interview, so he was very concerned about electoral trends, the mood of voters in his area, the nature of political advertising, and the like. On the other end of the sophistication continuum, there were informants who were quite knowledgeable about public affairs but not as focused on the political process and voter behavior. These interviews did help to illuminate some of the findings of the mail questionnaire and also gave me a better sense of what sorts of political activists become convention delegates.

Activists Think about Public Opinion

There were no significant differences between Democratic delegates and Republican delegates on questions of public opinion. And whether or not these activists had ever held elective office did not affect their answers to questions about public opinion, media, or representation in any statistically significant way. In general, these activists are of two minds about public opinion, believing that the aggregation of individual opinions (via surveys) *and* interpersonal dialogue within their social networks are both vital to understanding popular sentiments. When the survey respondents were asked in an initial open-ended question how they would "find out about public opinion on a certain issue," they tended to name three methods: looking at poll data, looking to the media, and talking to those around them (in the workplace or community). Many of the "look to the media" answers may mean "look to media polls," but this could not be determined from many of the mentions of mass media. Some respondents did mention the Internet as source for public opinion, a place where one finds poll data (during election season) and also many news group discussions and other such forums. In table 3, we see that nearly 35 percent of the surveyed activists mentioned polling as a way they would use to find out about public opinion on a certain issue, while 36 percent said they would turn to some form of media for such information. A large number (24 percent) noted that they would talk to people around them if they wanted to discern popular opinion on a political issue of interest to them.

While the media fare well as a source for public opinion in this open-ended question, subsequent forced-choice questions about the usefulness of individual methods make it clear that these activists prefer polling (aggregation of indi-

Table 3 Activists' Methods for Discerning Public Opinion (Open-Ended Question)

Method	Percentage of Activists Naming Method
Consulting mass media sources	36.2
Looking to polls	34.5
Talking and listening to people	23.5
Observing actions of state or federal agencies	1.2
Other	2.0
Don't know/no response	6.6

Note: The above data show responses to the following question: "If you wanted to find out about public opinion on a certain issue, how would you do so?" The numbers add up to more than 100 percent because some respondents listed more than one method.
$N = 528$

vidual opinion) and interpersonal dialogue within social networks to all other methods. Sixty-one percent of respondents either strongly agreed or agreed that "polls are an accurate indicator of public opinion." Sixty-seven percent believe that "what people say in the workplace" is an accurate indicator of public opinion and 58 percent count on conversations with friends in order to assess public opinion with some certainty. Other methods we asked about did not fare as well—none of the following indicators (listed in order of perceived accuracy) were viewed as accurate by more than 27 percent of respondents: newspaper articles, television news, statements by public officials, radio talk shows, and interest groups. The specific percentages are shown in table 4.

The figures in tables 3 and 4 are most interesting because they contrast greatly with the perspectives of staffers and journalists described in previous chapters. Staffers and reporters who covered the legislature are quite wary of polls, while these activists tend to believe in aggregative means of knowing public opinion. The activists share journalists' interest in interpersonal dialogue as a means of understanding public opinion, but activists are unlikely to mention the two means of opinion assessment closest to staffers' hearts: interest group communications and media (news and editorial) content. I will take up this contrast among the three groups—legislative staffers, journalists, and citizen activists—in the next chapter, but it is important to underscore the differences here. Activists seem to ascribe to the basic philosophy underlying survey research (one person, one vote), while our more sophisticated political professionals are more

Table 4 Activists' Preferred Indicators of Public Opinion (Closed-Ended Question)

Indicator	Percentage of Activists Deeming Indicator Accurate
Discussions in the workplace	66.5
Polls	60.7
Conversations with friends	58.4
Newspaper articles	27.1
Television news	26.2
Statements by public officials	23.9
Radio talk shows	22.1
Interest groups	15.9

Note: The above data show responses to the following question: "Please indicate whether you agree or disagree with the following statements: Television news [interest groups, polls, radio talk shows, etc.] is an accurate indicator of public opinion." Respondent choices for each item were "strongly agree," "agree," "disagree," "strongly disagree," and "don't know." The figures above indicate the percentage of respondents who responded "strongly agree" or "agree" to each item.

$N = 528$

likely to rely on other professionals or themselves (in the case of journalists' imaginative constructions of public sentiment) as indicators of public opinion.

In answer to our open-ended query about the way they personally would search out public opinion on an issue of interest to them, respondents often simply wrote "polls" or "surveys." Many wrote a bit more, like the Florida Democrat who said he would "obviously" use "a telephone or personal interview [with] properly structured questions." A female delegate from Alabama said, "If it was a political or popularly discussed issue, I would probably rely on CNN, C-Span, *USA Today* and their polling." And yet another delegate from Connecticut chose two methods, writing that she would "survey a defined population, or conduct a focus group." The depth interviews I conducted with the small group of ten activists turned up some very positive views of polling as well, although when probed at length about polls, they expressed a bit more skepticism about them than was indicated in the survey. One Republican activist who had been a journalist for a short time before establishing his own business said this about discerning public opinion:

> I guess the best way is to survey a particular group, depending . . . on what the project is. . . . If you were doing something on the stock market, I would certainly try to zero in on a group that was in a high income bracket, that bought and sold stocks. If I was just looking normally for a voter input, we would take a certain group and poll them to see what their reaction was to a certain statement made by a candidate. [We could] give the person that candidate's statement and say, "Hey, how do you think that statement deals with your lives?"

Upon closer questioning this respondent noted that people are not always honest with pollsters and that question wording is often a problem. I asked him how he knows when to believe polls, given these difficulties. In response he said:

> It's a real tough thing, when to believe polls. I think people have a tendency not to want to tell you exactly what they're thinking in regard to who they're going to vote for, for instance. I know that some polls have shown to be very inaccurate in some election campaigns where people say, "Hey, this is such a large majority," and then suddenly [at the election] you find out that the majority is not that large and the election is very close. . . . [B]ut I think polls are really the best way you have [of measuring public opinion].

Some of these activists had direct experience with opinion measurement and reflected on the value of polls. A Democratic delegate spoke of the superiority of polls over focus groups:

I'm not real happy with what I consider the overuse of focus groups. It seems to me that it's a cheap way for outfits to do it, and there are a lot of variables that enter into the use of focus groups, so that kind of makes me nervous. And I've seen some personal examples of how [focus group data are] a little misleading. . . . Some years ago, we had a focus group [that] our national organization ran here in Chicago for opinions on education and how the union was serving [it]. It came out very negative, and I think there were twelve or fourteen or fifteen or whatever the number was. . . . [They] got thirty bucks or whatever the amount was, and then they [gave] their opinions. Well, you have a selection process [bias] right there as you can see. . . . [We then] took a survey of the membership, and it was absolutely by a professional polling outfit, and it [the resulting attitudes toward education and unions] came out absolutely the opposite, and overwhelmingly so. . . . I think polls, when they're removed from the immediate vicinity of events like conventions . . . [are generally] the indicators that you have to pay attention to. But sometimes I think that those who serve the public spend a lot of time jumping around on issues to please some kind of electronic pollsters, and I don't think that's good.

Finally, one longtime Democratic activist said that polls are an accurate means for measuring public opinion and at the same time serve participatory democracy: Polled individuals "feel that they have some input, and that's a good feeling for them."

Not all the depth interview participants were positive about polling. Two informants mentioned a belief that poll respondents lie, and two others were bothered not by inaccuracy of polls but by their transitory nature. As his evidence of how people lie to pollsters, one informant said that people in his community have admitted to giving false statements in interviews just to have a good time. It is odd that some informants believe such lying is common, since motivating factors for this are unclear (and not very well articulated by either informant). The criticism that polls only measure a "snapshot" of public opinion was articulated quite eloquently by two informants. One of the Republican activists said:

I think [polls] sometimes do a disservice to the general public, particularly political events, because . . . polls are just a snapshot of a moment. But my goodness, if you listen to polls and listen to people who take the polls, whether you're on one side or the other [you can find a poll that leans in your favor] . . . and [you can use that as "gospel"]. Then the general public sits in the center and says, "What the hell's going on?" [with all these confusing and contradictory polls].

In answer to the question about how often public officials read poll data in order to gauge public opinion, an overwhelming 98 percent of the respondents answered either "often" (71 percent) or "sometimes" (27 percent). The sense I get from the answers to the open-ended questions, the forced-choice responses, and the depth interviews is that activists are attracted to the egalitarian and democratic nature of polling (one person–one vote) but are not entirely happy with the authoritative way surveys are used by politicians and journalists in public discourse. An interesting finding in this study is that many activists believe—despite a solid understanding of representative sampling—that public opinion can also be discerned through interpersonal dialogue with those around them. Polling numbers may provide some evidence about opinion in the electorate at large, but for activists, direct queries of those around them is also an important aspect of opinion surveillance. As noted above, in the open-ended question early in the survey 24 percent mentioned conversation within their networks as a way to gauge public opinion. Later in the survey, when respondents were given a list of methods for assessing public opinion, 67 percent and 58 percent respectively found discussions with colleagues and conversations with friends to be accurate indicators of public opinion. In the open-ended responses, a Democrat from Florida wrote that one should "spend time in schools, churches, and parks" in order to discern public opinion. Another delegate from Oregon said that he "calls friends and business associates" in addition to tuning in to talk radio programs. And a Democrat from New Jersey said that, in addition to perusing the mass media, she has "discussions with my 5 grown children, their friends, my friends, and acquaintances." She adds in parentheses, "My husband and I share the same general philosophy."

From the depth interviews I got a better sense of how these activists have come to think of interpersonal communication as a means for knowing public opinion. Informants get a textured understanding of public opinion and some sense of the intensity of public opinion from dialogue with people around them, just as journalists occasionally do. In fact, there is a real parallel between the two groups on this point, since both activists and journalists have a sense that public opinion surveillance must involve some meaningful dialogue with those in one's own community. After she complained about the mass media as a source for reliable information about public opinion, I asked one Democratic activist how she did locate the voice of the public, and she replied:

> I belong to a lot of different organizations, not just political [ones]. And I think that you can go and just [talk and] listen to people's reactions. In the grocery store, in the

doctor's office, riding the bus, just any kind of general public [setting]. . . . I think that just by communicating with the average neighbor group that you belong to—you know, the mailman. Just average people [whom you can ask]: "What do you think of this [issue]?"

When people mention these dialogues with friends, family members, colleagues, or strangers within their own communities, they are not making claims about the representative nature of these discussions. On the contrary, the informants seem to understand well that these conversations do not necessarily reflect the nature of public opinion in the nation at large. But this does not matter to them, and perhaps they see interpersonal dialogue as a supplement to poll data, which they do mention as an accurate source of public opinion.

This is a good place to pause and look back again to the concerns of our best theoretical and philosophical tracts on public opinion. In particular, work by Ferdinand Tönnies, so well known to sociologists and largely overlooked by political scientists, provides some resonance with the kinds of arguments activists are making about interpersonal dialogue and public opinion. Tönnies argues that in modern, complex societies (*gesellschaft*), public opinion serves the same functions that religion and customs did in older communal social structures (*gemeinschaft*).[15] Just as religion served to bind people together and limit their actions (e.g., by deeming certain behaviors or lifestyles nonnormative), so public opinion serves this function in the contemporary world. For Tönnies, public opinion actually *displaces* religion in the modern world, pushing it out as the glue connecting people to each other within societies. Indeed, as Gillian and Albert Gollin have pointed out, Tönnies believed religion and public opinion are in dialectical struggle with each other. This is not to say that the two cannot coexist, but that public opinion will inevitably dominate religion in emerging, complex societies. How does this view illuminate our findings here? I would argue that the activists in this study are very much aware of their *location* in communities—in neighborhoods, families, and towns. Activists generally carry with them a strong sense of community and connectedness with those around them because they are so intent on mobilizing and organizing. So it is natural for them to think of public opinion as something located in local community, something sewn into the fabric of interpersonal social networks. Public opinion is, for the activists, not simply about poll data that track the opinions of anonymous Americans. Public opinion is also present in the traffic of day-to-day life in one's community. Relatedly, in my depth interviews I found that informants were very quick to make clear and sophisticated distinctions between national media and local media, arguing often that the latter are more sincere and less biased than the former. Among activists, even those who find themselves in the ideological minority, there is a real communitarian spirit that inevitably affects the way they think about the nature of public opinion. This is not to say activists in this study do not have their cynical moments, but they are far more optimistic and hopeful about the value of public opinion than our legislative staffers and journalists.

What Public Opinion Is Not

The legislative staffers described in chapter 2 made reasoned arguments for interest groups and media content as conduits for public opinion. And they often went further to argue that lobbyists and editorialists are synonymous with public opinion. These notions, which come so naturally to staffers, are absent in the survey results and interviews with partisan activists. Only 16 percent of respondents agreed or strongly agreed that interest groups were accurate indicators of public opinion. At first this is not particularly surprising, since the public generally sees lobby groups in a harsh light. As I thought about these results, however, they seemed a bit odd since many of the convention delegates have themselves been involved in lobbying of various sorts. We failed to ask about participation in interest groups in the survey, but it is quite likely that a large number belong to such interest groups (e.g., the AARP for the retired delegates, the ABA for our large number of attorney respondents, etc.). In my sample of ten activists, several were active and dues-paying members of interest groups, and one has been a registered lobbyist in Springfield since the 1970s. Despite these memberships, activists are still unwilling to make the connection staffers do quite easily between public opinion and interest groups. When I queried depth interview informants directly about interest groups I received comments like this one, from a Republican activist: "[Interest groups] have their own agenda. They have their own doctrine, and they will spin a story, a situation, to whichever way they want to see it come out." And there was this statement from another Republican:

> If you are a paid lobbyist and you're a salesman for that particular group, you're gonna work your rear off to make sure that whatever the issues are that are paying for your overhead, your existence, are gonna be the things that you're gonna promote. And you can't truly be as objective as you'd like to be. Now, they sometimes say that a real good lobbyist is objective, knows when to push and when to step back. . . . [A] lobbyist's true essence, a true definition [of a lobbyist] would be one who speaks on behalf of the concerns and the issues of the group that they represent, and that's a prior deal—a primary issue with them.

Chapter Four

I questioned the activist who was a registered lobbyist at the state legislature about the link between public opinion and interest group communication: Did he feel as though, in his lobbyist role, he represented public opinion? He said

> I think there is a great deal of difference between interest groups. I think that teachers and teacher interest groups have the same interest at this point in time as the general public. I think everybody's interested in improving public education. . . . [B]ut there's a great deal of difference between teachers' unions' interests and the interests of the National Rifle Association, which is also an interest group. I think sometimes we tend to overplay the [power] of interest groups and not listen to the people who are doing the job [like teachers]. . . . They improve cars when they talk to the people who are on the line.

A common argument surfaces here: that some interest groups are broader and more seemingly tied to "the public good" than others. For this informant, teachers are a group who somehow represent public opinion, but this view is certainly not shared by all. As a matter of fact, one of 1996 GOP presidential nominee Bob Dole's most rhetorically successful moments at his party's convention involved his condemnation of selfish teachers' unions. Overall, among the partisan activists, I sense some ambivalence about interest groups, but they clearly do not see lobbies as synonymous with public opinion in the way many legislative professionals do.

Do our partisan activists find the media a useful indicator of public opinion? One-quarter of the delegates surveyed believed media to be an accurate indicator of public opinion. This again runs counter to our staffers' natural reliance on media, and also to the views of our journalists, who believe they do a fairly good job representing public opinion in their stories about public affairs in Illinois. Media bias is rampant, the activists claim, which is why it is not a reliable conduit for public opinion. Forty-five percent of activists agreed media were biased although they did not specify how. Twenty-five percent wrote of ideological bias (left or right wing) and 10 percent and 9 percent respectively mentioned biases toward sensationalism and corporate self-interest. Republicans often see liberal bias in the mainstream media and Democrats see conservative bias, but this is to be expected. And in the depth interviews I conducted, Republican activists were far more vehement about ideological bias of the media, which are liberal in their eyes. One specifically mentioned studies that show journalists to be Democrats, and others—since they were just coming from the Republican convention—focused on coverage of that meeting in San Diego. Here are two views of media bias, both from Republican delegates. The first informant backed away from "liberal" or "conservative" characterizations of media but also said:

> [J]ournalists have bias and they shine the light on what they perceive is reality. For instance, I will give you a very good example. When General [Colin] Powell was speaking [to the 1996 Republican convention], he was delivering a message to the entire convention floor. You could hear a pin drop because everyone was listening to what he had to say. Dan Rather cut away and in the middle of [Powell's] presentation, [Rather] began to tell people [viewers] what was being said and . . . that General Powell was delivering a divisive message and was being jeered. The only time there was any indication of negative response to anything General Powell said was when he said, "You know I am a firm believer in women's choice and affirmative action." At that point there were a few people—and I say a few—who had some bit of noise that emanated from their mouths, but that was it. . . . And so for the people that were watching that particular channel and heard what Dan Rather's perception of what reality was, was *not* what most people sitting in that hall had experienced.

Another said about convention coverage:

> I think the media's looking for a story. In San Diego there were 7.5 media people for every one delegate. I think that's overkill. I think the media is always looking, every reporter is looking, for a different story. There are only so many stories that come out of the convention. I think at times . . . the media make up stories on the littlest things so that they get a little different hook on it than the other reporters do. I sometimes think that media go very far to the Democratic side to reporting issues. I sometimes think that, as Republicans, we're not given a fair shot [to interpret] what's going on.

In the eyes of partisan activists then, media are unreliable as sources for public opinion evidence because they are biased—often ideologically and structurally as well (e.g., media are sensationalist or journalists are pressured to find a "hook," etc.). When I presented media content as an indicator of public opinion to informants in the depth interviews, they dismissed this connection with great confidence. This rejection of media content as useful in the assessment of public opinion is in direct conflict with our staffers, who see a connection and even a conflation between public opinion and media. So, here we find a fairly direct connection between location in the social/political world and lay theory about public opinion. Staffers and journalists, no matter how connected they believe they are to common citizens, are not embedded in community networks in the same way activists must be. Political professionals' lives—in this case, professionals connected to the state legislature—revolve around the political institution and each other. The pressures of their work make it very difficult to get outside of their networks, while partisan activists are more likely to deal with diverse groups of people within their own communities. What all this means is that many professionals look to the media for a connection to the public, while activists feel no need to depend on this function of media: They are connected to other citizens—indeed, to the public—through interpersonal contact and conversation. Mediated information on public opinion, while interesting to them, is not necessary because they still feel as though they can—through dialogue with those around them—discern public opinion when they want to. Staffers, more so than journalists, have some anxiety in this regard, and *know* that they are removed from the public. Several of the staffers looked forward to the end of the legislative session or anticipated campaign work, so they could get "connected" again with their constituents and with average citizens.

Activists Think about Representation

One important reason to study party activists is that they tend to think a lot about political representation. They do not share the complex concerns of our best contemporary political theorists, some of whom we visit with in the next chapter. Yet these partisans occupy a unique place in the political matrix, since they are part of the machinery of representation itself. Men and women who are active in the two major American parties are vital in two obvious respects. During election campaigns they volunteer at the phone banks, raise money, organize debates, attend rallies, and hand out leaflets. All of these activities help local, state, and national candidates get elected, so activists are key players in the placement of a particular man or woman in office. In addition to their roles during campaigns, party workers are vital in communicating constituent opinion to elected officials. Most elected officials, at one time or another, look to their constituent mail or to a survey (scientific or unscientific) of district or state public opinion. But most communication comes from constituent to elected official via far more informal routes: coffees at churches and synagogues, small meetings with businessmen or law enforcement officials, neighborhood barbecues, state fairs, and the like. This is the heart of representation in America, as so many political scientists—Richard Fenno among them—find, despite all the formal channels a leader might use. These informal, private, or even spontaneous interactions between elected official and constituent are perhaps the current-day equivalent to Abraham Lincoln's "public opinion baths"—small meetings he held at the White House with common folk who came to see him in Washington, about matters both weighty and trivial.[16] But Lincoln was not the only president who gained great insight and strength from such informal gatherings, as our large number of presidential memoirs and private papers indicate. Serving as the glue between the average voter and his or her state representative or congressman gives activists great pleasure. Representatives to local, state, and national office need activists for their knowledge of public sentiment, and activists look forward to their interactions with the men and women they often helped to elect.

The participants in our mail survey are not up-to-date about political theories of representation, but they are very thoughtful about one of the essential dichotomies in democratic theory: Edmund Burke's distinction between representatives and trustees.[17] A reading of all 528 answers to an open-ended question about representation and leadership reveals these partisan activists as both sophisticated about the nature of representation and hopeful about the possibilities of this process in the late 1990s. We turn to these brief but quite interesting "texts" momentarily, but first it is interesting to note how our respondents *believe* representation occurs. How elected officials *actually* assess public opinion is a rather complicated matter, studied by a variety of scholars using different methodologies.[18] That research is at present inconclusive given the variety and idiosyncratic nature of most public affairs issues at all levels of government, and I cannot offer new data about the content of linkages between elected officials and the people they represent. That said, let us look at respondents' answers to the following question on the mail survey: "Elected officials often try to gauge public opinion. Please determine to the best of your ability how you think public officials gauge public opinion" (see appendix C).

In table 5, we see that our activists' views of the representation process resonate with and depart from staffers' conceptions of that process discussed earlier in this book. These activists believe that leaders pay close attention to both interest groups and mass media, *in order to get a sense of public opinion*. Although they themselves do not see interest groups or lobbies as a reasonable stand-in for public opinion, they sense that their leaders do. Additionally, activists know that election result analysis is critical in discerning public opinion. And staffers (in keeping with legislative leadership) are of course quite attuned to election margins. In fact, these margins are so important that they hover over all policy debate and policy making at the legislature, guiding the sorts of issues the leadership pushes and the issues they avoid. Respondents are probably correct about lead-

Table 5 Activists' View of Public Officials' Methods for Gauging Public Opinion

	Perceived Frequency of Public Officials' Reliance on Method			
Method	Often	Sometimes	Rarely	Never
Listening to constituents	45.9	49.0	5.0	0.0
Reading poll data	71.3	26.6	1.7	0.4
Reviewing election results	78.6	20.6	0.6	0.2
Listening to interest groups/lobbyists	58.5	38.8	2.7	0.0
Paying attention to local news	47.3	44.8	7.6	0.4
Listening to talk radio	9.7	52.2	36.3	1.8
Making guesses	17.0	42.9	32.0	8.2

Note: The above data show responses to the following question: "Please determine to the best of your ability how you think public officials gauge public opinion: (*a*) Listen to their constituents back home; (*b*) Read poll data; (*c*) Review election results; [etc.]" Respondent choices for each item were "often," "sometimes," "rarely," and "never." Because of the effects of rounding, the sum of the figures in some of the rows is a bit more or less than 100 percent.

$N = 528$

ers' attention to poll data, although it is not clear that elected representatives or staffers at the state or national level *use* polling to guide actual policy choice.[19] Talk radio and "making guesses" also influence leaders' conceptions of public opinion, these activists believe, although not as much as other sources. In terms of sources for public opinion that public officials often turn to, "listening to constituents" ranked lower than four of the six other methods for gauging public opinion. Some readers might find this view somewhat cynical. Because activists believe so strongly in attention to local community dialogue, these results probably indicate that activists are somewhat disappointed with how much attention their own leaders pay to such interpersonal communications.

One of the more interesting aspects of the survey results concerns *when* activists want leaders to become "trustees" in the Burkean sense. All but 4 percent of respondents agreed that there were times when leaders *should not* be guided by public opinion. Table 6 lists the sorts of cases in which respondents believe their leaders should act as trustees and not reflectors of public opinion. These answers were given in response to an open-ended question, reproduced in the table.

Almost all (90 percent) of respondents who wrote a response in answer to this open-ended question agreed that there were cases when public opinion should not be considered. The responses activists took the time to write were very interesting, with some reflecting on the question more generally and others writing lists of issues where the trustee model of representation should hold. Some of the general answers supporting the trustee approach took the following form:

Table 6 Cases Where Trustee Model Is Appropriate

Case	Percentage of Respondents Mentioning Case
When issue concerns morality/principles/ethics	19.3
"Yes" only (no case specified)	15.3
When the public is badly informed	14.0
When issue concerns good of public as a whole	12.8
When issue concerns national security	7.3
When issue concerns constitutional law	7.3
When issue concerns civil rights	5.2
When issue concerns abortion	3.4
When issue concerns foreign affairs	2.9
When issue concerns budgetary matters	2.9
When issue concerns the death penalty	1.5
When issue concerns the military	1.3

Note: The above data show responses to the following question: "Are there cases when public officials should *not* be guided by public opinion in their decision making? Please list as many cases and examples as you like."
$N = 528$

I think people are elected to make good decisions. [Those decisions are] based on many factors. If an official only follows public opinion polls, they have no conviction or backbone. (Democrat, North Dakota)

Public officials have an obligation to listen to and solicit public opinion but ultimately must decide issues and act in the best interest of the public, using their own best judgment. (Democrat, Wyoming)

If someone is elected with a clear agenda, it is his/her duty to stick to that agenda. We elect representatives, not pollsters. Like Hamilton and Madison, I believe we live in a republic, not a direct democracy. (Republican, Utah)

Some of the respondents did provide lists of cases, like the Montana Republican who listed a large number of cases where public opinion should not be consulted: "Hillary's Medicare," partial birth abortion, abortion, immigration, welfare, taxes, education. Most respondents mentioned fewer cases, citing one or two.

The most frequently mentioned cases where delegates excused their leaders from the evaluation and representation of public opinion were the following: when the legislator has moral convictions that run counter to public opinion (19 percent), when the public is not sufficiently informed to make a judgment on an issue (14 percent), and when the *entire* public welfare is at stake and the leader must ignore factions (13 percent). Specific responses will help to clarify these categories, so let us look first to the mentions of morality and conscience:

[Leaders should ignore public opinion] when they think their position is right. But officials have a responsibility to go back to their constituents, report on what they did, and why they came to a particular decision. [The] role of leaders is not merely to follow, but to help shape and mold public opinion. (Democrat, Hawaii)

National Security, and where your strong personal, philosophical, and moral opinion and belief is in conflict [with public opinion]. (Republican, Florida)

When an issue is morally-based, [leaders should] listen to their conscience, not [look to gaining] votes. (Republican, Minnesota)

Public officials should not be guided by public opinion in their decision making when such opinion contradicts a strongly held belief of theirs, such as women's reproductive rights. (Democrat, Massachusetts)

Questions of ethics: e.g., the internment of the Japanese-Americans during WW II, war with Iraq in '91, questions of conscience (death penalty, decriminalization of drugs); in the end a public servant must vote his/her conscience after gathering the best information." (Democrat, Montana)

Typical responses from activists about public lack of knowledge as a basis for trustee behavior took the following form:

[Public officials should ignore public opinion] on complex issues where [the] public doesn't have all the details and on issues with long-term implications where [the] public is not thinking that far ahead. (Republican, Florida)

[Public officials should ignore public opinion] when knowledge of the situation or of consequences is limited to the officials. Public opinion is not informed well enough to know the best course. (Democrat, North Dakota)

We elect people who have a conscience and the ability to think. At least we try. They need to weigh all information that may or may not be known to the public. Given that, they should always consider that public opinion is a result of public knowledge. Without information opinion is just that. Trusting their judgment even when the public disagrees is a function of courage. Besides, public opinion is changeable. The right thing is constant. (Democrat, Massachusetts)

There are many potential cases when officials should not be guided by public opinion. Such a case would be when the public is obviously wrong according to the principles of truth, morality, or the Constitution. It is easy for the public to be swayed by media hysteria and gain a herd mentality. Public officials should have the guts to do what's right, no matter how unpopular it may be. (Republican, South Dakota)

Public opinion is often evenly or close to evenly split. Public officials must listen to constituents then make up his or her mind according to his/her best knowledge. The public is often under-informed or uninformed especially on complex or technical issues. In these cases, the official must make a decision that might be contrary to public opinion. (Democrat, Montana)

If the official has information which would change public opinion, their duty lies in providing leadership. (It is not enough for the elected official to take the moral high ground, asserting he/she is bucking public opinion because his/her morality is superior. [He/she should buck public opinion] only if his/her information base would change [or inform public] opinion. (Republican, Utah)

Finally, a large number of activists argued that leaders can often see "the big picture" and discern what is best for the public *as a whole*. In cases where public opinion seems not to recognize the long-term public good, elected officials must act in the fashion they deem most appropriate for all citizens. A typical response along these lines came from one Arizona Democrat who stated that "[Public officials should ignore public opinion] when the public official genuinely believes his position will serve the *public* interest best—but these instances should be extremely rare and not taken lightly."

These results are interesting because they are a bit at odds with popular and academic writings about the loss of trust in government and in public officials by the citizenry.[20] Most of these studies documenting loss of trust, many of which draw on large databases like the National Election Study, include samples of randomly selected citizens rather than activists.[21] There may, in fact, be a very real difference between the confidence that our most loyal party workers have and the much lower confidence levels among the citizenry at large. This makes perfect sense for a few reasons. First, activists may be among the Americans who most trust government, since they often want to hold public office or greatly respect those in such offices. Second, party activists are far more educated than the average citizen, and they do sense a significant gap between themselves and non-activists in terms of political knowledge. Activists realize just how poorly informed most Americans are, on various local, state, and national policy issues, and so realize that public officials have their hands tied: They cannot always respond to public opinion because public opinion is not always educated, engaged, or aware. Finally, party activists believe, although probably not to the same extent that our legislative staffers do, that it is difficult for the public to keep up with the intricacies of fast moving policy debate. Unlike staffers, these party activists do strongly believe in public opinion as an aggregation of individual opinions and as the content of interpersonal dialogue. Yet they realize that public opinion cannot and need not always be consulted, since citizens hold limited knowledge and insight about policy processes.

It would have been inappropriate to query activists in order to discover their causal theories of the policy process. They simply do not know as much as the staffers and journalists about the ways media, public opinion, and policy are connected. This is a function of their occupations, of course—the fact that they are not professionals who work in the policy-making arena. They are occasional visitors to that arena, however, because they do attend to politics between and during elections. They are a rare group of Americans, but their views are instructive as we try to build theory about public opinion processes and the nature of public opinion itself (the subject of the next chapter). Partisan loyalists are unwilling to argue for media content or interest group communication as indicators of public opinion. Instead, they fall back on a combination of social science and culture: They argue, in effect, that public opinion in a democracy is an aggregation of individual opinions, no matter how uninformed or flighty. Polls often allow for proper representation of individuals' opinions. Yet, it is interpersonal dialogue—the discourse we find in neighborhoods, churches, schools, and businesses—that helps us to realize the strength and subtlety of public opinion.

The empirical studies described in this chapter and the two previous ones were useful in exploring the nature of lay political theories and how they are tied to occupation and to one's place in the social matrix. Getting some sense of the arguments that nonacademics make about the political world—public opinion, media, and representation—opens up many questions about the meaning and limitations of public opinion. But how should scholars think about this elusive construct? The last chapter takes up some of the broader issues raised early in this book: the construction of public opinion, the conflation of media and public sentiment, and the role of organized interests in theorizing about public opinion. Yet the central goal of the concluding section is to fit various findings from previous chapters back into the context of public opinion theory and democratic theory more generally. How can we, in formulating theory and research projects about public opinion, learn from those who work in the thick of American political life?

5 Meanings of Public Opinion: Lay Theory Meets Democratic Theory

THIS BOOK HAS EXPLORED the lay theories of some extraordinarily thoughtful political actors, with a focus on their ideas about public opinion. Although these theories or "folk models" about public opinion are inherently interesting and enable us to gain some insight into political action, they are most important in how they resonate with—and also challenge—our ideas about democracy itself. There was, in the previous chapters, a sort of extended meeting between lay theory and democratic theory, and it is this connection I hope to illuminate here.

As we uncover lay theories of individuals across occupational categories we are reminded of the many oppositions which make the study of politics so interesting and so frustrating. Although I have not emphasized these oppositions in previous chapters, students of politics probably detected some chronic conflicts among people and ideas: Dewey versus Lippmann, Lane versus Converse, advocates of polling versus critics of polling, elitists versus populists, representatives versus trustees, and the like. One opposition we do not find is between liberals and conservatives since, on questions of public opinion and representation, party affiliation does not seem to affect the views of staffers and activists. This is not to say that ideology does not matter, of course, because it matters greatly even at a time when the two major parties are not always philosophically distinct. It is to say, however, that these engaged citizens, across occupational category and level of experience in politics, share at least some views of larger political processes and the mechanics of public opinion.[1]

One of the starting points of this book was the social construction of public opinion. Although scholars have tracked changing conceptions of public opinion across historical periods, it is apparent from the small studies reported here that meanings of public opinion are also greatly influenced by place in the political matrix: We conceptualize "public opinion"—the embodiment of our fellow citizens' concerns and ideologies—as it intersects with our own lives and goals. This book clearly demonstrates that public opinion is socially constructed—that not everyone shares a common view of this phenomenon. I need not belabor this point but will begin this chapter by briefly looking back at constructionist views in light of the data in this book. In this chapter I focus primarily on the relationship between lay public opinion theories and citizens' views of democracy more generally, and I also try to make links between this study and some of the important bodies of academic research that inspired it: literature on belief systems, on the aggregate match between opinion and policy in America, and on our leaders' behaviors in office. I shall take up larger theoretical and normative concerns as well, focusing on representation, the size of polities, and the connection between personal ties and political life. Finally I speculate on the future of public opinion research. With this book I hope to open up a few new avenues for research and remind scholars of some older approaches we have abandoned. Explorations into the nature of lay theory should help us to be better theorists and more acute observers of American political culture.

The Phenomenology of Public Opinion

Social constructivism as a paradigm has much support and elaboration in the academic literature—especially in sociology. From Berger and Luckmann's original treatise published thirty years ago to William Gamson's more recent research on the framing of social problems by citizens, we have scores of sophisticated theoretical statements and provocative empirical investigations. This particular way of viewing politics—as fluid, socially embedded, and connected to the mass media—is very much in the tradition of the Columbia School (of Lazarsfeld, Berelson, Merton, and others), but it also goes a bit beyond that tradition. Social constructivism is a framework that attends to the stimuli and the constraints all political actors face, but it draws much of its power from phenomenology. If we see politics as subjective reality, the methods of cognitive anthropology and European social psychology can all be brought to bear on questions of public opinion, its meaning, and its status in the policy making process.

It is clear that social constructivism as a theoretical frame is useful and interesting only if there is conflict—if political actors have differing ideas about public opinion or other democratic concepts. We found in the previous chapters that such conflict exists because views of public opinion are tied to one's position in the political world. Different actors do play different roles with different mindsets. What I believe social constructivism teaches us about public opinion, beyond underscoring the varying meanings of public opinion, is that occupation demands that informants come to view public opinion in utilitarian ways: They have found means to make public opinion work for them, helping them construct a political world that seems sensible from their distinctive vantage points in the democratic process. I could tell very clearly in the course of my depth interviews with staffers and journalists that they had *internalized* particular views of public opinion. Some of these views we recognize from the literature on democratic theory: Bentley and Truman's notions about groups or Tarde's discursive perspective on public opinion. Others seem more foreign to us, like the idea that media content might be seen as a useful artifact of public opinion. In any event, we need to be attuned to the fact that these internalizations of public opinion definitions play themselves out as staffers, activists, and journalists go about their business—designing legislation, campaigning for candidates, and writing about legislative activity for wide audiences. Informants have no reason to think or talk in the abstract terminology we use constantly—"public opinion," "deliberation," "representation," or even "democracy." Yet lengthy queries about their lay theories of politics reveal all sorts of definitions and constructions of public opinion that are enormously useful to the analyst trying to understand the policy process.

Seeing politics (and public opinion, more specifically) as subjective reality does help us link micro and macro levels of analysis. The actors—here staffers, journalists, and activists—are doing the work of their institutions: the legislature, the mass media, and the major political parties. In the lay theories of individuals we discover clues about institutional culture and how these cultures clash. We cannot query institutions or professions, but we can question their agents in order to understand how and why these large and diffuse bodies act as they do. For example, I found that journalists struggle with the notion of public opinion, treating the idea with both passion and anxiety: Many reporters have great respect for the collective wisdom of their readers but are often startled by the tremendous degree of ignorance about public affairs among these same readers. These feelings on the part of informants are a telling manifestation of the larger problems in American journalism, where mass media institutions debate about how to cover the political scene. Journalism as a profession must face simultaneous challenges: How proactive or reactive should reporters be in covering the legislature, the governor, or the president? How much knowledge should they ascribe to the average reader? Should they take cues from the party leadership, or should they work intently to avoid the spinning of communication directors and press secretaries, thereby risking the loss of exclusive stories or inside information? These institutional struggles are present at the micro level, and asking journalists to think aloud about public opinion illuminated new dimensions of these and other macro-level phenomena.

Finally, a focus on how occupation enables one to make sense of public opinion expands the study of political cognition. People may "process" the bits of public opinion information they find in the world, but they do so within very real constraints—professional and personal as well as ideological. We can manipulate many variables in the lab as we explore political cognition, of course. But studying political psychology in tandem with more sociological concerns sheds new light on when, how, and why public opinion matters to political actors.

Lay Theories of Public Opinion, Models of Democracy

The central reason we should care about lay theories of public opinion—those ideas citizens have about the meaning, measure, and value of public opinion—is that these theories give us some insight into how people think about democracy. We already know much about the content of citizen attitudes from the mass of survey data in the literature, from case study work about political behavior, and from experimental studies which have demonstrated how (in the short term) citizen attitudes can be altered by exposure to media or other stimuli.[2] And this information has been extraordinarily helpful in trying to assess people's beliefs on both transitory policy issues (e.g., affirmative action, particular environmental dilemmas, or U.S. military involvement in international conflicts) and on more fundamental issues (e.g., race relations, separation of church and state, etc.). We have some knowledge also of how the public feels about particular institutions, such as political parties, the presidency, and Congress. Yet we know far less about how citizens view contemporary democratic ideas and processes, in particular the relationships among media, opinion formation, representation, and policy. In this book I have posited that citizens do have arguments to make about these relationships and that their arguments are worth heeding.

We have gotten some sense of how different actors in the political process tend to think about public opinion. Our two small groups of political professionals—legislative staffers and journalists—proposed a variety of definitions of public opinion, and few of them chose aggregative ones. Let us put ourselves in these political actors' shoes for a moment, and try to view public opinion from their vantage points. First, elections matter, of course, but they provide limited information about policy preferences. It is difficult to "read" them as any sort of nuanced text about public opinion, although they certainly give us a sense of general ideological tendencies in the population. One difficulty is that we do vote for *candidates,* and this makes it challenging for office holders or their aides to discern whether voters were persuaded by their issue positions or their personas. Another aggregative scheme—opinion surveys—are more helpful and less helpful than elections for discerning public opinion. Well-executed surveys can provide nuance. And in theory, opinion polling can be done repeatedly if one has the great resources constant polling demands. Yet polling does not tell us whether people will or will not act on their opinions. We can ask survey respondents, and we often do, what sorts of activity they might hypothetically engage in. But this is not a very reliable approach for many reasons. Among them is fact that the opinions we have, and how we act (or fail to act) on them, are often separated by great expanses of time. And so it is difficult to connect the answers an individual gives to a pollster with the particular forms of action he or she might eventually take in the political world. It is no surprise then that busy legislative staffers and journalists find these methods problematic. In their world—a highly professionalized state legislature—aggregation does not help them address vital questions related to public opinion. Across policy issues these actors wonder which segments of the public will react to a legislative maneuver and how such reactions will become manifest. Staffers and journalists want to predict reaction, but they also need to understand *how informed* citizen opinions actually are. They want to know about *tradeoffs*—what citizens will give up for particular social goods. In general, staffers and journalists want to understand intensity of opinion, how opinions evolve from knowledge of an issue, and whether any of this opinion development leads to overt behavior. Aggregative means of assessing public opinion are limited in all these regards. This is not at all to say that elections and surveys are useless in the eyes of staffers or journalists, but it is to say that they have limited value in the context of fast-moving and complex legislative debate.

If these professionals do not rely on polls or election results, how do they assess public opinion in the public-policy-making arena? They choose local means of opinion evaluation that enable them to get some sense of the intensity of the opinion, the level of knowledge which produced the opinion, and the link between opinion and action. Staffers look to interest group communications, for one. Lobbyists tend to provide staffers and members with sharply defined views of their "side" of an issue and some sense of how parts of the public feel toward that issue. Using lobbyists as "surrogates" who report on public opinion may seem dangerous to scholars, but staffers are quite comfortable with this informal system. Committee staff in this large legislature are accustomed to dealing with lobbyists and feel they can listen to them—indeed, collect information about public opinion from them—without being in thrall to lobbyists intellectually or ideologically. Are staffers as critical and discerning about interest group communication as they say they are? This is hard to know (and to measure), but my sense is that—on conflictual issues—staff are forced to be skeptical because they typically hear different interpretations of the same issue from a variety of groups. They must find a way to assess them all, and this demands a critical approach. Crucially: Members rely on staffers *for exactly this type of removed and critical analysis.* Staffers believe they can treat lobbyists' reports on public opinion "with a grain of salt," judging for themselves whether the information is useful or suspect. Staffers do have other sources for assessing public opinion, so these can serve as "checks" on some lobbyist communication. And there are, as so many scholars cited in chapter 2 have pointed out, severe penalties when lobbyists lie. So while interest group representatives certainly use an array of rhetorical strategies to construct reality in particular ways, they cannot speak blatant untruths about public opinion if they are to maintain good reputations in the halls of the legislature. Again, interest groups provide many insights into public opinion that aggregative means cannot: They do provide succinct, crystallized information about public opinion (mostly qualitative, sometimes quantitative) and can speak about tradeoffs. They know what their constituencies and clients will and will not give up in the rough-and-tumble process of policy making.

Interestingly, we can detect some connections between "public opinion" and the activities of interest groups and lobbies in American political activity of the late nineteenth and early twentieth centuries. As sociologist Elisabeth Clemens notes, women's associations fighting for suffrage and a variety of other policies during the period from 1890 through 1920 joined forces at many crucial moments and successfully lobbied both Congress and state assemblies. The conglomeration of smaller associations into much larger entities was often viewed as "public opinion" by legislators, journalists, and citizens. In 1921, for example, the Sheppard-Towner Act, a health bill benefiting women and children, was passed as the result of work by fifteen national women's organizations, including the National Congress of Mothers, the Daughters of the American

Revolution, and the National League of Women Voters. In her analysis of this campaign and others like it, Clemens notes: "As in so many campaigns in so many states, group endorsement was taken as a signal of public opinion."[3]

In many ways the new female lobbyists of the early twentieth century and their more professional counterparts of today serve functions similar to those of party bosses in nineteenth- and early twentieth-century American politics. Bosses had such a good sense of their constituents that they could speculate about public reactions to legislation or candidacies before these items appeared on the horizon. This keen ability to understand public opinion was explicated rather elegantly for me in a previous study, where I interviewed congressmen and journalists who had worked in U.S. politics in the 1930s and 1940s. I asked one prominent journalist if he called on bosses in the large metropolitan areas he covered for information about public opinion, and he answered:

> Oh, very regularly. Because [bosses] were quite reliable. In a way they were more reliable than the polls because the polls can only tell you about current reactions. Now, the bosses had the kind of relationship with their constituencies whereby the bosses could predict what reactions [of their constituents] would be under a certain set of circumstances. . . . Today about the best you can do is do some demographic studies and go over some polls. And the trouble is, that's static, you know, it's sort of freezing society in one place. Now the boss understood how society was acting, not just where it stood, but how it was acting.[4]

I believe that staffers see interest group communication in much the same way as this experienced journalist viewed his party boss sources. One of the most valuable skills in politics is an ability to make predictions about public reaction, and bosses—with their thorough, highly textured understanding of their constituents—were able to make such predictions. Good lobbyists can do the same thing, and that is why their communications are so functional to many staffers.

It is important to note here, as a reminder, that this book has not addressed political campaigns. Members of the legislature and their staffers (when they are asked to leave their positions to work on campaigns) use polls often during the heat of an election campaign to adjust their rhetoric, plan campaign events, and the like. Polling is enormously helpful as a tool in these circumstances, and campaign-related polls are ignored in this book, which is largely about political life between campaigns. I have focused on staffers' and journalists' broader insights about their day-to-day activities, not on the brief, frenzied period of a tight reelection contest.

Chapter Five

In the interviews with committee staffers the mass media were mentioned as sources for information on public opinion. Staff members did not differentiate among types of media content as academics do, so when they spoke of influential media they moved easily across categories of "straight news," "news analyses," and "editorials." We might find this lack of distinction disturbing, since there are some important differences among categories of text in our daily newspapers, but staffers do it without hesitation.[5] Perhaps staffers, sophisticated about politics, believe that they can make their own judgments about statements in the newspaper regardless of whether an editor calls them "news" or "news analysis." In any event, the media are an important source of public opinion information for these individuals. My interviews with staffers reveal that media (*not* media polls, but news and editorials) are useful as public opinion indicators for several reasons. First, they provide citizen insights and quotations of value to the staff, who are somewhat insulated from the public. Media give staffers vivid examples of public reaction. Staffers talk about public opinion in abstract terms to each other all the time (what will X or Y constituency feel about an issue?), but they lack the colorful sorts of material journalists can provide as they canvass members of the public on an issue. Second, staffers believe that journalists are close to citizens—that newspaper content resonates with readers. So in the eyes of staffers there is often a close match between what readers think and what appears in newspaper stories. If viewed in this way (our own scholarly opinions on the subject aside), newspapers are a far more efficient public opinion surveillance device than talking directly to citizens. Beyond the vividness and efficiency of the newspaper stories, however, staffers believe that reading the media enables them to get a good sense of how media *shape* public opinion. So not only are newspapers repositories of fairly crystallized public attitudes, but scanning the media also gives staffers a sense of the opinion formation process *in action*. They believe that they can read the newspaper to ascertain what the mass of readers might be taking from particular news stories.

Journalists and political activists share at least one meaning of public opinion: the notion that public opinion can be located in conversation among citizens. Journalists may not seek out or cover these conversations as often as we might hope. In fact, the reporters studied here are most likely to "stumble upon" citizens in conversation instead of developing more systematic ways to locate such political talk. Activists, on the other hand, talk constantly because it is a vital part of what they do. While journalists like public talk for its flavor and (sometimes) the ideas it gives them about tendencies in public opinion, they can and do write stories about public opinion without data of any significant kind. Journalists in this study, as well as others I have interviewed for other projects, are confident in their knowledge about readers' preferences and tendencies. The "imaginary readers" discussed in chapter 3 are very useful for journalists who are pressed for time and unable to talk to citizens about all issues. And journalists are cynical about polling, so issue surveys are not a great help to them. Activists, on the other hand, are in perpetual surveillance of their own opinion enclaves. They are in near-constant discussion of national, state, and local politics with those around them. These activists also believe polling has some value, unlike the more jaded staffers and journalists. For them, polling provides a somewhat flawed "big picture" about public opinion, but polling carries with it an aura of democracy. When polling is paired with the textured public opinion insights activists get through interpersonal dialogue within social networks, the two methods give activists what they need to assess popular sentiments.

We might combine these lay theories about public opinion with informants' thoughts about media and the policy process, in order to try and discern some generalized models of democracy to which these informants subscribe. This is a tricky endeavor, no doubt. I might have asked staffers, journalists, and activists directly about the meaning of democracy—what a democratic public sphere looks like. But my previous work on meanings of public opinion led me to believe that this would be an unproductive approach. "Public opinion" is itself quite abstract, but at least—through probing and discussion of measurement—informants can begin to articulate rough definitions and theories. Asking them to define democracy would probably be an impossible task, given how difficult it is for academics to agree about a meaning. I will, however, take a look back to David Held's work, mentioned in chapter 1, to see if we can project from informants' lay theories of public opinion to their theories of democracy.[6]

Let us begin with the political activists surveyed and interviewed here. These men and women, who have served as party delegates to national nominating conventions, are our most classically democratic group. They devote an enormous amount of time and energy to politics, and while they know they are unusual in this regard, they maintain a certain confidence about the judgments of their fellow citizens. Thus, they place some trust in opinion polling, which recognizes all people (all survey participants) as having a valuable and indeed equal voice in politics. These activists also enjoy and find much value in the interpersonal dialogue within their own very unrepresentative social networks. So activists walk around with two competing visions of public opinion in their heads. These visions do not seem contradictory to activists, but complementary. Activists tend not to see just how unique their own communication networks really are or, if they do recognize this, do not care very much. For them, polling gives them a sense of what *all* their fellow citizens think despite the problems of the method. But interpersonal dialogue gives them the kind of vivid insight into the nature of public opinion that they seek.

Although many features of early, Athenian democracy are irrelevant in contemporary America, some of the basic characteristics of that governmental form resonate with activists' views in this study. The classical model, as described by Held and others, emphasizes equality among citizens as well as much direct participation in government. Voting does matter, but political participation extends far beyond voting, and citizens want to have a hand in many aspects of the polity's operation. Activists in this study are somewhat trusting of opinion polls because they have a fundamental belief in direct citizen participation. Although they note that surveys are narrow, occasional, and flawed, they do at least recognize the significance of citizen opinion. Activists also have confidence in their elected officials. They believe that citizens do the necessary cognitive work to elect the best candidates they can, so activists are willing to trust public officials to defy public opinion when they can justify doing so. Allowing elected officials to stray from public opinion is not at all contradictory to the general framework of classical theory. It actually fits quite nicely, since informed voters tend to choose candidates who they have examined carefully and indeed skeptically. Generally speaking, activists have a strong belief in the opinions of the common man and woman as well as a cautious trust in government officials, and these attitudes among activists cohere with the simple and rather inspiring tenets of early democratic theory. This makes perfect sense. To be a political activist is, in many ways, to be a democratic idealist. The activists I spoke with at length are not naive or unsophisticated. But they do have a fresh and compelling view of democracy as a system controlled by a citizenry that—in the end—knows what it wants from the state.[7]

In trying to link staffers' and journalists' views to models of democracy, we might argue that both of these parties fall closer to what Held calls "competitive elitism" or the "technocratic vision" of democracy. Held draws on Max Weber's work and also that of Joseph Schumpeter to compile a model of democracy many have deemed "appropriate" for a highly industrialized mass society. Democracy in this model is viewed as an efficient way of choosing and restricting leaders so that they serve the public interest. Key features of this model are strong political leadership, a somewhat autonomous and highly capable bureaucracy, strong competition between political party elites, and a relatively uninformed and unengaged citizenry. Weber and Schumpeter each had his own detailed vision of how to deal with the problems presented by a strong bureaucracy and conflict among elites, but both were convinced that more direct democratic schemes were unrealistic and dangerous. Schumpeter was eloquent on the subject of citizen knowledge, arguing, as have so many political observers, that citizens are uninterested in politics and incapable of knowing their own interests. In one of the stronger passages of *Capitalism, Socialism, and Democracy,* he notes that:

> [Citizen] ignorance will persist in the face of masses of information however complete and correct. It persists even in the face of the meritorious efforts that are being made to go beyond presenting information and to teach the use of it by means of lectures, classes, discussion groups. Results are not zero. But they are small. People cannot be carried up the ladder. Thus the typical citizen drops down to a lower level of mental performance as soon as he enters the political field. He argues and analyzes in a way which he would readily recognize as infantile within the sphere of his real interests. He becomes a primitive again. His thinking becomes associative and affective.[8]

None of the staffers or journalists in this study made such statements about citizens, but they did—directly and indirectly—speak to the uninformed nature of public opinion. Journalists were more cautious about this ignorance, tending to alternately defend the wisdom of their readers and express disappointment about their knowledge levels. Staffers were unlikely to defend constituents. Both groups understand what Lippmann did: that citizens are often occupied so thoroughly by their work, family, and personal concerns that they are unable or unwilling to apply their minds to the intricate nature of public policy debates. No doubt they have even less interest in state politics, the milieu in which my staff and journalistic informants labor. These political professionals are democrats all, but their model of democracy—about which we can speculate, given their notions and arguments about public opinion—emphasizes a strong and knowledgeable stratum of bureaucrats. If citizens are unwilling to learn about policy debates or get involved, staffers believe they must learn about public desires through the articulate spokesmen within their reach: interest groups and media content. Journalists too are well aware of citizen ignorance. But they still make attempts—rather unsystematic ones in the case of the small group studied here—to learn from citizens through conversation. Journalists also do a fair amount of speculation about public opinion without measuring it in any way. They believe they know their average reader and can project what that reader might want from government if he or she were informed on the issues. This is efficient, of course, because it does not demand the time-consuming process of opinion research. It instead demands that journalists keep their eyes and ears open, incrementally gaining a sense of what their audience is like.

This brief exercise in connecting arguments about public opinion to arguments about democracy is useful because it underscores just how important lay theories of public opinion are. Our notions about the character of public opinion are basic elements in our larger ideas about the democratic process. There is a conflict in democratic principles when we compare activists to our political professionals. These parties see the public sphere from different perspectives, and they demand different things from citizens. Staffers would like to see a citizenry familiar with more technical details of policy, but they are commonly disappointed. Journalists would like to see engagement as well, and they look for it, but they are also often disappointed. Activists do not make such high demands of their fellow citizens and tend to meet them at their own level, so they still maintain a belief in the wisdom of public opinion. Although it is difficult to sort through all the views of my informants on these rather complicated issues closely connected to democratic competence, it is clear that professionals lean toward democratic models that emphasize the role of professionals. And citizen activists cling to our classical models that emphasize an informed and engaged populace. These connections are worth further exploration: Who believes in democracy, and what type of democracy do they envision? Our cognitive models of democracy are undoubtedly built through our experiences in politics, but once these models are established, we probably formulate expectations of our fellow citizens based on these personal visions.

This discussion also brings us back to the "So what?" question: Why does lay theory matter at all? At the end of this chapter, I discuss how the particular lay theories in this book provoke us to ask some novel theoretical questions, revise some older ones, and also think in new ways about methodological approaches to understanding public opinion. But here I would like to emphasize one of the most important reasons for studying lay theory of public opinion as well as the larger theories people hold about democracy: People's notions of public opinion and indeed democratic practice are connected to action they take or fail to take. In the case of the activists, we see a very clear congruence between their high activity levels and their generalized beliefs in the value and importance of mass and local opinion expression. Direction of causality—whether becoming an activist makes one more optimistic about public opinion or whether trusting public opinion leads one to political activism—is obviously undetermined here. But we can see a comfortable fit between action and views of democratic practice, and this should be suggestive to us if we are interested in understanding and indeed predicting political behavior. My depth interview informants are longtime activists, who became involved out of a general interest in politics and a concern about the future of their local communities. Their sensibilities about public opinion and its role in democracy have developed over extended periods and their involvement in politics has seemed to grow steadily. Some of them have had very direct experience with policymakers and with journalists, while others are content to do significant work for their parties without making such connections. In any case, they seem to share some similar views about public opinion and its value during and between elections. Their activism would be an empty and unsatisfying type of involvement if they did not adhere to some of the more fundamental tenets of participatory democratic theory.

There is also a good fit between the way our political professionals view public opinion and the sorts of behaviors they engage in. Staffers do not go out of their way to meet with citizens or develop channels for constant contact with constituents. There are public meetings, and staffers listen to the occasional engaged citizen-caller or visitor. But on the whole, they see public opinion as sleepy and not particularly informed on policy issues—even those matters that affect voters' pocketbooks and their children, taxes and education. As a result the public voices they hear are those voices brought to them by interest groups and the media. These conduits are satisfactory for them; otherwise, staffers would have developed some other type of infrastructure for gaining knowledge about public opinion. And we can look at journalistic informants in much the same way. They too lack a systematic means for gathering public opinion. They attend, although quite skeptically, to the occasional relevant policy surveys they come across. And they listen to people—to editors, to lobbyists, to citizens. They enjoy conversation with citizens in particular because these dialogues help them get a sense of what people care about and why. Nevertheless, these ways of discerning public opinion are vague and inconstant, without much structure. Journalists, like staffers, worry about issue polls. The "one person–one vote" approach to opinion assessment, which has so much appeal to activists, is not particularly useful to them. Their skepticism of aggregative mechanisms runs high, for all the reasons discussed in previous chapters. Instead, staffers and journalists have found their own methods, and while their methods are not particularly well developed, these professionals find them functional. Their methods for evaluating public opinion ultimately affect the ways they do their work—which opinions "count" and which do not.

Occupation was key in this study, as staffers, journalists, and activists, with their unique vantage points, did differ in their views of democratic practice. I did not treat occupation as a demographic category, but as a window that people use to look out at the political landscape. And all three roles played by my informants here are critical ones on our political stage. Staffers provide the permanence, the collective memory, and the expertise that keep the legislature running smoothly. Journalists try to interpret the complex events of the assembly for their readers. And activists supply the manpower that enables political parties to function—to raise money, to educate citizens about candidates and issues, and to get out the vote. All three groups work under very different concerns and constraints, and this leads them to varying perspectives on basic political processes. It makes no sense to ask what individuals think of politics unless we know where they stand: what sort of experience they have in the political realm, what kinds of investments they have in political process, and what they hope to "get out of" their political involvements. In political cognition research, in contrast to this study, we could ask experimental subjects to take certain occupational roles or positions and act in accordance with those roles. But there is nothing like the real thing: When an individual's career and livelihood are at stake (in the case of journalists or staffers), or when an individual believes the future of his or her community is at stake (in the case of activists), the decision-making process is undoubtedly far more complex than it would be in the hypothetical world of the laboratory.

The three occupational groups in this study expressed different views of public opinion, and these views conflict with one another. Although this conflict in perspectives may not come to the surface in a conversation between a staffer and a journalist or between an activist and a journalist, it may be one important reason why these three groups view the political process and even particular issue debates so differently. Let us take, for example, the two parties in this book who are actually in the same physical locale—reporters and staffers at the state legislature. Staffers complained about journalists and media bias, arguing that journalists often do not understand the issues at stake in connection with the introduction of a particular bill. And journalists believe staffers (especially communication directors, who are the staff's voice to the world) are partisans who often spin information about legislation according to the ideological positions of the leadership. One thing these groups contest in many battles is "what the public wants." Yet each has different ideas about the nature of public expression and how it is best measured. Staffers, using interest group communication and media as indicators, may sincerely believe that they have firm evidence about public needs, but journalists may find these assessments wildly off base because they hear a different public voice in their conversations with citizens. So the contested nature of "public opinion" can manifest itself in very real battles where the public's desires must be interpreted. We see debates over "what the public wants" chronically in American politics, but as scholars we have not yet explored conceptions of public opinion as one root of the problem in many political controversies. It is clear that turning to the phenomenon described in this book—the social construction of public opinion—will illuminate why particular policy debates are often heated but at the same time unproductive.

Striking to me, besides the importance of occupation and how it influences views of public opinion, is the way this limited study underscores other researchers' ideas about ambivalence in the expression of beliefs. Several scholars have argued that individual citizens, when given the chance, will give rather complex and even contradictory answers to survey questions or to queries they receive in depth interviews. I saw this among my highly educated and experienced population of informants just as other researchers have found ambivalence in their studies of average citizens. Jennifer Hochschild is eloquent on this point. Near the end of her book about Americans' attitudes toward distributive justice, she argues that, "given the opportunity, people do not make simple statements; they shade, modulate, deny, retract, or just grind to a halt in frustration."[9] Even my very well-informed and highly engaged respondents have uncertainties about the ways they approach their work and think about democratic process. While Hochschild and others who have studied ambivalence focus on ambivalence in people's attitudes toward issues, I would extend this to argue that most of us are conflicted about the more fundamental terms and ideas of democracy itself. In my informants' statements I found scores of examples of ambivalence about public opinion, the role of media in democracy, and the nature of representation. But one of the more glaring examples comes from the political activists. Recall that activists queried through the mail survey chose *both* opinion polls and interpersonal dialogue with friends, neighbors, and colleagues as equivalent to public opinion. To my mind, choosing both of these meanings of public opinion is evidence of real ambivalence among activists about the nature of public opinion. Survey data are different from the dialogic "data" one receives by exchanging political opinions with a neighbor. Beyond the obvious differences (e.g., survey data represent many narrowly measured beliefs while conversation lets you hear from only a few people at great length), these two types of public opinion data are presented to us quite differently. We read poll data in newspapers and see them displayed on television, while interpersonal dialogue is something we ourselves shape and participate in. Activists feel they can have it both ways: They can see public opinion as the aggregation of atomized individual opinions while also viewing it as textured interpersonal discourse. The two are related, no doubt: Interpersonal dialogue helps us formulate the answers we give to survey researchers, for example. Yet the differences between the two are still immense, and they imply different portraits of how citizens should participate and what forms of citizen participation leaders should pay attention to. This sort of ambiguity in lay theories of public opinion deserves more scholarly attention.

One last implication of staffers' views of public opinion is in order before we move on, since these professionals are so rarely studied in political science. As I have noted, many of the staffers do not equate public opinion with either poll results or extensive, structured conversation with average citizens. This is not to say that they do not speak with voters or listen closely at public hearings, because they do. But public opinion for these legislative experts is more commonly conveyed through interest groups and media sources. I wondered, after the study was complete, whether members of the public itself actually sense this absence from staffers' models of policy making. In their study of Congress, John Hibbing and Elizabeth Theiss-Morse document a very high degree of contempt for the legislative process among citizens.[10] Average voters seem to find the democratic process itself—especially as manifested in legislative activity—messy, corrupt, and unfair. Interest groups are often singled out for critique and are viewed by many citizens as working against the public good. Although Hibbing and Theiss-Morse focus on Congress, they note that the distaste for legislatures *in general* (U.S. state legislatures and other national legislatures) is rampant. Interestingly, as the authors point out, as legislatures become more professionalized, disdain for them grows: Professionalization, in the eyes of citizens, simply creates larger, more complex bureaucratic infrastructures that are both inefficient and unresponsive to public needs. In this book I did not interview citizens about the legislative process, but it is interesting to consider the possibility that staffer cognitive models (and the actions they take as a result of these models) are part of the legislative practice which so irks the public—even though these models are hidden from direct view.

Lay Theory and Political Science

It is fairly easy to see how people's fundamental conceptions of democracy might affect their actions as political professionals or citizens. It is also conceivable that an individual's lay theories about the public sphere affect opinion formation on specific policy issues. For example, an individual's feelings about representation might affect the way he or she views the debate over term limits, and it is possible that exposure to that controversy may in turn alter citizens' basic notions about representation. With further study, we may be able to make links between lay theories of democracy and policy attitude formation. But we also need to try and connect the study of lay theory more directly to the scholarly literature in American politics. It is this literature which animated my own small project and so it is this literature we should turn back to, in order to make sense of some of the findings discussed in previous chapters. This is not a simple task, since there are no direct matches between this study of lay theory and the sorts of research programs it follows. For example, John Kingdon's work on congressional decision making is relevant—as we shall see shortly—but it is about congressmen's floor votes, not about day-to-day policy making in a state assembly. And much of the research in American political behavior is either survey-based or experimental, in contrast to the interpretive methods used in many parts of this book. I do not want to stretch the results of this study to argue that it addresses all the issues raised by outstanding works in our field. However, it is very useful to see if we can map out some parallels between the present work and existing literature in American politics. Are the findings about lay theories in dialogue with middle-range theory from American scholars who have studied policy making, public opinion, and the legislative process? I choose only a few works to address here, and my choice of works is not arbitrary: I simply look back to some modern "classics" which tend to be a beacon for many of us.

Richard Fenno's study of house members and their districts, mentioned in earlier chapters, helps us to illuminate findings about lay theories. In *Home Style,* Fenno argues that congressmen carry with them a mental map of sorts, which outlines the various constituencies they must serve. Members perceive their constituency as a "nest of concentric circles," and this view enables them to operate as efficient representatives for a variety of groups. It is also vital to their strategizing during election campaigns. Fenno posits that there is a large geographic constituency, a smaller reelection constituency, an even smaller primary constituency of loyal supporters, and then a tiny circle of close advisors that serve as a member's "intimates." The congressmen speaks differently to these varying constituencies and they have different functions for him as he strives for reelection. Seeing a lawmaker's perceptual map this way—as several nested concentric circles—makes the study of such actors more challenging, and on this point it is useful to quote Fenno:

> It complicates matters both conceptually and statistically. For example, political scientists have a heavy investment in role conceptions that distinguish between the "trustee" who follows his independent judgment and the "delegate" who follows the wishes of his constituency. But we now must ask, which constituency? . . . Similarly, the variables we have used as surrogates for "the constituency" in our statistical analyses (for instance, in relating roll calls to constituency characteristics) have described only the geographical constituency—typically derived from census data. Rarely have we used variables capable of differentiating the other three constituencies, individually or collectively. A perceptual analysis warns us of the hazards of these oversimplified conceptualizations and representations of "the constituency."[11]

Fenno's argument about varying constituencies is a good parallel to the multiple meanings of public opinion we locate among informants in this study. Although the word "public" is even more ill defined and complex than "constituency," we see that staffers, journalists, and activists in this study provide varying conceptions of the public. None of the participants in this project concern themselves directly with reelection the way that Fenno's congressmen do, of course. And so informants here may, as a result, have less well-articulated views about publics since they do not have strategic pressures associated with reelection every two years. Yet it is the multiplicity of publics that links these informants to Fenno's writings. It is instructive to try and think about my informant interviews with the concentric-circle model of constituencies in mind, even though we are removed from the electoral context. Staffers certainly have intimates—the members they serve and their own close colleagues. Their next group of concern includes the lobbyists and media they depend on to get a sense of public opinion. Finally, they do think about citizens of the state of Illinois, although in a very vague and unfocused manner. This is not to say that they disregard the public at large, but that in their nested concentric circles, the geographic constituency is still furthest out and most "theoretical" as they go about their day-to-day policy-related activities.

Journalists and activists may also see their worlds in the concentric pattern Fenno develops as he describes his group of congressmen informants. Correspondents at the state legislature have a clear picture of who their intimates are.

Beyond their closest friends and colleagues, their editors are closest to them in terms of a constituency or audience. The next concentric circle out from the center, for the typical legislative journalist, is most likely the local journalistic and legislative community—the people in Springfield who make politics, the "movers and the shakers" in the arena of state government. Staffers and journalists noted that Springfield is the sort of place where one is constantly running into other policy professionals going about their errands and recreational activities, so there is a casual flow of people moving from work to play environments. But I got the sense that these political professionals have very concrete notions of whose opinions really matter to them. For journalists, the largest and indeed vaguest constituency is their readership at large. It is a constituency so diverse and so difficult to describe that it holds a fair amount of mystery for reporters. The journalists in this study work for large newspapers and media outlets, and so their audiences tend to be more heterogeneous and difficult to describe than are the readerships for smaller regional papers.

Finally, we have political activists, and we may speculate on their concentric circles of constituents as well. Activists in this study are quite articulate about the importance of their intimates—the tight social networks they use to gather ideas and information about the nature of public opinion on issues of the day. The next circle out from the center for them is undoubtedly the party—the local organization and then the national party, which activists connect with only during presidential campaigns and nominating conventions. Finally, there are the voters at large, whom the activists think about and talk about. But these are largely faceless beings, who are present to activists as poll statistics and television images.

This speculation about informants' constituencies is useful for two reasons. First, it underscores how the views of those in one's closer circles become equated with "public opinion" in one's eyes. For example, staffers spoke about interest group communication as public opinion—what the lobbyists, who are part of everyday life at the capitol, articulate the popular mood to be. I need not emphasize here that both parties (staffers and lobbyists) are "insiders" working in a very insular community. So here we see an odd convergence of a fairly intimate constituency *and* a conception of public opinion. Lobbyists are indeed connected to a larger world—to their often huge membership. Lobbyists spend much of their time at the capitol, but they do leave to consult with national headquarters or with their clients outside of the Springfield city limits. But to call this group a conduit for public opinion is still surprising, because staffers and lobbyists are so alike in the worlds they know and their professional conceptions of the political realm. Another reason why links to Fenno's work are provocative is that, for policymakers (congressmen, in Fenno's study), voters form the farthest constituency in terms of cognitive distance from the center of policymakers' concerns. The voters in their districts at large are important, but it is more strategic and informative to pay attention to intimates, loyal supporters, and reelection constituencies than to the mass of people within the geographic confines of the district. And thinking about the mass public is difficult for staffers and journalists in this study. Staffers hope to learn about these folks from lobbyists' communications, from media reports, from the occasional poll, and from their interactions with friends and neighbors. Journalists rely on conversations with a variety of sources and on their own deep and textured notion of what the "average reader" is like. Both parties tend not to speak about citizens of the state at large even though they work for or report on a state legislature whose mission is to serve Illinois residents. The public, as a mass of atomized individuals, is quite difficult to conceptualize for my informants here, and the central reason is clear: The state is far too large and diverse to allow anyone to really "get a handle" on public opinion, when public opinion means mass opinion. Surveys and elections are the best tools available for knowing mass opinion of this sort, and these two methods are both occasional and limited in the sorts of information they provide.

From the perspectives of journalists and staffers, especially, issues of great interest to their "inner-ring" constituency or public are likely to receive the most attention. This point of Fenno's is elaborated by David Whiteman in his study of members of Congress and their staffs.[12] Staff members interviewed by Whiteman did not have the time or inclination to monitor issues of interest to distant publics: Instead they focused their energies on monitoring policy matters of concern to the inner ring—in many cases the interest group leaders with whom they had the most frequent contact. This phenomenon is undoubtedly present in committee work at the state assembly as well, since the staffers I spoke with did seem most attuned to the issues presented by the publics "closest in" to them. Staffers are able to keep track quite easily of the concerns of inner-ring constituents because these groups and individuals (largely representing lobbies) share the staffers' physical space. Interpersonal communication characterizes the relationships between staffers and members of the inner-ring public. Monitoring state issues of concern to distant publics (the outer-ring public) demands attention to the media, since citizens of Illinois rarely come to the capitol and staffers rarely see them. What is worrisome, of course, is that the different communication modalities used to monitor the concerns of inner-ring versus distant publics result in inequitable quality of dialogue. Face-to-face communication is, as so many researchers have demonstrated, enormously persuasive, and lobbyists have the advantage of being "the public" closest in to the staffers and *therefore* the public most able to use the wide array of personal and rhetorical tactics associated with interpersonal communication.[13] Citizens at large across the state (the vague public, farthest away) do not have the tools of face-to-face communication at their disposal, and instead are represented—either well or badly—by the mass media.

Relevant also to this study is John Kingdon's work on the way congressmen vote on bills. Kingdon evaluates each source of pressure on a congressman—his constituencies, colleagues, party leadership, staff, and the like—in order to build a model of how members make their decisions.[14] Since he focuses on Congress, it is dangerous to draw too many parallels between this work and my interviews with staffers. But there are some useful connections to make. Kingdon emphasizes that interest groups do tend to concentrate on committees in trying to argue for their side in a policy debate. And in this study, by interviewing committee staff, I may have heightened the role of interest group opinion as synonymous with public opinion. Had I interviewed office staff, interest groups might not have loomed so large. But committees are where much of the important work on bills occurs, so it is best to focus on them if one is to study the actual design of policy. Kingdon recognizes quite clearly what I have called the "crystallizing" function of interest groups. He notes that such lobbies

> serve as attention-focusing mechanisms or filters for information. They bring matters to the attention of sympathetic congressmen who would not otherwise have taken any action. . . . Much of lobbying, furthermore, is aimed not at obtaining a specific output, but rather at simply keeping a subject on the decision agenda.[15]

It is important to note that lobbyists bring matters to a policymaker's attention, but they also provide information on public opinion and on the technical matters associated with a bill. Kingdon plays down the influence of interest groups a bit, and that may be a function of the era in which the study was conducted. During the early 1970s there were far fewer interest groups operating at the state and national levels. Since Kingdon's book was written, the number and diversity of lobbyists has expanded greatly. In Illinois during the 1990s there is particular worry about the role of lobbyists at the legislature since there are no limits on campaign spending or on political contributions. Former Senator Paul Simon led a reform group called the Illinois Campaign Finance Task Force, whose recent report noted that the amount of interest group contributions—just over the course of the last few years—has jumped dramatically. The gambling lobbies, the report noted, contributed $50,000 to Illinois leaders in 1990. By 1994 they were contributing more than $1 million to politicians in the state.[16] Whether the lack of restrictions on giving directly influences policy *to the detriment* of average or underprivileged citizens is a more complex issue not addressed here. This is obviously one of the most important research topics in the study of interest groups and legislatures. Congressmen, state legislators, and the staff who assist them must, as David Mayhew puts it, "service the organized." But how they do this is still often mysterious to students of politics.[17]

Kingdon does devote some effort to outlining the influence that media have on congressmen's voting decisions, but finds journalism's impact to be quite limited. This again may be a function of his specific research period, a time when media were less omnipresent and less powerful in most legislative environments than they are now. Kingdon mentions a crucial dimension of media power in legislatures: agenda setting. Media do have the unique ability to bring an issue to the attention of leaders, and if they deem it important, they keep shining light on the issue until it is finally addressed by policymakers. Kingdon notes that media may have direct influence, as when a congressman actually reads a news article that makes him think about an issue. And there were staffers who mentioned getting ideas for legislation from the press. But there is also indirect influence of media, which we now know—after decades of communication research—is vital to understanding the impact of journalism on politics. Media can shape the communication environment in which policymakers operate, by highlighting information, framing an issue, using symbols, providing visual imagery, and the like. I believe Kingdon is hinting at such powerful media effects, which loom large in this age of technologically sophisticated journalism. In his book, Kingdon does not address the notion that media content is construed by leaders as synonymous with public opinion, since concepts and meanings of public opinion were not his focus. One can ask now, though, after thinking about the lay theories of staffers, whether Kingdon's congressmen informants would indeed place more emphasis on media as conduit of the public sentiment if they were queried at greater length today.

One particularly important effect of media in state and national politics is their ability to create both the frames and the language we use to discuss issues.

As Shanto Iyengar puts it, "people are exquisitely sensitive to contextual cues when they make decisions, formulate judgments, or express opinions."[18] And while party leaders and their communication directors try very hard to spread their favored contextual cues or frames in the heat of policy debate, journalists have enormous power to pick and choose among these frames according to their news sense. Some frames make for better coverage than others, and journalists have their own rules of thumb about what appeals to their readers and viewers. Staffers in this study are, as we saw in chapter 2, very attuned to the content of media and to the sorts of frames and contextual cues reporters used to describe legislative debate. The clipping service at the capitol allows them to keep abreast of coverage on issues of import to their committees and to monitor the ways issues were framed. Often there are major tax and education bills that staffers—across committees and houses—attend to quite closely. One substantive and symbolic issue that several staffers discussed (because it had been debated so recently with such great emotion) was proposed legislation that would have created prisoner chain gangs wearing shackles to work on the state's roadways. In the debate over this bill, framing was vital as various members, staffers, and communication directors sparred over the meaning and impact of the legislation. Was it a productive means for punishing criminals while simultaneously deterring more crime? Or was the bill a throwback to the particular style of racism found in the south during mid-century? One staffer noted that the public seemed very much keyed in to this particular issue, perhaps for its racial resonance but certainly because it was so hotly debated by their representatives. This staffer—an attorney and expert in criminal matters—said that the chain gangs bill "got a lot of press in the papers once the bills [one in the House and one in the Senate] were filed. People [the public] really liked it. I think . . . public opinion—the public—liked the idea that we do not coddle these criminals anymore." Note here the tendency (documented in chapter 2) to mix talk of public opinion with talk of media coverage: The great press attention is a signal to this staffer about the content of public opinion. But also note the media frame—the alleged tendency of the penal system to "coddle prisoners." The frame was present in the members' debate about the legislation at the capital certainly but, due in part to the media, it also became the language staffers and others used to think about this particular proposal.

Another now classic work in American politics that helps to illuminate the findings in this book is E. E. Schattschneider's *The Semisovereign People.* In this provocative essay, the author argues that understanding politics entails the study of conflict and the spread of conflict. One incentive that leaders have to containing a policy conflict within small circles is that diffusion of information about the debate leads to uncertainty and even chaos: "So great is the change in the nature of any conflict likely to be as a consequence of the widening involvement of people in it that the original participants are apt to lose control of the conflict altogether. . . . Therefore the contagiousness of conflict, the elasticity of its scope and the fluidity of the involvement of people are the X factors in politics."[19] Although I did not query staffers about contagion of conflict—something easier to do with narrow legislative issues than broader ones—they are probably well aware of the problem. It may be that the reason staffers pay such close attention to media, as conduit of public opinion, is that media play a crucial role in setting the scope of conflict. If journalists choose to take up an issue and focus on it, they can widen the scope of conflict quickly and easily. They can also shrink the scope of conflict, by portraying an issue debate as relevant to only a small segment of the population. Journalists must of course make the conflict interesting and relevant to readers; otherwise it will be ignored. But they certainly have the potential to influence processes of "contagion." Since media have this power, staffers must attend to it in order to get a sense of how large a conflict has become and which parties are now part of the conflict.

Many of the conflicts journalists are attracted to, at the national level and in Springfield, are conflicts of personalities. Battles among party leaders greatly interest journalists, who like to put a human face on conflict and (in the best case) educate their readers about ideological contrast in this manner. This is not exactly the sort of conflict Schattschneider had in mind. Yet, this is the way conflict tends to emerge in American political media. Some of the journalists interviewed in this book spoke quite specifically about the need to focus on personalities in order to pique readers' interest. Whether this journalistic technique—addressing issue and ideological debate using personality conflict among leaders as a vehicle—is effective for newspapers is unaddressed here. But it is believed to be a more general problem in American political communication, as some of our premier scholars of media have pointed out.[20] The role of the media in generating conflict and public interest in conflict cannot be underplayed: When members of the mass public enter onto the scene they do not spread out equally across policy positions. As Schattschneider puts it:

> It is extremely unlikely that both sides [in a policy conflict] will be re-inforced equally as the scope of the conflict is doubled or quadrupled or multiplied by a hundred or a thousand. That is, the balance of the forces recruited will almost certainly not remain

constant. This is true because it is improbable that the participants in the original conflict constitute a representative sample of the larger community; nor is it likely that the successive increments are representative. . . . It follows that conflicts are frequently won or lost by the success that the contestants have in getting the audience involved in the fight or in excluding it, as the case may be.[21]

Media, then, are critical in expanding scope of a conflict. So while staffers in this study do not attend to mass opinion in any particularly systematic way, they do attend quite closely to mass media to see how the scope of conflict is emerging. It is possible that lobbyists help them understand the scope of conflict as well, but such actors tend to be insiders and so likely also turn to the media for such purposes.

Schattschneider also raises for us the possibility that it is conflict and controversy that pull people into political debate, that awaken an inattentive public. Conflicts create the aperture for common citizens to pay heed and even get involved on rare occasions. Journalists in the study, and journalists in general, seem to have a fundamental understanding of this notion: They see that conflict—either ideological rifts or the personality clashes of men and women in power—generates interest and excitement about public affairs. Staffers, on the other hand, find conflict more worrisome: They know they cannot avoid it and they have become adept at dealing with controversy in their policy areas, but the fact that conflict inevitably increases the number of participants in a policy debate makes their work exceedingly difficult, complex, and uncertain. Because he is so hopeful about the ways conflict can spur political attention and participation, Schattschneider is our antidote to Lippmann's negative characterization of the sleepy public (discussed below). The sleepy, reactive public of staffers' and journalists' causal models is not to be scorned, in Schattschneider's view, because it can and will be awakened through real, vital conflict. In fact, the missing piece in Schattschneider's theory is the mass media, and this study underscores how the media may expand the scope of conflict (drawing people into issue debate) or largely ignore a conflict, letting experts, staffers, and lobbyists serve the public while serving *as* the public.

The last major works in American politics I would like to address before moving on to grand theoretical notions about public discourse and representation concern the knowledge level or "rationality" of the common citizen. In his widely known article, "The Nature of Belief Systems in Mass Publics," Philip Converse gives us reason to worry about citizen information levels. He demonstrates that a large portion of the population have belief systems which exhibit very little consistency or "constraint" among attitudes. And since he wrote, we have heard from other scholars who argue much the same thing.[22] Recently, some social scientists have argued for "low information rationality" or have noted that aggregation of unstable opinions can lead to rather stable mass opinion over time (an argument made by Benjamin Page and Robert Shapiro).[23] Whether American citizens are informed enough to act in their own best interests is still a matter of research and debate in political science, but it is clear to me that the political professionals interviewed here are very much in Converse's camp. They deem people to be largely ignorant about politics—particularly the ideological content of debate over bills and the technical issues associated with most legislative action. They do not think people stupid, but they see them as distracted from the political world by their work, family, and personal concerns. Both staffers and journalists have deep worries about citizens' knowledge levels and about their general conceptions of the political scene. Some very seasoned journalists whom I interviewed could still be surprised by public ignorance and could still become depressed about areas of ignorance. Staffers and journalists are among our most sophisticated citizens, when it comes to politics, and they feel the gap between themselves and the public quite intensely. Activists were less likely to complain about mass ignorance or unsophistication among the citizenry, since they are our most optimistic and indeed classically democratic group. They are optimistic about their party's ability to educate people and mobilize them when necessary. Activists would feel comfortable in the Page and Shapiro camp, undoubtedly, since they are our champions of aggregate opinion. Again, they are skeptical of polls, but they still see some value in this form of mass opinion evaluation.

Page and Shapiro find that, while there is often a "match" between public preferences and the direction of public policy, these two entities are "out of sync" in one-third of all policy cases. They argue that government responsiveness is less likely when public attention and knowledge are low. On issues where the public does not make itself heard, in other words, leaders may often do what they please—what is expedient for themselves or their parties. And here Page and Shapiro agree with Schattschneider: When the scope of conflict is narrow, leaders need not worry about accountability to constituents. Looking at the findings in this book through Page and Shapiro's lens is provocative. If state politics has a fairly good match between public opinion and policy, (and there is some demonstration of this very fact in the literature), I hypothesize that it may not be due to the abundance of polling. In this study, we found that staffers pay little attention to opinion polls as they research and write legislation, and there is now some confirmation of this in at least one national policy instance as well. Perhaps policy and opinion frequently match because media and interest groups do give staffers a fairly good sense of what people prefer (if we assume that Page and Shapiro's surveys measure such preferences accurately). On the other hand, the many cases of mismatch demonstrate that faulty communication between leaders and the public is evident. Then there is the possibility as well that leaders are actually leading and are purposefully avoiding the consultation of public opinion. These are complex issues, which I am in no position to address here with my limited data set. However, they are stimulating ones raised by the lay theories articulated by political professionals in this book. We academics may care about citizen knowledge levels because we care about democracy, but staffers, journalists, and political activists care as well for their own varied reasons. How do their actions reflect their views of citizens, what they know and what they are capable of?[24]

Lippmann versus Dewey, Large Polity versus Small

Early in this century Walter Lippmann argued that public opinion was a phantom, that citizens had neither the time nor the inclination to engage in political debate with each other or to attend to all the controversies swirling around the public sphere at any moment in time. And it is Lippmann who wrote some of the most haunting and troubling passages of twentieth-century political thought. He observed that

> The private citizen today has come to feel rather like a deaf spectator in the back row, who ought to keep his mind on the mystery off there, but cannot quite manage to keep awake. He knows he is somehow affected by what is going on. Rules and regulations continually, taxes annually and wars occasionally remind him that he is being swept along by great drifts of circumstance. Yet these public affairs are in no convincing way his affairs. They are for the most part invisible. They are managed, if they are managed at all, at distant centers, from behind the scenes, by unnamed powers. As a private person he does not know for certain what is going on, or who is doing it, or where he is being carried. . . . In the cold light of experience he knows that his sovereignty is a fiction. He reigns in theory, but does not govern.[25]

And Lippmann maintained this perspective over the course of his long career, which spanned much of the twentieth century. In his roles as journalist, political thinker, and advisor to statesmen, Lippmann would always question the ability of the common citizen to reason or participate properly in the political realm. An enormously depressing view of democratic competence, no doubt, but a realistic one according to a man who spent a great deal of time reflecting on politics.

The staff informants and journalists in this book made many remarks that indicate an affinity to Lippmann's paradigm. They move in and out of his worldview, and they would undoubtedly reject many of Lippmann's stronger statements about citizen competence. Yet their models and notions of public opinion seem built on a foundation of weak citizens. Staffers often rely on experts—on lobbyists and journalists—to help them understand public opinion. These conduits are interpreters, or translators, who tell these busy policy managers what they can expect from the public or what the public expects from the legislature. Journalists, on the other hand, have a highly developed rhetoric and mindset about the public: In many instances they put the public on a pedestal, as they know they must serve their readers and speak to readers' interests. Yet journalists in this small study did not make a concerted effort to systematically gather or assess citizens' opinions. Instead, they relied on many of the traditional techniques journalists have always used to gain a sense of public opinion—talking to many sources, observing their environments, speaking with their colleagues, and imagining possible public reactions to events and policies. Academics may not be happy with these approaches to assessing public opinion, but they are methods that Lippmann would deem quite reasonable. If the public is a sleepy and uninformed mass, exacting consultation with citizens is not a useful expenditure of one's time or resources. One can always get people to talk, but if what they say is not based on an informed worldview, what are such opinions worth?

Lippmann's views are often discussed in contrast to those of his great philosophical opponent, John Dewey.[26] And most thinking people prefer the more optimistic Dewey to the more skeptical Lippmann, whose dark and brooding prose makes us wonder whether we will ever see a highly engaged populace in American politics. Among the informants in this study, the political activists, those partisans who devote so much time and emotion to organizing and mobilizing their fellow citizens, are most in line with Dewey. Are the staffers and journalists drawn to Lippmann's depressing picture because they know more about politics and the potential for citizen action? That is possible. Their occupations do force them to take a close look at citizen action across many issues, and so they have a broad experience in politics that activists tend not to have. Our partisan activists are highly engaged, but they are not full-time political workers, so their involvement is more limited. Yet activists know a kind of politics as well, and their experience draws them closer to Dewey, to a progressive and even sunny view of politics and public opinion. I found, in this analysis of activists' lay theories, that they see public opinion as both an aggregation of individual opinions and the discourse of people interacting in local communities. It is the latter, of course, that Dewey prized as the basis for citizen participation and the fundamental force that drives democracy itself. Dewey tells us: "Regarded as an idea, democracy is not an alternative to other principles of associated life. It is the idea of community life itself."[27] Partisan activists seem to see community *and* the conversations that actually form community as vital parts of a working democracy. Staffers do not dismiss conversation, but they do not think of it in connection with "public opinion." Journalists are more discursive in their conceptions of public opinion, but they do not provide evidence that they have thought about conversation in any rigorous matter: None of the journalist informants in this study have formal or informal systems for seeking out conversation, even though they know conversation provides very valuable information about the nature of public opinion on particular topics. Our activists, on the other hand, cling quite closely to conversation as a staple of democracy. They see the connection between local community dialogue and that towering, yet slippery concept of "public opinion."

When activists spoke or wrote about social network discussion as public opinion, their ideas seemed to resonate with some of our oldest theoretical work: speculation on the relationships among friendship, community, and polity. In *The Nicomachean Ethics,* for example, Aristotle argues that close personal friendships are the basis of the city-state itself:

> [F]riendship] appears to be the bond of the state; and lawgivers seem to set more store by it than they do by justice, for to promote concord, which seems akin to friendship, is their chief aim, while faction, which is enmity, is what they are most anxious to banish. And if men are friends, there is no need of justice between them; whereas merely to be just is not enough—a feeling of friendship is also necessary. Indeed the highest form of justice seems to have an element of friendly feeling in it.[28]

Here Aristotle recognizes that there is something beyond the simple contract citizens make with each other to form the state. Personal feeling is vital if the machine of democracy is to operate smoothly, since it paves the way for alliance and consensus. Where there is friendship binding people together, a variety of judicial mechanisms become superfluous because there is trust and goodwill motivating people's actions.

The notion of friendship as the basis for equal citizenship and democracy is one of the most interesting and most neglected ideas from classical democratic theory. Classics scholar David Bolotin argues that although friendship was vital to ancient theory, contemporary theorists avoid the issue. He speculates that "[O]ur hopes for universal, or even national, brotherhood tend to make us lose sight of so private and exclusive a relationship."[29] Connections among friendship, community, and politics have been explored most often by theorists, although we have a handful of empirical research projects that try to make such links as well.[30] One such study was conducted by Jane J. Mansbridge, who described and analyzed a variety of small-scale "unitary" democracies. These are communities where friendship is one axis or operating principle around which people organize, argue, and make policy. Important for us is Mansbridge's argument that "any polity based on friendship must be a democracy, for it is based on a fundamental equality among its members."[31] It is this link we find in the comments of political activists studied in this book. Partisan activists seem to have a very clear sense of equality among citizens in a democratic state. They acknowledge the problems associated with opinion polling, but they prefer it to many other means of assessing public opinion *because it assumes equality of opinions.* Yet the texture and indeed joy they get from their friendships must play a part in their conceptions of public opinion as well; hence they mention the opinions of those around them as vital to their own assessment of popular sentiment on public affairs. Equality and friendship, then, loom large in activists' very classical models of democracy. These partisan activists are not naive: They know that citizens vary in terms of their interest in and knowledge of politics. But these men and women still, at base, believe that all Americans deserve a hearing in the court of public opinion.

In contrast to activists, who make these connections among friendship, equality, and public opinion—which cohere very neatly with their goals of organizing and mobilizing those around them—are the staffers and journalists. In my conversations with these policy professionals, informants did mention their friends and colleagues repeatedly in various contexts. Yet when it came to judging public opinion, to getting a sense of popular sentiment, they were reluctant to emphasize their social networks as strongly as did activists. This is to be expected, though, since professionals would be unlikely to admit that the friends' opinions are "data" to employ for designing policy or reporting on important legislative issues. Yet despite this reluctance, I saw traces of friendship or reference to social networks as staffers and journalists spoke about public opinion.

Even these professionals, with their resources and contacts, still value the vivid interpersonal dialogues they find in everyday conversation with people they know. How often these dialogues play a role in their conceptualization and action on legislative matters is an interesting issue to explore, since I have not given it nearly the attention it deserves here.

Closely related to the notions of friendship, equality, and public opinion is the issue of polity size. In their thoughtful study on the subject, Robert Dahl and Edward Tufte address one of the most troubling issues in democratic theory: What is the ideal size for a democratic state?[32] This question is very closely linked to sociological concerns about networks, since talk in one's neighborhood or community matters most when these units have some power as well. Dahl and Tufte consider a variety of models for democracies, noting that for two thousand years the city-state was thought to be the ideal size. By contrast, it is only during the last few hundred years that the nation-state has been theorized as the ideal-typical democratic unit. The authors struggle with the question of size, but in the end cannot argue for an "optimal" size of polity. Instead they urge theorists and statesmen to consider the issue of size in the formulation of participatory structures. Large nations, like the United States, will not maximize citizen participation until smaller units for governing are recognized and enhanced. And there are movements afoot in this regard. We have witnessed a variety of experiments in "teledemocracy" such as cable-access community programming and televised town meetings. Here the mass media are used to "de-massify" and enable people to participate in politics or at least build some connection to others in their local communities. One of the more important experiments in democracy, which deals directly with issues of size and public opinion formation, is James Fishkin's "deliberative democracy" program. In his theoretical work and empirical investigation, Fishkin demonstrates the powerful benefits of political discourse among small groups of citizens. Indeed Fishkin organizes people for the express purpose of political talk, argument, and opinion formation, and finds that interpersonal dialogue is extraordinary effective in getting people to think about their ideological frameworks.[33] Despite this work, however, we still know very little about how people talk about politics—and act on that talk—in local communities. This book's finding that many people actually define public opinion as local talk within social networks should give us added incentive to study such enclaves. This sort of work will necessarily be ethnographic in part, and therefore labor-intensive. But it will bring together sociology and political theory in useful ways.

Issues of Representation

In this book we uncovered three different views of representation. Although representation was not the central focus of my interviews or the central focus of the activist survey, themes and problems associated with representation were omnipresent. And if one is interested in public opinion—particularly in its basic conceptualization—representation obviously matters greatly. Public opinion, no matter how intense, must be captured in a format we can grasp; otherwise, it can never be represented or acted upon. Let us take our groups—staffers, journalists, and activists—one by one, and see how their comments touch on debates in the area of representation.

Our staffers believe that interest groups and media often represent public opinion effectively. They have no evidence for this, but then again, it is not clear what sort of evidence would help them figure out whether or not these agents are properly representing mass opinion. Opinion surveys might enable staffers to compare aggregated individual opinions to the portraits of public opinion gathered through lobbyists or media. Yet, as noted earlier, opinion polling has very obvious problems when it comes to specific legislative debates—particularly when they are complex, fast moving, and technical. There are large areas of ignorance among members of the public, and staffers know this, which is why survey data do not carry much weight with staffers as they work on bills during session at the statehouse. Using "surrogates" like lobbyists and media to assess citizens' views is very close to a client-oriented view of representation. A. Phillips Griffiths has called this "ascriptive representation": It is a model whereby agents represent people even though they are not necessarily *similar* to those people (demographically or ideologically).[34] Our staffers feel comfortable with this ascriptive representation system when common citizens are indeed clients of lobbyists and media. This is not an unproblematic model, of course, since citizens never "hired" these clients to represent them. Lobbyists are hired, but by interest group leaders. And although subscribers buy newspapers, they certainly do not hire journalists to represent them to legislative staffers, or members, for that matter. So the ascriptive model may be in place for the staffers, but not for the represented. Since we do not have any small or large-scale studies that probe citizens at length about representation—their views of the process and whether they find media or lobbyists to be up to the task—it is hard to know whether there is a mismatch between staffers' and citizens' models of representation. We can speculate, though, that citizens would feel a bit uncomfortable with lobbyists and media representing their opinions: After all, Americans are accustomed to voting for their representatives.

Unlike staffers, journalists are not public servants, so we should not evaluate their views of public opinion representation in the way we view legislative actors' attitudes. Journalists would rightly defend their work as interesting and useful to readers, but they would not try to argue that in all issue debates they represent various segments of public opinion. Yet it is fascinating to note that they also have models of representation even if representation is not their central task. Journalists have their sources on various issues, but they also carry with them imaginary portraits of their audiences. These stereotypes, to use Lippmann's word, enable journalists to go about their work efficiently. Such imaginary figures are internal, and often very vivid, representations of large and diverse constituencies who read a major newspaper or listen to a radio station. Political leaders undoubtedly have these sorts of "pictures in their heads" as well but, because they are elected, they need more concrete evidence of public opinion before they act, whether they attend to this evidence or not. In any case, these images of average voters or newspaper readers are important and scholars need to recognize that these images, in addition to other forces, may very well drive the actions of public officials and journalists.

Partisan activists in this study seem to recognize what John Stuart Mill called the "aggregate of the community," which is why they are accepting of opinion polls, flaws and all.[35] They would like their leaders to consider the aggregation of individual opinions as embodied by elections, referenda, polls, and other such mechanisms, yet they realize these are problematic as communication devices. And beyond the inability of such quantitative indicators to relay all aspects of public opinion from citizen to representative is the fact that legislators often need to act without consultation of public opinion. As we noted in the last chapter, activists are comfortable with an element of the Burkean perspective: They realize that there are many cases where representatives feel compelled to use their own judgment because they are better-informed than the public or have personal opinions which they cannot abandon (e.g., opinions about moral issues, such as abortion). The activists' model of representation asks leaders to both consider aggregate opinion and act independently. Many of the activists noted that representatives can and should act in defiance of public opinion at times, but they must always explain and justify such an action to their constituents.

So we do see differences among groups in terms of representation. Our activists come closest to embracing classical, direct participation forms of democracy, but they see the need for representation in a mass society as large as our own. Journalists feel, justifiably so, that it is not their job to represent public opinion, but they do try to describe it as best they can. And whether they realize it or not, their perspectives on public opinion are often taken up by staffers as evidence of popular sentiments. Staffers find the media enormously useful and evocative as they try to get a sense of the climate of opinion. And, as we saw, lobbyists help them with this task as well. There was a glaring absence in my discussion with staffers of endorsement of systematic, aggregate devices for assessing public opinion. Such approaches to assessing public opinion do cost money (e.g., conducting issue polls on a regular basis), and their results might be difficult to staffers to interpret in the heat of complex legislative debate, but their *absence* undoubtedly helps shape the nature of politics in this large American state.

The Future: Theory and Research on Public Opinion

There are several theoretical and methodological implications of the research presented in this book, and this section is devoted to the future: How should our knowledge of staffer, journalistic, and activist lay theory about public opinion affect our scholarly approaches to public opinion and politics more generally? My research is not conclusive: On the contrary, like most of our work, it does tend to raise more questions than it answers. This may be due to my choice of method—depth interviews and extensive probing/conversational research techniques instead of more survey work, which allows for great generalization with less depth. Yet sample size seems less problematic than some of the other limitations. Although Illinois is a large and diverse state with a professionalized legislature, it is still one state in fifty. This study deserves expansion in other environments, including the U.S. Congress. Access to staffers and journalists becomes more problematic as one moves to the federal level, but I hope I have demonstrated that probing these actors is quite useful to us as we try to gain knowledge about the democratic process. Beyond exploring different levels of government, one could include other categories of actors in future research, including legislators themselves, agency bureaucrats, interest group leaders, party officials, and the like.

These obvious qualifications aside, let us step back to evaluate how public opinion theorizing and research might proceed given the findings in this book. One very important implication, to my mind, concerns the study of mass media as artifact of public opinion. Staffers mention media as artifact of public opinion without hesitation, and perhaps there is much value in following up on their views. Scholars in the interdisciplinary field of Cultural Studies have long argued that media tell us quite a bit about the climate of opinion in a mass society.[36] There are several reasons why such researchers are confident that media illuminate mass opinion, and indeed many scholars even find survey research or depth interviewing of citizens unnecessary, since media texts are so rich in information about public opinion (the extreme position). The most important reason why media texts are valuable public opinion sources is that the most popular ones (hit television programs, newsmagazines with high circulation, or talk radio programs with a large listening audience) *are* popular because they resonate with the attitudes and norms of the public at large. When it comes to media consumption, people vote with their feet: They have limited time and limited finances, so they are drawn to media content that "clicks" with what they believe. In media studies there is substantial evidence that people choose media selectively, and they choose it according to what they already like and believe. It is clear that this close relationship, between people and the texts they search out and enjoy, can be exploited by students of public opinion. Systematic content analysis is labor-intensive and challenging, since the measurement of manifest content is a complex process. Yet, we need to think more systematically and rigorously about content analysis as a window to understanding public opinion. Must one always study flesh and blood citizens, through surveys, depth interviews, or experimentation, in order to understand public opinion? This is a question that the Cultural Studies scholars have already considered, and a question to which they have resoundingly answered "no." Political scientists are slower to consider this, given the long history of attitude research in the field. It is, of course, optimal to employ multiple measures of public opinion, but media might be considered with more respect (and caution, of course) as a very textured and very plausible means of understanding public opinion.

But what do our most popular news media or entertainment media—and granted these categories are empirically conflated—tell us that surveys and experiments cannot, as we try to understand public opinion of the past or of the present? Perhaps, because they are vivid and structured as narrative, media texts provide a more complex sort of information about ideology and attitudes. Media can give us a sense of the range of attitude intensity, for example. Analysis of media cannot tell us how *many* people register highly intense or emotional attitudes toward an issue and how many do not, but textual analysis may give us some clues about attitude/action linkages that we might not gather through opinion surveys. Let us take as an example media directed at African Americans, and focus specifically on the O. J. Simpson verdict—an extraordinary event in the recent history of race relations. Survey research before the verdict, which found Simpson innocent of murder charges, indicated a split in public opinion between blacks and whites: Blacks leaned toward an innocent verdict and whites toward a guilty one.[37] We can infer great differences in feeling of blacks versus whites from these data, but they certainly did not prepare most white Americans for the very intense, positive reactions of many blacks after the verdict of innocence was revealed. Surveys could tell us, before the verdict, how people saw the case in very narrow terms: innocent or guilty. But the fact that the case was a focus point for great emotion, and for concern about racial injustice in America, was not revealed by survey data. Such facts were revealed by black talk radio, however.[38] Attention to that medium, before the verdict was released, did uncover such intensity of feeling and foreshadowed the celebratory reactions of many African American citizens. So in this case, the highly ideological and marginal nature of at least one black talk station in a major city revealed an aspect of public opinion that was not evident from survey results. Could survey researchers have done a better job measuring intensity of feeling among blacks and whites about this high-profile court case? Perhaps. But survey research has its limits, as our staffers of chapter 2 pointed out. And even in a wealthy nation like America, few news outlets, political organizations, government agencies, or academic research institutions have the resources to engage in constant survey research on all political and social controversies of the day. Survey research has its advantages, and they are clear. But gaps in our understanding and predictive capacity, when it comes to public opinion, may be filled through experimentation with new methods and new public opinion artifacts.

Even though careful, critical historians have long relied on media as artifact of public opinion, contemporary social scientists are more dismissive of this source. The notion that media might serve as one repository of public opinion is typically a controversial one, I have found, and we rarely take the time to reflect on it because it feels so undemocratic and indeed repulsive. In fact, when the idea is mentioned in academe today it seems to get the same negative reaction as one of its proponents, Walter Lippmann. How could the American mass media, so full of inane, "infotainment," possibly manifest any useful clues about the somber and hallowed democratic concept, public opinion? It is difficult to pair discussion of our (less-than-ideal) newspapers, broadcast programs, and magazines with discussion of public opinion. Yet in all contemporary democracies, we cannot escape the unrelenting sights and sounds of the mass media. There are no issues of public import which do not receive massive media coverage—some of it reflecting the tastes of the educated and highbrow and some of it far more superficial and verging on incompetent. But we must put our own preferences for media content aside if we can. An opinion researcher who ignores the media, our constant companions who reflect, crystallize, and distort the ideas of our times, is engaging in an incomplete form of social science. Decades ago, social scientists argued that the study of media content would be vital in the *reconceptualization* of public opinion as an idea, and they recognized media as *one* wonderfully rich archive full of public opinion indicators. Edited volumes and essays about public opinion in the 1940s, 1950s, and 1960s regularly included discussions of the media as both manipulators and *representatives* of public attitudes.[39] The study of media and the study of public opinion, these scholars believed—very much in the spirit of Bryce, Tarde, and Lippmann—should not be separated. The world is a different place now, with more media outlets of varying type and quality, but these complexities should entice opinion researchers who are devoted to the comprehensive study of popular sentiments.

The search for artifacts of public opinion is important for political scientists if they are to understand or predict political behavior, since there are so many movements of public opinion we have not detected through surveying. Who could have predicted, for example, that Bill Clinton would fail in the particular ways he did, in reforming national health care policy? Perhaps no means of measuring public opinion can help us predict idiosyncratic policy failures, but we can certainly do better in the future with a broader methodological spectrum in mind. Historians have thought about this problem in more sophisticated ways than social scientists have, in fact, because their choices for measuring public opinion are so constrained. When studying polities of the past and trying to understand the climate of opinion, historians typically cannot use surveys since potential respondents are long gone. So creative historians look to available archives and read the documents in them with great care and skepticism, hoping to weave together a "story" about public opinion that illuminates their period of interest. Along these lines, historians have used newspapers, legal briefs, letters to newspaper editors, personal correspondence, and letters to public officials, in addition to many other types of documents.[40] One example of using letters to public officials to understand political action is Taeku Lee's analysis of constituent mail about the American civil-rights movement.[41] Lee finds, in a systematic evaluation of both letters to presidents and survey research data, that the analysis of such letters is extraordinarily useful in understanding and anticipating social movements. Constituent mail is both robust, when compared with survey data, and it provides texture on public attitudes that surveys fail to capture. Lee notes that, in the case of the civil-rights movement, letters illuminate differences between (what he labels) "elite" and "nonelite" influences on mass mobilization. And letters are rich in symbols, tropes, and themes that social historians have found invaluable in understanding this vital period in American political history. Public opinion researchers would find them valuable as well, no doubt.

This brief mention of alternative public opinion measures, which historians have already utilized to great effect, is not simply a call for triangulation of methods. It is also an argument for a broader and richer conceptualization of public opinion itself among researchers. People who work in politics, who spend much of their lives thinking about policy, mobilization, and public opinion, have already realized that public opinion means different things in different contexts. And different contexts—whether the state legislature, Congress, or a local school district—demand different meanings and measures of public opinion. We give lip service to this notion, but the social and methodological construction of public opinion is often lost in our rush to measure the public mood. Media, interest group communication, and the interpersonal dialogues of citizens were all mentioned by informants in this study as useful measures of public opinion. Can scholars find value in them as well? A notion worth exploring, highlighted by the lay theories of working political professionals and activists.

Beyond methodological diversity and the need to reconceptualize public opinion in different political milieus, there are other more narrow implications of lay theory findings for public opinion research. This study makes clear, for example, that we still know very little about the use of various opinion assessment techniques within government or in journalism. When do legislators or their key staffers use polls in construction of or debate about bills? For example, do polls affect the way these men and women think about issues, even though they are not cited in formal documents, speeches, or committee discussions?[42] Or, crucially, when a poll and some other form of public opinion evidence are in conflict, which takes precedence in strategic calculations of our leaders? These instances of conflict are potentially fascinating, and studying them might give us some insight into basic policy-making processes. The same questions might be applied to the practice of journalism: What do reporters do with multiple, conflicting reports on public opinion? Academics may have their own choices of opinion assessment techniques, but what do political actors themselves do to assess public moods? We can complain all we want about the unsystematic approaches they use, but legislators, staffers, journalists, party officials, lobbyists, and activists are the groups who formulate policy, educate the public about current affairs, and mobilize citizens for political action.

One interesting implication of this study concerns rationalization—the Weberian trend toward increasing quantification and systematization in our social, political, and economic practices. I have argued elsewhere that the lengthy history of public opinion measurement is in fact a narrative of increasing rationality, as a variety of political actors have tried to find more rigorous and predictive measures of public opinion.[43] This book is not a historical study, but it does make us wonder about the trend toward rationalization. Will the proliferation of polling, which is so clear during election campaigns, eventually affect day-to-day policy making? Or will policymakers continue to resist surveys, despite the diffusion of survey research methods and the growing number of polling organizations? In other words, is rationalization—in this case the increasing tendency to try to quantify public opinion—slow to spread, or is it unlikely to spread much further, across political environments? Max Weber wrote about rationalization as a linear process, but one with stops and starts. It is an uneven process, and it can be interrupted by influential individuals (e.g., charismatic leaders), by institutions, or by unexpected events. In this study, the state legislative staff and the journalists who cover the legislature for major news outlets are somewhat resistant to the drive toward quantification. But without more study, it is hard to know whether this situation is common in other states or in Congress. At this writing it is difficult to tell just exactly *where* we are in the historical development of public opinion. It is an important issue to ponder, though, as we think about the historical context of our work and the future of democratic process itself.

The conflation of media and public opinion, which was raised by staffers and—less directly—by activists, is methodologically provocative for us, but troubling as well. Some staffers believe that media and public opinion are synonymous, that they can detect public opinion not through media polls but through the narrative content of journalism. Should we consider public opinion and media as so thoroughly intertwined that they can—theoretically and methodologically—be treated as one entity? We have not, in media studies or political science, been particularly successful in demonstrating sustained effects of media on public opinion or vice versa.[44] There are some dramatic cases where the two seem separable and we can detect effects: Media can be very effective, for example, in rallying people in times of war or in stimulating Americans to raise money for famine relief in foreign nations. Yet on the whole we have trouble determining the effects of media on public opinion, just as early Columbia School researchers did in a period of far less mass media penetration. We certainly are far from forming grand theories of effects that outline how, when, or why media move public opinion. Finding law-like propositions in this area may be an impossibility, but we do not seem to be much closer to this goal than we were in the early part of the century, when radio was introduced on the American scene. I am not arguing here for the elimination of all theoretical models that put "media" and "public opinion" in different "boxes" (e.g., "agenda-setting" research). But I think that we might consider the notion that the two entities of media and public opinion are often largely conflated: Together they may be quite powerful in the formulation of policy or the start of a social movement, but when we separate them we become distracted from the study of larger trends and phenomena.

Again, this is an issue about which many postmodern theorists and Cultural Studies scholars have already come to consensus. They would find the separation of media and public opinion, so common in political science and communication studies, simply bizarre. In their eyes, institutions and actors go about their business in a completely media-saturated environment: We swim in a sea of ever changing symbols and ideas, and media affect our every thought and consideration. At this point, public opinion researchers have been almost entirely resistant to theoretical claims of this sort, and indeed such ideas wreak havoc with most of our hypotheses and methodologies. But this is the sort of provocative thinking about media and politics that will ultimately enhance public opinion work. After all, public opinion is one concept in political theory that is *thoroughly connected to concerns of culture.* Public opinion analysts need to think more about culture—about symbols, religion, the arts, and so forth—because citizens are not one-dimensional political animals who attend to the news (or not) and vote (or not). They are people who move in and out of politics, as they move in and out of other realms, and our avoidance of this fact makes public opinion study far less rich than it should be. Those of us who are interested in public opinion cannot master every field that touches on it. None of us can manage it all—history and aesthetics in addition to sociology and psychology. But we can demonstrate more sensitivity to the cultural context in which people live, work, play, and ultimately form opinions. Cultural Studies analysts have been fearless in trying to discern the mix of ideas in American culture, and these ideas are ideological, aesthetic, religious, stylistic, gendered, and infused with race. We may not like their methods, and we may cringe at some of the more fantastic tenets of postmodernism, but Cultural Studies critics are working on many of the same problems public opinion researchers grapple with. So, we have yet another call for more interdisciplinary work. Acknowledging the need for more interdisciplinary work seems uncontroversial on the surface, but can we actually broaden the field of public opinion in fundamental ways, so that we may begin to address the concerns of culture?

This book began with the idea that public opinion is a social construct, dependent on the historical, political, and technological contexts in which we labor. Thinking about public opinion in this manner is not a squishy or unrigorous approach. We can utilize survey methods, experimentation, depth interviews, content analysis, and other methods in our existing repertoire to conduct research which admits to the fluctuating nature of public opinion itself. The exploration of lay theories, across occupational groups, is just one route to understanding the nature of public opinion constructs. And it has its problems and blind spots. But I hope this work underscores the flexibility and openness of the concept of "public opinion" itself. We should not throw up our hands, admit to multiple meanings and measures of public opinion, and simply continue to work in the ways we always have. And we certainly should not eliminate that elusive phrase "public opinion" from our scholarly or popular vocabularies. However, we do need to think harder and longer about the meaning of public opinion if we are to follow up on the thoughtful legacies of Lippmann, Dewey, Blumer, Lazarsfeld, and other early twentieth-century analysts of public opinion.

Appendixes

....

Appendix A: Notes on Interviews and Building Grounded Theory

I began all interviews with questions about the informants' backgrounds—where they grew up, went to school, and eventually settled. I was particularly interested in socialization issues with the political activists and asked all of them whether they grew up in activist or partisan households and how they became politically involved. The legislative staffers and journalists also had interesting backgrounds; many of them had come to Springfield after beginning other careers or (for the journalists) covering other beats. After asking about their pasts, I asked them to tell me about their current work. Staffers noted which committees they served and also explained—often at length—what their work on those committees entailed. Journalists recounted their daily routines in the press office, both during session (January through May) and during the summer and the brief governor's veto session in the fall. The background queries were quite useful to me since they gave me some clues as to the approaches and goals of informants. One of my last interviews was with a longtime Democrat in his seventies who had been a pro-labor, but socially conservative, activist as long as he could remember. I did get the sense that his view of the political world was his father's (also a Democratic activist) view, and that changes in political culture and media had very little effect on his model of politics. His resistance to recognizing change as well as his "cut and dried" approach to political action came through in his substantive responses later in the survey, and it was helpful to know how and where his perspective originated.

Questions about informants' backgrounds often bled into the more specific queries that followed. After asking about their paths to political or journalistic careers, I presented a variety of concepts and phrases to informants and asked for definitions of these concepts. Among the terms were *public opinion, ideology,* and *media bias.* In my early interviews, I experimented with a few other terms (*public deliberation* and *citizen participation*) that turned out to be too abstract, even with patient probing. When asking about public opinion, the term I probed about most, I also asked informants how they evaluated public opinion on particular topics and whether their approaches were effective or not. The activists had difficulty answering the open-ended question about public opinion evaluation, and I needed to bring up some specific methods (e.g., polling, reading newspapers, etc.) for informants to reflect on to enable them to articulate their ideas more clearly. The more sophisticated legislative staff and journalists, by contrast, knew precisely what I was asking when I posed an open-ended question about public opinion evaluation.

In my interviews with journalists and staffers, I asked about recent policy debates they had covered (in the case of reporters) or had played a large role in. This was a very productive sort of questioning because it demanded that informants apply their general thoughts about public opinion and media to a specific, illustrative case. It allowed me to explore their "theories" more rigorously, with a special eye to issues of causality (e.g., "What moved public opinion, in this case?"). Some of the cases they brought up were important and very widely publicized, so I asked them whether the media and public-opinion dynamics were different in this instance than in most others in order to figure out whether informants held different theories in varying political contexts. I did not use this line of questioning with party activists because they tend not to focus on particular policy issues in the same intense and technical ways that staffers and journalists do. Instead, I asked them for specific examples and illustrations within the more general queries. Because these activists are very much embedded in the politics of their local communities, the specific issues of concern for them were not always comparable to the larger state and regional topics offered by the journalists and staffers. For example, several activist informants mentioned debates over taxes in municipalities. While these debates are critical in the lives of most citizens, they are somewhat narrow and are not as interesting as issues that have more ideological complexity.

One of the most nagging concerns in the conduct of depth interviews and ethnographic work more generally is the nature of intervention by the interviewer. I had given this issue considerable thought in previous studies and, based on past experience with depth interviews, had decided to be very conservative in this regard. I tried to help the less articulate informants (who were mostly activists) explicate their ideas and theories, but I was careful not to push them in any particular direction. If I sensed any sort of confusion or resistance to a probe, I abandoned that line of questioning in order not to lead them in any particular direction. As with survey respondents, informants participating in depth interviews want to be helpful to the researcher and tend to be agreeable. I was very much aware of this since all of my conversations were friendly exchanges, so I avoided any revelation of my own opinions or theories about the relationships among media, public opinion, and public policy. After some of the interviews ended, informants—particularly staffers—wanted to know more about academic theories in the area of public opinion and media, and I was happy to oblige by discussing current research. The methodology I used here, often referred to as "elite interviewing," is challenging and also intensely gratifying: Informants are highly trained and have fascinating insights for the researcher. Informants can also be quite persuasive, drawing the researcher into their conceptual frameworks and distracting the interviewer from the task at hand. So it is incumbent upon the researcher to follow informants to some extent but also to guide them back to the protocol in order to complete the interview within the promised time limits. All the staffers and journalists in this study were busy people despite the break in legislative session. Many reporters were working on deadline, and staffers were engaged in special projects that they wanted to complete before the fall campaigns began and before the governor's fall veto session.

A common complaint about depth interviews is that the interviewer—engaged by the persuasiveness or eloquence of the informant—fails to maintain critical distance from the interview and therefore from the data. In this study I was sensitive to the need to find a balance between what informants told me and how they might be construing their past behavior and opinions in order to *appear* more cynical, more naive, more democratic, or less democratic than they actually are. This is a complex issue, no doubt, because our self-presentation changes from one situation to the next: The staffers I talked to probably assume one persona in their conversation with an academic researcher but use another in conversation with an influential legislator or lobbyist. My approach to this problem was to be on the alert for artificiality or posturing on the part of informants—something I found very little of. On the whole, informants spoke naturally, used examples, and made their points without much hesitation. But the best defense against posturing (which leads to gathering data that makes informants look good) was my own lowly position. Staffers, journalists, and political activists are accustomed to contact with the powerful, so speaking with a college professor was not nerve-wracking or even mildly exciting given their other activities. The informants were not particularly interested in my reactions to their remarks, which I was keeping to a minimum in all cases. All informants knew that my findings would be published eventually, but that did not seem impressive to them since their remarks are often published in widely distributed texts rather than obscure academic studies. Journalists are of course accustomed to this wide distribution of their thoughts, but staffers are comfortable as well with the diffusion of their memos and analyses. The activists I spoke with—often simply because they were national convention delegates—had had significant contact with journalists, so they were a bit weary of interviews and appeared to this interviewer to speak their mind without hesitation.

I chose depth interviews in addition to survey research (used in chapter 4) for a variety of reasons, but mostly because this study is an attempt to build what Barney Glaser and Anselm Strauss have called *grounded theory*.[1] As Strauss and Juliet Corbin note, grounded theories are reached inductively, with the researcher engaged in multiple tasks simultaneously—data collection, analysis, and theorizing. The intent is to build theory in an incremental way, with constant collection of empirical data (interviewing in this case). Over the course of the study certain findings become solidified and others fall by the wayside, so the researcher is able to collect data more efficiently and with greater ease. This was certainly the case in this study, where initial interviews were much longer than subsequent ones.[2] By the last interviews, I had gathered a comprehensive set of categories, lay theories, and approaches to politics, so the final interviewees were repeating (though in their own idiosyncratic terms) much of what I had already heard. This is an important point in any theory development project, as anthropologists know, because it is at this point that the researcher realizes he or she has spoken with an adequate number of informants. While in qualitative research there are no strict directives about sample size, methodologists agree that theory development halts when the interviewer is no longer hearing anything novel.

Strauss and Corbin, like others working inductively to build theory in their respective fields, emphasize the importance of several aspects of good qualitative research. For one, the interviewer must display a certain degree of "openness" and "flexibility." Researchers need to be patient with the more verbose or inarticulate informants, and they must also be ready to shift gears if a line of questioning is unproductive. As noted above, building grounded theory demands reciprocity between theorizing and data collection; nevertheless, I was forced to make only minimal changes in my interview protocol over the course of the study. Sensitivity and listening are vital, of course, for obvious reasons: Such close attention to the words of informants makes probing more directed and more effective.

Notes on Interviews

One question often asked about qualitative research is this: How is building grounded theory different from simply *describing* a phenomenon or group of informants? Strauss and Corbin, as well as a variety of other qualitative methodologists, believe that building grounded theory certainly demands description but moves far beyond that. First, building grounded theory involves the employment of concepts that tie anecdotes, examples, and narratives together in a coherent fashion. Even the best descriptive studies shy away from construct development, which is so useful in the inductive-theory building process. Second, the development of grounded theory involves the search for relationships, causal or not. In this study I was concerned with an informant's place in the political matrix and his or her conception of public opinion, among other relationships. Last, development of grounded theory involves sustained and intensive interpretation of data, something that we normally do not find in a purely descriptive study. And, of course, interpretation must be done with care in order to avoid reading too much into minor statements by informants or stretching their remarks in inappropriate directions.

The explication of lay theory through survey research or experimentation is certainly possible, although it has not been attempted in the area of media, politics, and public opinion. It is my feeling that these sorts of methods are inappropriate until we get a more general sense of what such theories look like. Studying people who work in politics, many of whom have devoted most or all or their professional lives to politics, is one very direct way to collect and analyze lay theories of the public sphere because such informants have elaborate and well-articulated ideas. And they think about causality (when pressed), which is absolutely essential in our search for mental models of public opinion. Depth interviews enable us to discover the relationships among context, ideology, professional constraints, and lay theories about the public sphere, since there is time and linguistic space for such exploration. As we have seen in the preceding chapters, and as other scholars have noted—particularly the British social psychologists and cognitive anthropologists cited in chapter 1—mental models are full of specifics: They are textured and subtle at times. Yet, despite the existence of such idiosyncratic characteristics across interviews, there are many commonalties. It is the commonalties, in fact, that allow for development about grounded theory.

Those who need to conduct depth interviews to explore topics of interest to them have the benefit of a fairly sophisticated methodological literature on which to draw. There are now scores of useful and compelling tracts on the value of such interviewing practices in the area of political-attitude research and behavior, although most who write on the topic acknowledge their debts to anthropologists: Ethnographers struggled with the problematics and challenges of depth interviewing long before political scientists considered them useful. Yet students of politics have, I believe, enhanced the methodological literatures established by anthropologists and sociologists. I have in mind, for instance, Jennifer Hochschild's thoughtful notes as preface to her own depth interview study *What's Fair? Americans Beliefs about Distributive Justice,* published over fifteen years ago. Unlike anthropologists, who need not contend with a tradition of survey research and experimentation in their own field, Hochschild discusses the unique contributions of depth interviews relative to other available methods for studying political attitudes and beliefs. She argues that depth interviews can, of course, enable us to develop theories we can test using quantitative methods and large samples. But she believes this assessment badly underestimates the value of depth interviewing with small samples: Intensive interviewing can generate data that we simply cannot generate through survey research or experimentation. In survey research (as in experimentation, I should add), "the *researcher infers* the links between variables; in intensive interviewing, the researcher induces the *respondent* to *create* the links between variables as he or she sees them."[3] I hope it is clear in this book that the sorts of lay theories and definitions of public opinion I unearthed among informants could not have been revealed with any alternative methodology. As Hochschild quips about depth interviewing, "The proof is in the reading."

One can, as mentioned earlier, study lay theories through survey research, experimentation, content analysis of documents produced by individuals and organizations, or even focus group research, although the latter is clearly our most underdeveloped and unwieldy methodology at this point. What is the real "value added" one obtains by conducting depth interviews as an alternative to other methodological choices? In this study of political professionals it was clear to me—both before and (even more so) after the research was conducted—that we do not know much about how legislative journalists and staffers think or act. We are not quite starting from scratch: We do have some studies of these individuals in the literature, as the notes in previous chapters indicate. But we still have a very dim picture of their mental frameworks and have not queried them closely about public opinion, its meaning, or its manifestations. When researchers know so little about a topic and realize that the particularistic nature of informants' working environment (the state legislature, in this case) will matter in the research, depth interviews are vital. Depth interviews do not just give the researcher lots of "quotes" and anecdotes to make for a colorful report: They enable the researcher to enter the informant's world and see it through his or her eyes, to hear it through his or her choice of language. This need to probe in depth was not as necessary with political activists (chapter 4) because they are—as the large number of activist studies in the literature indicate—far better understood than political professionals like journalists and legislative staffers. Survey research, which includes open-ended questions, can often provide opportunities for respondent creativity, but the data are far less complex than those derived from the depth interviews. The interviews I conducted with ten delegates helped me to understand the survey results more fully, but as has been noted by so many researchers with experience in the use of multiple methods, one does clearly give up something in the pursuit of population coverage. One need only look at a good depth interview transcript to see this.

There is no need to belabor the benefits of depth interviewing with small samples, since the contributions of this method to the study of human attitudes and behavior have been developed so many times by so many important scholars since the early decades of the twentieth century.[4] But it is vital to keep in mind the most significant difference between this method and survey research or experimentation: In depth interviewing, meaning of phenomena is *jointly constructed* by interviewer and respondent.[5] This is simply not the case in the survey interview or the experimental situation, where protocols are formalized and rigid. To say that meaning is jointly constructed means that the relationship between informant and academic questioner is characterized by a great deal of equality. Survey research and experimentation have their important uses, but there is no doubt that the researcher has the authority and the experimental subject or survey respondent is there to cooperate. When interviewing political sophisticates it is essential that the researcher allow informants the freedom and intellectual autonomy they are accustomed to, given their great experience in the political world. As I began the research, and as I completed the analysis, it was obvious to me that surveying informants with only the conventional closed-ended question form or putting them through an experimental protocol would have been inappropriate and even perhaps offensive (if they would have cooperated at all). And in these short interviews building rapport with informants was very important if I was to discern lay theories. I tried to take a lesson in building rapport from one of our premier rapport builders and conductors of depth interviews, Richard Fenno. Fenno spent many days with informants, as compared to an hour or so in my own case. But his reflections about the struggle to build relationships with informants are helpful to all who do interpretive work with political professionals. In his methodological essay, which serves an appendix to *Homestyle,* he writes

> Rapport refers to the state of the personal relationship—of compatibility, of understanding, of trust—between researchers and researched. It cannot be prescribed or taught. Sometimes it is a matter of luck. Always, it is a challenge and a preoccupation. Because you must constantly evaluate the quality of the data you are getting, you must, perforce, constantly evaluate the quality of your relationship with the person who is giving it to you. . . . Mostly, of course, the way you establish good rapport is by being nice to people and trying to see the world as they see it. You need to be patient, come on slow, and feel your way along.[6]

I tried to do just this in my interviews: make the informant feel comfortable and free to speak his or her mind, without losing sight of my own research agenda.

Appendix B: Interview Protocols

The following model protocols were used for the qualitative interviews, which were all conducted from June through September 1996. The protocols served as guides only, and the protocol was refined over the course of the study. In addition, the probes and questions related to specific policy issues do not appear in the forms reproduced below. Although the forms appear brief, informants did answer at length to many queries, and I probed them extensively as well on matters of importance. The formal, recorded part of the interview lasted approximately 45–50 minutes, although a few were shorter and some ran well over an hour.

I should note that queries about "public deliberation" were dropped soon after the study began because they proved unproductive and confusing, despite my attempts to describe this concept from political theory to informants.[1] I did ask all informants about the meaning of "ideology" and their answers were quite interesting, but those data are not discussed in this book.[2]

I. Interview Protocol: State Assembly Staff

Thanks again for participating in this study—I really appreciate it. As I explained in my letter, this study concerns the way that committee staffers think about the policy making process, about the media, and about public opinion. Some of the questions are specific, asking for examples of your experiences. But most are fairly general: Not much is known about the attitudes and opinions of policy makers or staffers—particularly at the level of state government.

This interview has 3 parts, and I'll give you a sense of where we're at as we move through these 3 categories: (1) background about yourself, (2) your reflections on some basic democratic concepts, and (3) an example of a recent legislative initiative you've been involved with.

All of your answers to my questions will be kept entirely confidential. In other words, your name and answers will never be linked, your name never revealed.

It will be too difficult for me to write down all that you say, and want to make sure I get your exact remarks recorded. So is it all right if I tape record our discussion?

A. Questions about Background

1. Just to make sure my records are correct, could you tell me which committees you are currently working on?

2. I'm wondering if we can take a few minutes to discuss your background—how you came to work at the Capitol and on this committee(s). Perhaps you could start by telling me where you are from and where you went to school.

3. How long have you been working in your current role?

4. Previous roles inside or outside state government?

5. I'm wondering if you can talk in generalities about your work on this committee? What do you spend most of your time doing? (e.g., cycle of work following the demands of the legislative cycle).

6. Could you talk a bit about the relationship of the staffer to the committee members, then specifically about the kinds of support and research you do for the members?

7. Which mass media publications or broadcasts do you attend to on a regular basis, in order to keep up with the news?

8. Do you have much contact with the media? With whom and how often? Are there particular journalists you know well/have regular professional contact with?

B. Questions about Basic Concepts

There is a lot of interest in political science right now about how different sorts of people think about basic, fundamental concepts in democratic theory. I've done a lot of work tracing the meaning of public opinion, from the 19th century to present, for example. In the context of your work, I'd like to ask you to define or reflect on some of these concepts:

1. Let's start with public opinion. How would you define it?
[*A sample of the types of probes included:*

(a) Who is included in "the public"?

(b) Are their opinions stable or easily changed?

(c) How do you evaluate/measure it? Polls versus other forms?]

2. Citizen participation. How would you define that phrase?
[*Sample probes:*

(a) What does it look like?

(b) Where does one find it?]

3. Public Deliberation. Is that a meaningful phrase in your work?
[*Sample probes:*

(a) What does it look like?

(b) Where do you see/hear it?

(c) Do you think of the mass media as related in any way to public
deliberation? How so?]

4. Ideology
[*Sample probes:*

(a) What is it?

(b) Do you think of it is a positive, neutral, or pejorative term?]

5. Media bias

Some scholars believe the mass media are biased in certain ways, while others are
not particularly concerned with bias. Thinking about the media outlets you deal
with on state matters, do you believe they are biased in any way, ideologically,
stylistically, structurally, or otherwise? How so?

C. Questions about Causal Models

1. Can you recall for me an important project in the recent past where you and
the committee had to deal with both media coverage and public opinion?

2. Which media were covering this? Was coverage fair or biased?

3. How did you assess public opinion in this case?

4. Did/How did media affect your thoughts and work?

5. Did/How did public opinion affect your thoughts and work?

6. Did you feel like either force (public opinion and media coverage) was helpful
in gaining knowledge or direction for the committee? Or did they simply add
constraints as you thought about legislative action?

7. Did you feel as though there was *public* deliberation in this case? What did it look like? Where did it take place?

8. Do you feel like this is an unusual case, in terms of the interaction of media, policy, and public opinion?

9. If unusual, what is the more typical linkage?

[Thanks and closing discussion.]

II. Interview Protocol: Journalists

[Introductory remarks same as those used for Staff Protocol above.]

A. Questions about Background

1. I'm wondering if we can take a few minutes to discuss your background—how you came to cover the legislature. Perhaps you could start by telling me where you are from and where you went to school?

2. Years as a journalist _____

3. Years covering the legislature _____

4. I'm wondering if you can talk in generalities about your day to day work covering the legislature, the sorts of issues and sources you tend to focus on. Also, how does your work follow the legislative cycle?

5. I'm going to name a few categories of people, and ask how important they are to you as you write stories in Springfield. Perhaps you could make a brief comment about each:
    (a) Press officers?
    (b) Communication directors/press secretaries?
    (c) Members themselves?
    (d) Lobbyists?
    (e) Any other important sources or contacts I have not named?

6. Beyond your own paper/broadcasts, which mass media publications or broadcasts do you attend to on a regular basis?

7. Can you describe the general culture of the press corps covering the legislature? In what respects is it collegial, for example, and in what respects is it competitive? How are collegiality and competition manifested?

8. Which of your journalistic skills are most important when covering the legislature?

B. *Questions about Basic Concepts*

[Same as used in Staff Protocol above.]

C. *Questions about Causal Models*

1. Can you recall an important policy issue in the recent past that was of great concern to the public and your media organization?

2. What were the challenges associated with covering this issue, if any?

3. How did you assess public opinion in this case?

4. Did other journalists influence your thoughts and work? In other words, was there a lot of discussion among the Springfield press corps? And did these interactions affect your thoughts and work?

5. Did/How did public opinion affect your thoughts and work?

6. Did you talk to Members about the issue? How did their ideas affect your work?

7. What about press secretaries/communication directors?

8. What about lobbyists?

9. Did you feel as though there was *public* deliberation in this case? What did it look like? Where did it take place?

10. Going back your definition of public opinion, can you link this definition with this particular example of a policy debate?

[Conclusion same used in Staff Protocol above.]

III. Interview Protocol: Delegates

Thanks again for participating in this study—I really appreciate it. As my assistant explained, this study concerns the way that convention delegates in Illinois think about the policy making process, about the media, and about public opinion. Some of the questions are specific, asking for examples of your experiences. But most are fairly general: Not much is known about the attitudes and opinions of delegates to the national conventions from Illinois or any of the other states.

This interview has 2 parts, and I'll give you a sense of where we're at as we move through these 2 categories: (1) background about yourself, and (2) your reflections on some basic democratic concepts.

All your answers to my questions will be kept entirely confidential. In other words, your name and answers will never be linked, your name never revealed.

It will be too difficult for me to write down all that you say, and want to make sure I get your remarks recorded accurately. So is it all right if I tape record our discussion?

A. *Questions about Background*

1. I am wondering how you got involved in Democratic/Republican politics? Can you tell me how this occurred—how you came to be a delegate?

2. Did you come from a family interested in politics? Were they Democrats/Republicans as well?

3. How long have you lived in Illinois?

4. What is your occupation?

5. Do you now, or have you ever, held elected public office?

6. What is the highest grade in school you've completed? Any college or advanced degrees?

7. How do you see the role of delegate in a national convention? (Are you representing your community or a particular group, for example? How so?)

B. *Questions about Basic Concepts*

I'm going to list some democratic ideas and concepts that I often discuss with students in my class, and with my colleagues. I'm wondering if you could define or tell me what comes to mind when you hear the following phrases. Let me preface this section by saying that there are no right or wrong answers, only opinions:

1. Public Opinion

(a) If you wanted to find out about public opinion on a particular issue, how would you do so?

(b) I'd like to list some indicators of public opinion, and I'm wondering if you can tell me whether you think they are accurate ways to evaluate or measure public opinion.

(1) Television news
(2) Interest group opinions/statements
(3) Radio talk shows
(4) People in your community, family, workplace (who?)
(5) What elected officials say
(6) Polls
(7) Newspaper articles

2. Here's another concept. What comes to mind when you hear the phase "media bias"?

3. What about "ideology"?

4. What about "public deliberation"?

[Thanks and concluding remarks.]

Appendix C: Survey Form

[The survey form was preceded by a cover letter explaining the purpose of the study.]

1. If you wanted to find out about public opinion on a certain issue, how would you do so?

2. How would you define the phrase "public opinion"?

3. We are interested in how you think about the assessment of public opinion. Please indicate whether you agree or disagree with each of the following statements: *[Respondent choices for each item were: strongly agree, agree, disagree, strongly disagree, don't know]*

  (a) Television news is an accurate indicator of public opinion.
  (b) Interest groups are an accurate indicator of public opinion.
  (c) Polls are an accurate indicator of public opinion.
  (d) Radio talk shows are an accurate indicator of public opinion.
  (e) Newspaper articles are an accurate indicator of public opinion.
  (f) What people say in the workplace is an accurate indicator of public opinion.
  (g) What friends say is an accurate indicator of public opinion.
  (h) What public officials say is an accurate indicator of public opinion.

4. Elected officials often try to gauge public opinion. Please determine to the best of your ability how you think public officials gauge public opinion. *[Respondent choices for each item were: often, sometimes, rarely, never.]*

  (a) Listen to their constituents back home.
  (b) Read poll data.
  (c) Review election results.
  (d) Listen to interest groups and lobbyists.
  (e) Pay attention to local news.

Survey Form

(f) Listen to talk radio.

(g) Make guesses by the "seat of their pants."

5. Do you think that the news media are biased in any way, or do they present the news in an even-handed fashion?

6. Are there cases when public officials should <u>not</u> be guided by public opinion in their decision-making? Please list as many cases and examples as you like.

7. We hear a lot of talk these days about liberals and conservatives. Think about a ruler where we are measuring political views that people might hold. On this ruler, which goes from one to seven, the number 1 means very liberal and the number 7 means very conservative. Just like a regular ruler, it has points in between at 2, 3, 4, 5, and 6. Where would you place yourself on this ruler, or haven't you thought much about this?

1	2	3	4	5	6	7

Conclusion

What year were you born? _____

In addition to being American, what do you consider your main ethnic or nationality group?

Gender (please circle)   M   F

Do you work outside the home? (please circle)   Y   N

　　If yes, what is your occupation? _____

Do you now, or have you ever, held elected public office?
(please circle):   Y   N

　　If yes, was it a local, state or national office (circle all that apply):

　　Local   State   National

What is the highest grade in school or academic degree you have received?

_____

Are you a delegate, alternate delegate, or neither (please circle):

　　Delegate   Alternate   Neither

Please return the survey in the enclosed, self-addressed stamped envelope. Thank you.

Notes

Introduction

1. See Francis Graham Wilson, *A Theory of Public Opinion* (Chicago: Henry Regnery Company, 1962); Paul Palmer, "The Concept of Public Opinion in Political Theory" (Ph.D. diss., Harvard University, 1934); Wilhelm Bauer, "Public Opinion," in *The Encyclopaedia of the Social Sciences,* ed. E. Seligman (New York: Macmillan, 1930); David Minar, "Public Opinion in the Perspective of Political Theory," *Western Political Quarterly* 13 (1960): 31–44; Paul Lazarsfeld, "Public Opinion in the Classical Tradition," in his *Qualitative Analysis: Historical and Critical Essays* (Boston: Allyn and Bacon, 1972) 300–317. A few contemporary researchers are exceptional in their attention to the meaning of public opinion. See Elisabeth Noelle-Neumann, *The Spiral of Silence: Public Opinion—Our Social Skin* (Chicago: University of Chicago Press, 1993); Vincent Price, *Public Opinion* (Newbury Park, Calif.: Sage, 1992); and John Zaller, "Positive Constructs of Public Opinion," *Critical Studies in Mass Communication Research* 11 (1994): 276–87.

I should note here that before the application of sampling to the study of public opinion—before Jerzy Neyman and others did the statistical groundwork for stratified random sampling in the 1930s—sociologists and political scientists struggled with the meaning and measure of public opinion. Some interesting articles that illustrate early debates in American social science are Francis G. Wilson, "Concepts of Public Opinion," *American Political Science Review* 27 (1933): 371–91; Francis E. Merrill and Carroll D. Clark, "The Money Market as a Special Public," *American Journal of Sociology* 39 (1934): 626–36; Robert C. Binkley, "The Concept of Public Opinion in the Social Sciences," *Social Forces* 6 (1928): 389–96; and Carroll D. Clark, "The Concept of the Public," *The Southwestern Social Science Quarterly* 13 (1933): 311–20. On Neyman's contribution, see William Kruskal and Frederick Mosteller, "Representative Sampling IV: The History of the Concept in Statistics, 1895–1939," *International Statistical Review* 48 (1980): 169–95.

2. Susan Herbst, *Numbered Voices: How Opinion Polling Has Shaped American Politics* (Chicago: University of Chicago Press, 1993). See also Robert H. Wiebe, *Self-Rule: A Cultural History of American Democracy* (Chicago: University of Chicago Press, 1995), which is a study of our changing definitions of "democracy." Beyond a discussion of the shifting meanings of democracy, Wiebe takes on—from a historical perspective—some of the other very nebulous terms associated with democracy, such as the composition of "the people."

3. This book is very much inspired by Murray Edelman's works, which are cited throughout the notes to this text. Readers unfamiliar with his approach might begin with *The*

Symbolic Uses of Politics (Urbana: University of Illinois Press, 1985). A team of researchers in Germany is conducting micro-level research on how people in government think about polling and public opinion. The approach in this book is different from this European work, but many similar questions are raised. See the very provocative working paper, "The Observation of Public Opinion by the Governmental System," by Dieter Fuchs and Barbara Pfetsch. The manuscript is available from the Wissenschaftszentrum Berlin für Sozialforschung GmbH, Berlin.

4. See Jürgen Habermas, *The Structural Transformation of the Public Sphere: An Inquiry into a Category of Bourgeois Society*, trans. Thomas Burger (Cambridge: MIT Press, 1989).

5. I take as a model of recent information processing work in politics the excellent volume edited by Milton Lodge and Kathleen M. McGraw, *Political Judgment: Structure and Process* (Ann Arbor: University of Michigan Press, 1995). When I write in this book about political cognition, I am referring to the type of work contained in Lodge and McGraw's book. There are, of course, many other routes for studying political psychology. Some of these are represented in Diana C. Mutz, Paul M. Sniderman, and Richard A. Brody, eds., *Political Persuasion and Attitude Change* (Ann Arbor: University of Michigan Press, 1996), and Ann Crigler, ed., *The Psychology of Political Communication* (Ann Arbor: University of Michigan Press, 1996).

6. When I speak here of Robert Lane's work, I am referring to his general interpretive approach to political psychology, but most particularly to his interview study of fifteen working class men, *Political Ideology: Why the American Common Man Believes What He Does* (New York: Free Press, 1962).

7. See the citations in note 1 above.

8. While there is little research addressing the ways people conceptualize public opinion, there is a small body of literature concerning how citizens think about polls and polling. Two scholars working in this area are Ellen Dran and Anne Hildreth. See their papers, including "What the Public Thinks about How We Know What It Is Thinking," *International Journal of Public Opinion Research* 7 (1995): 128–44; and "Polling on Polls: History and Issues" (paper presented at the annual meeting of the American Association for Public Opinion Research, St. Charles, Ill., 1993).

9. See Alexis de Tocqueville, *Democracy in America*, ed. J. P. Mayer (New York: Anchor, 1969); James Bryce, *The American Commonwealth* (New York: Macmillan, 1891); Herbert Blumer, "Public Opinion and Public Opinion Polling, " *American Sociological Review* 13 (1948): 242–49; and Arthur Bentley, *The Process of Government* (Chicago: University of Chicago Press, 1908).

10. Indeed, one of our best textbooks on public opinion contains a chapter on group opinion, which displays national survey data on what categories of people ("working class" versus "upper class" or "blacks" versus "whites") think about particular policies. Later in the book, in a chapter on parties and interest groups, the authors bemoan the lack of research on whether interest groups represent public opinion or not, but there is no sustained discussion of the ways public opinion and interest group activity might be linked. See Robert Erikson and Kent Tedin, *American Public Opinion: Its Origins, Content, and Impact*, 5th ed. (Boston: Allyn and Bacon, 1995).

11. These authors' ideas are discussed at length in chapter 1. See Michael Billig, *Arguing and Thinking: A Rhetorical Approach to Social Psychology* (Cambridge: Cambridge University Press, 1996), and Deanna Kuhn, *The Skills of Argument* (New York: Cambridge University Press, 1991).

12. See Michel Foucault, *Power/Knowledge: Selected Interviews and Other Writings, 1972–1977,* ed. Colin Gordon (New York: Pantheon, 1980). For an introduction to Foucault's theorizing about power, see Barry Smart, *Foucault, Marxism, and Critique* (London: Routledge and Kegan Paul, 1985), or Hubert Dreyfus and Paul Rabinow, *Michel Foucault: Beyond Structuralism and Hermeneutics* (Chicago: University of Chicago Press, 1983).

13. One notable exception is the area of race and equality, where researchers have provided sophisticated analyses shedding light on individuals' attitudes and even on their "lay theories" about these important subjects ("lay theories" is my language). See, for example, Donald Kinder and Lynn Sanders, *Divided by Color: Racial Politics and Democratic Ideals* (Chicago: University of Chicago Press, 1996). Another project of note here is Pamela Johnston Conover, Ivor M. Crewe, and Donald D. Searing, "The Nature of Citizenship in the United States and Great Britain: Empirical Comments on Theoretical Themes," *Journal of Politics* 53 (1991): 800–832.

14. I am interested in the causal models informants articulate—how *they* see connections among media, policy, and public opinion. I do not explore their causal arguments about particular issues, although this is obviously an interesting and important topic. For research on "reasoning chains," see Paul M. Sniderman, Richard A. Brody, and Philip E. Tetlock, *Reasoning and Choice: Explorations in Political Psychology* (New York: Cambridge University Press, 1991).

15. For an example of journalistic debate see Jay Rosen, "Making Things More Public: On the Political Responsibility of the Media Intellectual," *Critical Studies in Mass Communication* 11 (1994): 362–88.

16. On legislative staffers as professional actors, see Barbara S. Romzek and Jennifer A. Utter, "Congressional Legislative Staff: Political Professionals or Clerks?" *American Journal of Political Science* 41(1997): 1251–79.

17. Lawrence Jacobs and Robert Shapiro, "The Politicization of Public Opinion: The Fight for the Pulpit" (paper presented at the annual meeting of the Midwest Political Science Association, Chicago, April 1997). A study of how state policymakers navigated among different sources for understanding public opinion, in the context of welfare reform, is Greg Shaw's "Social Policies and the Transmission of Public Opinion in the American States" (Ph.D. diss., Columbia University, 1997). His findings, from a cross-state survey of governors' office staffers, social service agency administrators, and state legislators themselves, differ somewhat from my findings discussed in chapter 2. His respondents report much more rigorous attempts to understand citizen opinion than do my informants. This may be due to the subject matter: The spotlight on welfare reform in the late 1990s may lead policymakers to solicit more public opinion information than they do on other topics (or lead them to *say* they solicit public opinion). Shaw does find that governors' aides, as compared to legislators themselves, are more likely to "keep in touch with constituents on issues of social policy" by "an intuitive sense based on [their] own knowledge of the state." Ibid., 12. We will see many

instances of this "intuitive sense for public opinion" in the comments of staffers and journalists in this book.

18. I refer mainly to *Numbered Voices,* cited above. On critical work about public opinion see Philip E. Converse, "Changing Conceptions of Public Opinion in the Political Process," *Public Opinion Quarterly* 51 (1987): S12–S24, and Converse, "The Advent of Polling and Political Representation," *PS* 29 (December 1996): 649–57.

Chapter One

1. Blumer, "Public Opinion," 243.

2. See Samuel L. Popkin, *The Reasoning Voter: Communication and Persuasion in Presidential Campaigns* (Chicago: University of Chicago Press, 1991).

3. See the following by Lawrence R. Jacobs and Robert Y. Shapiro: "Issues, Candidate Image, and Priming: The Use of Private Polls in Kennedy's 1960 Presidential Campaign," *American Political Science Review* 88 (1994): 527–40, and "The Rise of Presidential Polling: The Nixon White House in Historical Perspective," *Public Opinion Quarterly* 59 (1995): 163–95.

4. This conversation and others with activists are reported in my article, "The Meaning of Public Opinion: Citizens' Constructions of Political Reality," *Media, Culture and Society* 15 (1993): 437–54. .

5. David Held, *Models of Democracy* (Stanford, Calif.: Stanford University Press, 1987), 70.

6. See both Max Weber, *Economy and Society: An Outline of Interpretive Sociology,* ed. Guenther Roth and Claus Wittich (Berkeley and Los Angeles: University of California Press, 1978), and Joseph Schumpeter, *Capitalism, Socialism, and Democracy,* 3d ed. (New York: Harper and Row, 1950).

7. Held, *Models of Democracy,* 184.

8. See Walter Lippmann, *The Phantom Public* (New York: Harcourt, Brace, 1925), and Walter Lippmann, *Public Opinion* (New York: Free Press, 1965).

9. See Aristotle, *The Politics,* ed. and trans. T. A. Sinclair (Baltimore: Penguin Books, 1962), and Herbst *Numbered Voices,* chap. 3.

10. Throughout this book, I refer to "ideal types" and "ideal-typical" conceptions. I use these phrases very much in the spirit of Weber's methodological tracts on the subject. Weber found ideal types an efficient and creative way to build theory and collect empirical data. See his introductory passage, "The Definition of Sociology and of Social Action," in *Economy and Society,* 4–24.

11. *Numbered Voices,* chap. 3.

12. Presidential speech has been the form of political rhetoric studied most rigorously by political scientists and rhetoricians. Beyond the collections of speeches and addresses of presidents that can be perused for talk about public opinion, such as the well-indexed serial *Public Papers of the Presidents of the United States* (Washington, D.C.: GPO, 1929–1995), readers should consult Jeffrey Tulis, *The Rhetorical Presidency* (Princeton, N.J.: Princeton University Press, 1987); Roderick Hart, *The Sound of Leadership: Presidential Communication in the Modern Age* (Chicago: University of Chicago Press, 1987); and Karlyn Kohrs Campbell and Kathleen Hall Jamieson, *Deeds Done in Words: Presidential Rhetoric and the Genres of Governance* (Chicago: University of Chicago Press, 1990).

13. Clinton's speech can be found in Bill Clinton, *Public Papers of the Presidents of the United States: Bill Clinton* (Washington, D.C.: GPO, 1994), 1:155. Ronald Reagan was of course masterful in the use of personal anecdote and narrative for the purposes of persuasive communication. See Kathleen Hall Jamieson's *Eloquence in an Electronic Age: The Transformation of Political Speechmaking* (New York: Oxford University Press, 1988).

14. See Leila Sussmann's wonderful study, *Dear FDR: A Study of Political Letter Writing* (Totowa, N.J.: Bedminster, 1963).

15. Murray Edelman, *Political Language: Words That Succeed and Policies That Fail* (San Diego: Academic Press, 1977), 50.

16. See Herbst, *Numbered Voices,* or an earlier study of journalists' use of polls, David Paletz et al., "Polls in the Media: Content, Credibility, and Consequences," *Public Opinion Quarterly* 44 (1980): 495–513.

17. Hart, *The Sound of Leadership,* 128.

18. Shanto Iyengar, *Is Anyone Responsible? How Television Frames Political Issues* (Chicago: University of Chicago Press, 1991).

19. On what makes good news, see Herbert Gans' classic, *Deciding What's News: A Study of the* CBS Evening News, *the* NBC Nightly News, Newsweek, *and* Time (New York: Pantheon, 1979). Also see Michael Schudson, *The Power of News* (Cambridge: Harvard University Press, 1995).

20. See W. Lance Bennett's essay, "Constructing Publics and Their Opinions," *Political Communication* 10 (1993): 101–20.

21. For cases where media help to construct public opinion, see W. Lance Bennett and David Paletz, eds., *Taken By Storm: The Media, Public Opinion, and U.S. Foreign Policy in the Gulf War* (Chicago: University of Chicago Press, 1994), or W. Russell Neuman, Marion R. Just, and Ann N. Crigler, *Common Knowledge: News and the Construction of Political Meaning* (Chicago: University of Chicago Press, 1992).

22. See William Gamson, "A Constructionist Approach to Mass Media and Public Opinion," *Symbolic Interaction* 11 (1981): 161–74, and his more recent *Talking Politics* (New York: Cambridge University Press, 1992).

23. Aristotle, *The Politics,* 107.

24. There are classic studies of political behavior from the nineteenth century, including Tocqueville, *Democracy in America,* and Bryce, *American Commonwealth.*

25. Peter L. Berger and Thomas Luckmann, *The Social Construction of Reality: A Treatise in the Sociology of Knowledge* (Garden City, N.Y.: Anchor Books, 1967), 1.

26. Ibid., 3.

27. Gamson, *Talking Politics;* Neuman, Just, and Crigler, *Common Knowledge.*

28. Although political cognition as a field is growing and diverse, one exemplar of current work in this field is Lodge and McGraw, *Political Judgment.* Work in this area has become increasingly methodologically sophisticated as the years have passed, but one of the earliest, precedent setting volumes on political cognition, containing a variety of interesting findings is Richard R. Lau and David O. Sears, eds., *Political Cognition: The 19th Annual Carnegie Symposium on Cognition* (Hillsdale, N.J.: Lawrence Erlbaum Associates, 1986).

29. Lodge and McGraw, *Political Judgment,* 1–3. See also Lippmann, *Public Opinion.*

30. Jerome Bruner, *Acts of Meaning* (Cambridge: Harvard University Press, 1990), 2.

31. Ibid., 5.

32. Clifford Geertz, *The Interpretation of Cultures: Selected Essays* (New York: Basic Books, 1973), 49.

33. Bruner, *Acts of Meaning*, 19.

34. See Philip E. Converse, "The Nature of Belief Systems in Mass Publics," in *Ideology and Discontent*, ed. David Apter (Glencoe, Ill.: Free Press, 1964), but more recently Michael X. Delli Carpini and Scott Keeter, *What Americans Know about Politics and Why It Matters* (New Haven, Conn.: Yale University Press, 1996).

35. Richard E. Nisbett and Lee Ross, *Human Inference: Strategies and Shortcomings of Social Judgment* (Englewood Cliffs, N.J.: Prentice-Hall, 1980).

36. Fritz Heider, *The Psychology of Interpersonal Relations* (New York: Wiley, 1958).

37. See Charles Antaki, *Explaining and Arguing: The Social Organization of Accounts* (London: Sage, 1994). Chapter 2 contains the critique of Heider, and the book also presents interesting evidence about the structure of claims and explanations in everyday conversation.

38. Much of this work is cited in Adrian Furnham's volume, *Lay Theory: Everyday Understanding of Problems in the Social Sciences* (New York: Pergamon Press, 1988).

39. Kuhn, *Skills of Argument*, 7.

40. See Alice H. Eagly and Shelly Chaiken, *The Psychology of Attitudes* (Fort Worth: Harcourt Brace Jovanovich, 1993), for an introduction to the field.

41. John Dewey, *The Public and Its Problems* (Athens, Ohio: Swallow Press, 1954).

42. See Michael Billig, *Ideology and Opinions: Studies in Rhetorical Psychology* (London: Sage, 1991), and his *Arguing and Thinking*.

43. See George Herbert Mead, *Mind, Self, and Society* (Chicago: University of Chicago Press, 1934), and Serge Moscovici, *Social Influence and Social Change* (London: Academic Press, 1976). Also note R. M. Farr and Serge Moscovici, eds., *Social Representations* (Cambridge: Cambridge University Press, 1984).

44. Billig, *Ideology and Opinions*, 42–43.

45. Ibid., 43.

46. Michael Schudson, *Watergate in American Memory: How We Remember, Forget, and Reconstruct the Past* (New York: Basic Books, 1992).

47. Robert A. Dahl, *Who Governs? Democracy and Power in an American City* (New Haven, Conn.: Yale University Press, 1961); James David Barber, *The Lawmakers: Recruitment and Adaptation to Legislative Life* (New Haven, Conn.: Yale University Press, 1965); Doug McAdam, *Freedom Summer* (New York: Oxford University Press, 1988).

48. For one recent definition of "elites," see John Zaller, *The Nature and Origins of Mass Opinion* (New York: Cambridge University Press, 1992), 6. This definition works well for Zaller's purposes but is a bit too all encompassing for mine here.

49. See Dorothy Holland and Naomi Quinn, eds., *Cultural Models in Language and Thought* (New York: Cambridge University Press, 1987) or Furnham, *Lay Theory*. Deanna Kuhn, on the contrary, does not find that sophisticates in her study used better reasoning or evidence than her nonexperts. Her study is a bit different than the one reported on here, however, since I am taking a more constructivist model of what does and does not constitute proper "evidence." See Kuhn's *Skills of Argument*, chap. 9.

50. I randomly selected staffers from the official list published in the 1996 Roster of *Illinois Issues*, a periodical published in Springfield by Sangamon State University.

51. David H. Everson, "COOGA *Redux?*" in *Almanac of Illinois Politics 1996*, ed. Craig Roberts and Paul Kleppner (Springfield: University of Illinois Press), 1–6.

52. For an informational perspective on legislatures, and particularly on committees, see Keith Krehbiel, *Information and Legislative Organization* (Ann Arbor: University of Michigan Press, 1991), especially chaps. 3 and 4.

53. I owe my education about the enterprise perspective to David Whiteman. His book is a good explication of this approach, and he uses it in his study of congressional decision-making processes. See his *Communication in Congress: Members, Staff, and the Search for Information* (Lawrence: University Press of Kansas, 1995). Earlier works on the enterprise perspective are Robert H. Salisbury and Kenneth Shepsle, "U.S. Congressman as Enterprise," *Legislative Studies Quarterly* 6 (1981): 559–76, and John Kingdon's *Congressmen's Voting Decisions*, 3d ed. (Ann Arbor: University of Michigan Press, 1991).

54. Whiteman, *Communication in Congress*, 4.

55. The official name of the Illinois legislature is the "General Assembly," and in this book I use the words "legislature" and "assembly" interchangeably.

56. There are some differences between the responsibilities of press secretaries and communication directors, particularly in the area of staff size. For the purposes of this study, I group them together since my concern was their duties as mediators between staff and journalists. Press secretaries and communication directors both have many responsibilities in this regard. I cannot specify which informants held which title ("press secretary" or "communication director") due to my promises of anonymity.

57. This statistic was compiled by a count of female and male journalists listed by the Illinois Legislative Correspondents Association, an organization formed in 1946 to represent the needs of journalists covering the capitol.

58. Another group I might have interviewed, besides legislators themselves, is interest group officials. I avoided this only because there are already some fine studies of lobbyists' ideas and behaviors at the state level—many of which are cited in my notes. Yet it would be undoubtedly quite useful to query lobbyists directly about public opinion issues. Such a study should focus on the many different types of pressure groups, distinguishing citizen-oriented lobbies from professional group lobbies (e.g., the AMA), manufacturers, lobbyists for government agencies, etc.

59. See Carl E. Van Horn, ed., *The State of the States* (Washington, D.C.: Congressional Quarterly Press, 1989); Alan Rosenthal, *Governors and Legislatures: Contending Powers* (Washington, D.C.: Congressional Quarterly Press, 1990); Anthony Gierzynski, *Legislative Party Campaign Committees in the American States* (Lexington: University Press of Kentucky, 1992); Malcolm E. Jewell and Marcia Lynn Whicker, *Legislative Leadership in the American States* (Ann Arbor: University of Michigan Press, 1994); and Malcolm E. Jewell, *Representation in State Legislatures* (Lexington: University Press of Kentucky, 1982). Aside from studies of multiple state legislatures, there are studies of particular state bodies, such as Malcolm E. Jewell and Penny M. Miller, *The Kentucky Legislature: Two Decades of Change* (Lexington: University Press of Kentucky, 1988).

60. Alan Rosenthal, "The Legislative Institution: Transformed and at Risk," in Van Horn, *State of the States*, 69.

61. Carl E. Van Horn, "The Quiet Revolution," in *State of the States*, 2.

62. Ibid., 2–3.

63. Rosenthal, "Legislative Institution," 94.

64. Robert S. Erikson, Gerald C. Wright, and John P. McIver, *Statehouse Democracy: Public Opinion and Policy in the American States* (New York: Cambridge University Press, 1993).

65. James B. Lemert, "Picking the Winners: Politician vs. Voter Predictions of Two Controversial Ballot Measures," *Public Opinion Quarterly* 50 (1986): 208–21.

66. David H. Everson, "Illinois as a Bellwether: So What?" *Illinois Issues* (February 1990): 9.

67. Ibid., 10.

68. Jane J. Mansbridge, *Beyond Adversary Democracy* (Chicago: University of Chicago Press, 1980).

69. Weber, *Economy and Society*, 5. I was reminded of the Caesar quote while reading Frank Parkin's fine introduction to Weber's methods, *Max Weber* (London: Tavistock Publications, 1982).

70. An excellent and succinct introduction to Weber's methods, to *verstehen*, to the use of ideal types, and even to his views on positivism is Dirk Käsler's *Max Weber: An Introduction to His Life and Work* (Chicago: University of Chicago Press, 1988).

71. Weber, *Economy and Society*, 14.

72. For a study exploring how individuals conceptualize "citizenship," see Conover, Crewe, and Searing, "Nature of Citizenship."

73. Interviews lasted anywhere from thirty minutes to ninety minutes, but most took forty-five minutes or an hour. All interviews were conducted by the author during July, August, and September of 1996. Two legislative staffers were available for in-person discussions, but the other forty-two interviews were conducted over the telephone. I saw no significant difference between the two methods, in terms of the styles of staffers, their desire to be candid and helpful, the substantive answers to questions, or the length of the interviews. All interviews were tape-recorded and later transcribed by a professional transcription service. Participants were assured confidentiality and anonymity, although most were not concerned with these conventions because they were accustomed to speaking with journalists or were themselves journalists.

A note on quotations from the interviews used throughout this book: Ellipses are used to make the informants' comments more comprehensible in written format. While none of the informants were difficult to understand, the transcribing secretaries and I had to make decisions about punctuation, the start and end of sentences, and other grammatical issues. Bracketed explanations or notes are my own and are intended to make informants' remarks clearer to the reader. In cases where I need to underscore a particularly important section of an informant's remarks, I clearly note where emphases are my own.

Chapter Two

1. See Bruce Altschuler, "Lyndon Johnson and the Public Polls," *Public Opinion Quarterly* 50 (1986): 285–99; Jacobs and Shapiro, "Rise of Presidential Polling"; and Robert Eisinger, "The Illusion of Certainty: Explaining the Evolution of Presidential Polling" (Ph.D. diss., University of Chicago, 1996).

2. See Loïc Blondiaux, "Comment rompre avec Durkheim? Jean Stoetzel et la sociologie française de l'après-guerre (1945–1948)," *Revue française de sociologie* 32 (1991): 753–91. See also Blondiaux, "La Fabrique de l'opinion" (doctoral diss., Institut d'études politiques, Paris, 1994). For a brief introductory history of polling across nations see my essay "Surveying and Influencing the Public: Polling in Politics and Industry," in *The Cambridge History of Science,* ed. David C. Lindberg and Ronald L. Numbers (New York: Cambridge University Press, in press).

3. See Herbert Blumer's now classic critique of opinion research, "Public Opinion and Public Opinion Polling." The interest group literature is large and varied, with many fine studies of individual issue areas and broader attempts to characterize lobbying practices at the national and state levels. A few examples are Mark P. Petracca, ed., *The Politics of Interests: Interest Groups Transformed* (Boulder: Westview Press, 1992); Robert H. Salisbury, *Interests and Institutions: Substance and Structure in American Politics* (Pittsburgh: University of Pittsburgh Press, 1992); John Mark Hansen, *Gaining Access: Congress and the Farm Lobby, 1919–1981* (Chicago: University of Chicago Press, 1991); Kay Lehman Schlozman and John T. Tierney, *Organized Interests and American Democracy* (New York: Harper and Row, 1986); Allan J. Cigler and Burdett A. Loomis, *Interest Group Politics,* 4th ed. (Washington, D.C.: Congressional Quarterly Press, 1995); and Jack L. Walker, *Mobilizing Interest Groups in America: Patrons, Professions, and Social Movements* (Ann Arbor: University of Michigan Press, 1991). At the level of state legislatures, see Alan Rosenthal, *The Third House: Lobbyists and Lobbying in the States* (Washington, D.C.: Congressional Quarterly Press, 1993), or Jewell and Miller, *The Kentucky Legislature.*

4. Bentley, *Process of Government,* 236–37. See also David B. Truman, *The Governmental Process: Political Interests and Public Opinion* (New York: Alfred A. Knopf, 1960). There has been both much support and much critique of Bentley and Truman, as representatives of the group theory of politics. See, for example, Mancur Olson's discussion of the group he labels "analytical pluralists" in his *Logic of Collective Action: Public Goods and the Theory of Groups* (Cambridge: Harvard University Press, 1971). For our purposes here, we need not take sides in the debate between group theorists and Olson, since we are most interested in how our staffers understand the place of groups vis-à-vis public opinion. Nonetheless, many of the controversial points in this debate are provocative and indeed crucial for the general theoretical project I advocate we pursue: Research which attempts to pinpoint the (albeit shifting) relationship of public opinion communication to the actions of pressure groups.

5. On nonresponse rates in surveys, see Tom W. Smith's recent analysis of the problem, "Trends in Non-Response Rates," *International Journal of Public Opinion Research* 7 (1995): 157–71.

6. Petracca, *The Politics of Interests,* p. xx.

7. See Richard Hall and Frank Wayman, "Buying Time: Moneyed Interests and the Mobilization of Bias in Congressional Committees," *American Political Science Review* 84 (1990): 797–820, about the role of money in interest group politics, and Jack L. Walker's *Mobilizing Interest Groups in America: Patrons, Professions, and Social Movements* (Ann Arbor: University of Michigan Press, 1991), on monied interests and the problems of mobilization among the poor and unemployed.

8. Salisbury, *Interests and Institutions,* chap. 17. For another very comprehensive look at interest groups and their abilities (and inabilities) to influence policy outcomes, see John P. Heinz, Edward O. Laumann, Robert L. Nelson, and Robert H. Salisbury, *The Hollow Core: Private Interests in National Policy Making* (Cambridge: Harvard University Press, 1993).

9. Schlozman and Tierney, *Organized Interests,* chap. 15.

10. Jane J. Mansbridge, "A Deliberative Theory of Interest Representation," in Petracca, *The Politics of Interests,* 32–57.

11. See Allan J. Cigler and Dwight C. Kiel, *The Changing Nature of Interest Group Politics in Kansas* (Topeka: University Press of Kansas, 1988), cited in Rosenthal, *The Third House.*

12. George Gallup and Saul Rae, *The Pulse of Democracy: The Public Opinion Poll and How It Works* (New York: Greenwood Press, 1940), 28.

13. Perhaps this is a good place for a semantic note about political cognition. To say that people make arguments and in fact *think* in argumentative formats is not simply saying that people have attitudes. Attitudes are typically believed to have cognitive and evaluative components, and they can be directed toward the social world or one's own internal state. Arguments contain attitudes, certainly, but they also involve articulation, organization, attention to evidence, and reconstitution during the course of debate. Arguments are dialogic forms that are meant to be used as part of persuasion strategies. Forms of argument vary, of course, and have been the focus of rhetoricians since argumentation was first discussed in ancient Greece.

Some political scientists have labeled a cognition plus an evaluation of that cognition a "consideration." On attitudes, see Eagly and Chaiken, *Psychology of Attitudes.* On considerations, see Stanley Kelley, *Interpreting Elections* (Princeton: Princeton University Press, 1983), or Zaller, *Mass Opinion.*

14. Richard F. Fenno, *Home Style: House Members in Their Districts* (Boston: Little, Brown and Co., 1978).

15. See V. O. Key, *Public Opinion and American Democracy* (New York: Knopf, 1961), but also more recent work such as Jon A. Krosnick, "Government Policy and Citizen Passion: A Study of Issue Publics in Contemporary America," *Political Behavior* 12 (1990): 59–92.

16. E. E. Schattschneider, *The Semisovereign People: A Realist's View of Democracy in America* (New York: Holt, Rinehart and Winston, 1960). And although Grant McConnell's arguments about the American states are a bit out of date, given the professionalization of legislatures and changes in journalism since he wrote, his similar points about scope of conflict in states are relevant here as well. See his *Private Power and American Democracy* (New York: Vintage, 1966), chap. 6.

17. Schattschneider, *Semisovereign People,* 27 (emphasis in the original).

18. For a recent review of the "agenda setting" literature, see the multiauthored symposium, Maxwell E. McCombs and Donald L. Shaw, eds., "Agenda-Setting Revisited," *Journal of Communication* 43 (1993): 58–128.

19. The scholars associated with the Columbia School, for example, most certainly believed public opinion and media content to be related, but still distinctive. See, e.g., Elihu Katz and Paul Lazarsfeld, *Personal Influence: The Part Played by People in the Flow of Mass Communication* (Glencoe, Ill.: Free Press, 1955).

20. Lemert, *Does Mass Communication Change Public Opinion After All?* (Chicago: Nelson Hall, 1981); Benjamin I. Page, Robert Y. Shapiro, and Glenn R. Dempsey, "What Moves Public Opinion," *American Political Science Review* 81 (1987): 23–43.

21. See Jay Rosen, "Making Things More Public: On the Political Responsibility of the Media Intellectual," *Critical Studies in Mass Communication* 11 (1994): 362–88.

22. See Leila Sussmann, *Dear FDR: A Study of Political Letter Writing* (Totowa, N.J.: Bedminster, 1963).

23. Although Harold Innis and Marshall McLuhan are the earliest technological theorists of media, a more recent and more accessible argument for media effects (above and beyond the effects of content) is Joshua Meyrowitz, *No Sense of Place: The Impact of Electronic Media on Social Behavior* (New York: Oxford University Press, 1985).

24. See, e.g., Diana C. Mutz, "The Influence of Perceptions of Media Influence: Third Person Effects and the Public Expression of Opinion," *International Journal of Public Opinion Research* 1 (1989): 3–24.

25. See Robert Entman, *Democracy without Citizens: Media and the Decay of American Politics* (New York: Oxford University Press, 1989).

26. In this chapter I have, in two separate discussions, explored the ways that staffers define public opinion in terms of interest groups and in terms of the media. Yet there is an added complexity: Interest groups tend to speak to media—to journalists covering state politics—while simultaneously pressuring legislators and staffers. So one might argue that in many cases there is a fusion of interest group opinion and media content. Take the case of riverboat gambling, which is a chronic issue in Illinois state politics since a variety of legislators believe that this potential source of revenue for the state cannot be ignored. Interest groups on this issue—both casino companies and antigambling religious groups—speak to the media continuously when gambling bills are being debated in the legislature. So, both staffers and assembly members hear from interest groups through interpersonal contact *and* through the mass media. This is an important point because it underscores the two important modalities of communication (face-to-face and mediated) interest groups may work through. I thank Bob Shapiro for impressing the value of this point on me.

Chapter Three

1. See, for example, the papers from the symposium on journalistic behavior and norms organized by Lance Bennett and introduced by him in "Journalism Norms and News Construction: Rules for Representing Politics," *Political Communication* 13 (1996): 371–482.

2. Timothy E. Cook, *Making Laws and Making News: Media Strategies in the U.S. House of Representatives* (Washington, D.C.: The Brookings Institution, 1989).

3. An example of an issue that took many by surprise was the fallout over the Richard Speck videotapes in the spring of 1996. These videotapes showed mass murder convict Speck engaged in sexual intercourse with other inmates, and the tapes were given to a Chicago journalist, who later released them. The films were viewed by assembly members in highly publicized hearings that had been organized to discuss prison reform. Intense coverage by television broadcasters of events at the state legislature is rare, but in this case, all news media covered the story in a detailed fashion because they viewed it as lurid.

4. The White House press corps, for example, is often described as fairly closed and difficult to permeate.

5. I should underscore one limitation of this study: I do not evaluate *all* influences on journalists, simply the way their notions of public opinion impact their work. I do not, for example, scrutinize the way economic pressures affect the ways they report on the legislature. And I do not evaluate media content, one possible route for understanding journalistic behavior. These are potentially very useful avenues for exploration.

6. Staffers and journalists I spoke to are probably unaware of just how low citizen knowledge levels are when it comes to national politics. On this subject see Delli Carpini and Keeter, *What Americans Know About Politics.*

7. This is a study of journalists who cover the legislature for elite papers and news services. It is possible that inclusion of journalists for smaller newspapers and radio stations would have changed the results, but for this study I was interested in journalists with the largest audiences. I thank Lewis Friedland for reminding me of this.

8. *Illinois Blue Book 1995/1996* (Springfield: State of Illinois, 1995), 48.

9. James B. Lemert has argued that journalists can do a much better job reporting on lobbying practices than they currently do. He notes that, "Journalists covering the U.S. Congress and federal executive agencies, as well as journalists covering state government, are far more likely to report the *results* of interest group lobbying than they are to cover the lobbying *process* itself." Lemert finds this problematic, since citizens tend not to understand pressure politics on an issue until it is too late to act. See Lemert's essay, "Effective Public Opinion," in *Public Opinion, the Press, and Public Policy,* ed. J. David Kennamer (Westport, Conn.: Praeger, 1992), 57.

10. See my *Numbered Voices,* chap. 4.

11. On the sheer number of political polls found in media, as well as the use of polling by journalists, see Paul J. Lavrakas, Michael W. Traugott, and Peter V. Miller, eds., *Presidential Polling and the News Media* (Boulder: Westview Press, 1995).

12. See Philip Meyer, *Precision Journalism: A Reporter's Introduction to Social Science Methods* (Bloomington: Indiana University Press, 1973).

13. See my *Numbered Voices,* chap. 4.

14. Perhaps the best place to begin reading the theoretical debate on this subject is Nancy Fraser's critique of Habermas in *Unruly Practices: Power, Discourse, and Gender in Contemporary Social Theory* (Minneapolis: University of Minnesota Press, 1989). I discuss it as well in my *Politics at the Margin: Historical Studies of Public Expression Outside the Mainstream* (New York: Cambridge University Press, 1994).

15. On *salons,* see work by Deena Goodman, who has produced a large number of fasci-

nating studies on the subject. Interested readers might begin with her article, "Governing the Republic of Letters: The Politics of Culture in the French Enlightenment," *History of European Ideas* 13 (1991):183–99. In *Structural Transformation* Jürgen Habermas discussed the *salons* in less detail and without the benefit of recent social historical work. I have collected and analyzed much of the English language literature about *salons* of prerevolutionary France in my *Politics at the Margin* (chap. 2).

16. A summary and analysis of Tönnies' work in the area of public opinion is found in the essay by Gillian Lindt Gollin and Albert E. Gollin, "Tönnies on Public Opinion," in *Ferdinand Tönnies: A New Evaluation,* ed. Werner J. Cahnman (Leiden, Germany: E. J. Brill, 1973), 181–203.

17. See Gabriel Tarde, *Gabriel Tarde: On Communication and Social Influence,* trans. and ed. Terry N. Clarke (Chicago: University of Chicago Press, 1969). This is a book of Tarde's essays. Elihu Katz has been extending Tarde's theorizing, writing about how we might use Tarde's work in current-day mass communication research. Among his papers on the subject is "Mass Media and Participatory Democracy" (paper presented at the Series on Political Communication, Northwestern University, 11 October 1996).

18. James Bryce, a contemporary of Tarde's, used the word "weathervane" to describe the many functions of the nineteenth-century American newspaper. There are, in fact, many parallels between Bryce's *American Commonwealth* and Tarde's work, although Tarde's work is more philosophical and erudite than Bryce's.

19. See Noelle-Neumann's *Spiral of Silence.* Noelle-Neumann's work is controversial. For one critique, see Carroll Glynn and Jack McLeod, "Public Opinion du Jour: An Examination of *The Spiral of Silence,*" *Public Opinion Quarterly* 48 (1984): 731–40.

20. J. L. Austin, *How to Do Things with Words* (Cambridge: Harvard University Press, 1975).

21. Clyde Lyndon King, "Public Opinion as Viewed by Eminent Political Theorists," *University of Pennsylvania Free Public Lecture Course* (Philadelphia: University of Pennsylvania Press, 1916), 418.

22. See, for example, Robert Darnton's essay recounting his days as a young reporter at *The New York Times.* This piece about the sociology of journalism is "Writing News and Telling Stories," *Daedalus* 104 (spring 1975): 175–94.

23. On reception theory and its views of the reader, see Robert C. Allen, "Audience-Oriented Criticism and Television," in Robert C. Allen, ed., *Channels of Discourse, Reassembled: Television and Contemporary Criticism* (Chapel Hill: University of North Carolina Press, 1992).

24. See, for example, Herbert Gans' pioneering study of journalistic behavior, *Deciding What's News.*

25. On Watergate in journalistic and popular culture, see Michael Schudson's fine study of collective memory, *Watergate in American Memory.* On the social history of American journalism, see his *Discovering the News: A Social History of American Newspapers* (New York: Basic Books, 1978). A good and encyclopedic textbook on journalism history is Michael Emery and Edwin Emery, *The Press and America: An Interpretive History of the Mass Media* (Englewood Cliffs, N.J.: Prentice-Hall, 1988).

26. The premier book on cynicism and media is now Joseph N. Cappella and Kathleen Hall Jamieson, *The Spiral of Cynicism: The Press and the Public Good* (New York: Oxford University Press, 1997).

27. See Doug Underwood's *When MBAs Rule the Newsroom: How the Marketers and Managers are Reshaping Today's Media* (New York: Columbia University Press, 1993).

28. Deliberation is treated in chapter 5, but see James S. Fishkin, *Democracy and Deliberation: New Directions for Democratic Reform* (New Haven, Conn.: Yale University Press, 1991), or Benjamin I. Page, *Who Deliberates? Mass Media in Modern Democracy* (Chicago: University of Chicago Press, 1996).

Chapter Four

1. While I use first person singular throughout much of this chapter, I must note that the survey of party activists was conducted in a collaboration with Robert Eisinger. I conducted the depth interviews with activists myself, but the survey was a joint project, from start to finish.

2. Basic information on party activists can be found in Samuel Eldersveld's work, from his early projects in the 1960s onward. See *Political Parties: A Behavioral Analysis* (Chicago: Rand McNally, 1964) and *Political Parties in American Society* (New York: Basic Books, 1962). The delegates studied here are, of course, a very narrow segment of political activists. On political activism in general, see Sidney Verba, Kay Lehman Schlozman, and Henry E. Brady, *Voice and Equality: Civic Voluntarism in American Politics* (Cambridge: Harvard University Press, 1995).

3. See Robert Herrera's work, which has been enormously useful to me in understanding convention delegates. In terms of the heterogeneity of party convention delegates, see his article, "Are 'Superdelegates' Super?" *Political Behavior* 16 (1994): 79–92.

4. In this section on political elites, I draw on a very large literature and it is impossible and perhaps unnecessary to discuss or list all these works without taking us far from the rather specific subject of this book. Among the works used are: Herbert McClosky, Paul J. Hoffmann, and Rosemary O'Hara, "Issue Conflict and Consensus among Party Leaders and Followers," *American Political Science Review* 54 (1960): 406–27; Robert D. Putnam, Robert Leonardi, and Rafaella Y. Nanetti, "Attitude Stability among Italian Elites," *American Journal of Politics* 23 (August 1979): 463–94; Converse, "Nature of Belief Systems"; Norman R. Luttbeg, "The Structure of Beliefs among Leaders and the Public," *Public Opinion Quarterly* 32 (1968): 398–409; Robert W. Jackman, "Political Elites, Mass Publics, and Support for Democratic Principles," *Journal of Politics* 34 (1972): 753–73; Hans D. Klingemann, "Ideological Conceptualization and Political Action," in *Political Action*, ed. Samuel H. Barnes and Max Kaase (Beverly Hills, Calif.: Sage, 1979); Robert Luskin, "Measuring Political Sophistication," *American Journal of Political Science* 31 (1987): 856–99; Warren E. Miller and M. Kent Jennings, *Parties in Transition: A Longitudinal Study of Party Elites and Party Supporters* (New York: Russell Sage Foundation, 1986); Robert Putnam, *The Comparative Study of Political Elites* (Englewood Cliffs, N.J.: Prentice-Hall, 1976); Herbert M. Kritzer, "Ideology and American Political Elites," *Public Opinion Quarterly* 42 (1978): 482–502; and Robert E. Agger, Daniel Goldrich, and Bert E. Swanson, *The Rulers and the Ruled* (New York: Wiley, 1964). On "issue publics" see Krosnick, "Government Policy and Citizen Passion" or Jon A.

Krosnick and Shibley Telhami, "Public Attitudes toward Israel: A Study of the Attentive and Issue Publics," *International Studies Quarterly* 39 (1995): 535–54. More recent work and research specifically on convention delegates is cited below. On activism and race issues, see chapter 4 of Edward G. Carmines and James A. Stimson, *Issue Evolution: Race and the Transformation of American Politics* (Princeton, N.J.: Princeton University Press, 1980).

5. Luttbeg, "Structure of Beliefs," is an example.

6. Lane, *Political Ideology.*

7. After the 1996 presidential nominating conventions, journalists and television network executives expressed great disgust at what they believed were simply "media events" with no real substantive ideological or policy content. It remains to be seen whether the major networks cover the conventions in any significant way during the 2000 campaign.

8. The literature on delegates at presidential nominating conventions is large and interesting. Here I draw on the following works: Herbert McClosky, *Political Inquiry: The Nature and Uses of Survey Research* (New York: Macmillan, 1969); Jeane Kirkpatrick, "Representation in the American National Conventions: The Case of 1972," *British Journal of Political Science* 5 (1975): 265–322; Howard L. Reiter, *Selecting the President: The Nominating Process in Transition* (Philadelphia: University of Pennsylvania Press, 1985); William Crotty and John S. Jackson III, *Presidential Primaries and Nominations* (Washington, D.C.: Congressional Quarterly Press, 1985); Warren E. Miller, *Without Consent: Mass-Elite Linkages in Presidential Politics* (Lexington: University Press of Kentucky, 1988); Thomas Roback, "Motivation for Activism among Republican National Convention Delegates: Continuity and Change, 1972–1976," *Journal of Politics* 42 (1980): 181–201; John W. Soule and James W. Clarke, "Issue Conflict and Consensus: A Comparative Study of Democratic and Republican Delegates to the 1968 National Conventions," *Journal of Politics* 33 (1971): 72–91; Steven Greene, "How Convention Delegates Perceive the Political World: A Study of the Delegates to the 1992 National Conventions" (paper presented at the annual meeting of the Midwest Political Science Association, Chicago, April 1997). Herrera has produced many articles on convention delegates and they are largely based on surveys of convention attendees available from the Inter-University Consortium for Political and Social Research, University of Michigan. See his "Cohesion at the Party Conventions: 1980–1988," *Polity* 26 (1993): 75–89; "The Crosswinds of Change: Sources of Change in the Democratic and Republican Parties," *Political Research Quarterly* 48 (June 1995): 291–312; "The Understanding of Ideological Labels by Political Elites: A Research Note," *Western Political Quarterly* 45 (1992): 1021–35; and his article with Melanie K. Taylor, "The Structure of Opinion in American Political Parties," *Political Studies* 42 (1994): 676–89.

9. Herrera, "Cohesion," 87–88.

10. Greene, "Convention Delegates," 16–17.

11. The Barbour quote is from James Bennet, "The Delegates: Where Image Meets Reality," *New York Times,* 12 August 1996, p. 1. This article also includes results of the *Times/CBS* poll on Republican delegates. A similar study of Democratic delegates was published in James Bennet, "In Poll, Ardor for President," *New York Times,* 26 August 1996, p.1. All data in my discussion here are drawn from these two articles, each of which includes some methodological notes on the surveys.

12. This range is based on studies of delegates in the literature. The major studies are cited above. We initially chose twenty states—four from each region. But one state party organization provided an incomplete list of delegates and was therefore eliminated from the sample.

13. We are grateful to the state party organizations that provided delegate lists for us, but many lists either were incomplete or did not specify who was actually a delegate and who was an alternate delegate. The mail surveys were sent from September 17 to September 26 of 1996, shortly after both conventions. Of the 1181 surveys mailed to Democratic delegates, 327 were returned and usable. Of the 706 surveys mailed to Republican delegates, 197 surveys were returned. Four survey respondents sent the questionnaire back but did not state their party affiliation. There was only one mailing and we did not pursue nonrespondents: We did not want to survey delegates too long after the conventions were held, because the political environment changes so quickly during the campaign season. We were afraid that answers to the survey might be affected by the idiosyncratic climate of the moment during the campaign season, which changes rapidly and is certainly the most intensely *political* period in American politics.

There are many more Democratic convention delegates than Republican convention delegates, which is why more Democrats are included in the sample. In analyzing the data, we found no statistically significant differences between Democrats and Republicans on any of the survey questions.

14. Delegates in this sample represented the following states at the conventions: Alabama, Arizona, Connecticut, Florida, Hawaii, Kansas, Maine, Maryland, Massachusetts, Minnesota, Montana, New Jersey, North Dakota, Oregon, South Dakota, Tennessee, Utah, Vermont, and Wyoming. We deliberately omitted the Illinois delegation, so that I could call these men and women for depth interviews.

15. I draw here on the Tönnies book translated by Charles Loomis—Ferdinand Tönnies, *Community and Society,* trans. and ed. Charles Loomis (East Lansing: Michigan State University Press, 1957)—but also on the fine article by Gillian Lindt Gollin and Albert E. Gollin, "Tönnies on Public Opinion." The article by the Gollins is particularly useful because it interprets Tönnies' often obscure ideas and because much of his work on public opinion has not been translated into English. Also excellent is Paul A. Palmer's "Ferdinand Tönnies Theory of Public Opinion," *Public Opinion Quarterly* 2 (1938): 584–95.

16. See "My 'Public Opinion Baths,'" in *Lincoln on Democracy,* ed. Mario Cuomo and Harold Holzer (New York: Harper Collins, 1990), 284–85.

17. Edmund Burke, "Speech to the Electors of Bristol (3 November 1774)," in *The Works of the Right Honorable Edmund Burke* (Boston: Little, Brown and Co., 1889).

18. Most recently, see Jacobs and Shapiro, "Politicization of Public Opinion." There are scores of earlier studies on the subject, however. As far back as 1945, we can find articles like the one by George W. Hartmann, "Judgments of State Legislators Concerning Public Opinion," *Journal of Social Psychology* 21 (1945): 105–14. I am grateful to Kathy Frankovic for this citation. A few helpful articles in this literature are Bryan D. Jones, "Competitiveness, Role Orientations, and Legislative Responsiveness," *Journal of Politics* 35 (1973): 924–47, and Ronald Hedlund and H. Paul Friesema, "Representatives' Perceptions of Constituency

Opinion," *Journal of Politics* 34 (1972): 732–52. More recently we have works like Benjamin I. Page and Robert Y. Shapiro's *The Rational Public: Fifty Years of Trends in Americans' Policy Preferences* (Chicago: University of Chicago Press, 1992); James A. Stimson, Michael B. Mackuen and Robert S. Erikson, "Dynamic Representation," *American Political Science Review* 89 (1995): 543–65; and Erikson, Wright, and McIver, *Statehouse Democracy.*

19. This is still an issue of some debate, as mentioned in previous chapters and notes. See Jacobs and Shapiro, "Politicization of Public Opinion." Jacobs and Shapiro do find that, during the national health care debate of the early 1990s, leaders and their staffs used poll results to shape their rhetoric—to "sell" their ideas to a skeptical public. This use of polls is far different than using surveys to decide among policy options. There are some historical studies as well as popular books (insider accounts) of poll use in the White House. See Jacobs and Shapiro's articles, "Rise of Presidential Polling" and "Issues, Candidate Image, and Priming." See also Eisinger, "Illusion of Certainty."

20. There are a variety of scholarly works on the subject of increasing distrust and alienation among American citizens. One place to begin is Seymour Lipset and William Schneider, *The Confidence Gap* (Baltimore: Johns Hopkins University Press, 1987). More recently, see Scott Keeter's discussion of trust drawing on a variety of large national surveys, "Public Opinion and the Election," in *The Election of 1996: Reports and Interpretations,* ed. Gerald Pomper et al. (Chatham, N.J.: Chatham House, 1997), 107–34.

21. See, for example, Paul R. Abramson, *Political Attitudes in America: Formation and Change* (San Francisco: W. H. Freeman and Co., 1983).

Chapter Five

1. Although I did not detect important differences in public opinion views between Republican and Democratic staffers or Republican and Democratic activists on the very narrow concerns in this project, I was not focusing on partisanship. I do not believe I have definitively dismissed the possibility that such partisan differences exist, and it is possible that future research that focuses on partisanship might turn up differences in public opinion conceptions.

2. On citizen knowledge levels see Delli Carpini and Keeter, *What Americans Know about Politics.* For experimental work on media and citizen attitude change through priming and agenda setting see Shanto Iyengar and Donald R. Kinder, *News That Matters: Television and American Opinion* (Chicago: University of Chicago Press, 1987).

3. Elisabeth S. Clemens, *The People's Lobby: Organizational Innovation and the Rise of Interest Group Politics in the United States, 1890-1925* (Chicago: University of Chicago Press, 1997), 307.

4. Herbst, *Numbered Voices,* 107.

5. How people attend to different forms of newspaper content is a complex issue. For an overview of research in this area, see Jack McLeod, Gerald Kosicki, and Douglas McLeod, "The Expanding Boundaries of Political Communication Effects," in *Media Effects: Advances in Theory and Research,* ed. Jennings Bryant and Dolf Zillmann (Hillsdale, N.J.: Lawrence Erlbaum Associates, 1994).

6. Held, *Models of Democracy.*

7. Although I did not probe on this topic, and citizen information levels are not a central

focus of this book, one might argue that activists share a belief in "low information rationality." On this subject, see Popkin, *The Reasoning Voter.*

8. Joseph Schumpeter, *Capitalism, Socialism, and Democracy,* 3d ed. (New York: Harper and Row, 1950), 262.

9. Jennifer Hochschild, *What's Fair? American Beliefs about Distributive Justice* (Cambridge: Harvard University Press, 1981), 238. For a thoughtful view of ambivalence in survey responses and a discussion of how researchers need to theorize around this phenomenon, see John Zaller and Stanley Feldman's article, "A Simple Theory of the Survey Response: Answering Questions versus Revealing Preferences," *American Journal of Political Science* 36 (1992): 579–616, as well as Zaller's *Mass Opinion.*

10. John R. Hibbing and Elizabeth Theiss-Morse, *Congress as Public Enemy: Public Attitudes toward American Political Institutions* (New York: Cambridge University Press, 1995).

11. Fenno, *Home Style,* 28.

12. Whiteman, *Communication in Congress,* chap. 4.

13. For an introductory discussion of communication modalities and persuasion, see Richard E. Petty and John T. Cacioppo, *Attitudes and Persuasion: Classic and Contemporary Approaches* (Dubuque, Iowa: Wm. C. Brown Co., 1981). There are many complex questions about the conditions under which interpersonal persuasion and mass media persuasion are effective. On this topic, see Diana C. Mutz, "Mass Media and the Depoliticization of Personal Experience," *American Journal of Political Science* 36 (1992): 483–508. For a discussion of different mass media channels and their characteristics, see Neuman, Just, and Crigler, *Common Knowledge,* chap. 3.

14. John Kingdon, *Congressmen's Voting Decisions,* 3d ed. (Ann Arbor: University of Michigan Press, 1991). The original work was published in 1973, and a second edition was published in 1981.

15. Ibid., 172.

16. Don Terry, "Illinois is Attacked on Election Laws," *New York Times,* 30 January 1997, p. 12.

17. David A. Mayhew, *Congress: The Electoral Connection* (New Haven, Conn.: Yale University Press, 1974), 130.

18. Iyengar, *Is Anyone Responsible?*

19. Schattschneider, *Semisovereign People,* 3.

20. See, for example, Thomas E. Patterson, *Out of Order: How the Decline of the Political Parties and the Growing Power of the News Media Undermine the American Way of Electing Presidents* (New York: Alfred A. Knopf, 1993).

21. Schattschneider, *Semisovereign People,* 3–4.

22. Recent work on citizen knowledge appears in Delli Carpini and Keeter, *What Americans Know about Politics.*

23. Popkin, cited above, is a good spokesman for the "low information rationality" school. The argument about aggregation of unstable opinions is forcefully made by Page and Shapiro in *The Rational Public.*

24. The work on states I refer to here is Erikson, Wright, and McIver, *Statehouse Democracy.* On what leaders do with policy polls at the national level see Jacobs and Shapiro, "Politi-

cization of Public Opinion." For an interesting view of polling and how it affects leadership, see John G. Geer, *From Tea Leaves to Opinion Polls: A Theory of Democratic Leadership* (New York: Columbia University Press, 1996).

25. Lippmann, *The Phantom Public*, 13.

26. An excellent essay on the Dewey versus Lippmann debate is John Durham Peters, "Why Dewey Wasn't So Right and Lippmann Wasn't So Wrong" (paper presented at the annual meeting of the International Communication Association, Montreal, 1997).

27. Dewey, *The Public*, 148.

28. Aristotle, *The Nicomachean Ethics*, trans. and ed. H. Rackham (London: William Heinemann, 1975), 453.

29. David Bolotin, *Plato's Dialogue on Friendship: An Interpretation of the Lysis, with a New Translation* (Ithaca, N.Y.: Cornell University Press, 1979), 9. Why do contemporary researchers shy away from taking friendship more seriously in studies of politics, both local and national? It may be that such friendships—tight bonds created through shared history and affect between two or more people—are suspect in modern democracy: They seem to fly in the face of fairness and objectivity in policy making. We are, for example, dubious of our president's "cronies." And the notion that friendship patterns among legislators might determine policy outcomes seems downright repulsive to us in the late 1990s. Relatedly, it may be that our worries about friendship and bonds of affect corrupting democratic process may be one reason why women—traditionally associated with close friendship and emotion—have been suspect as political beings. See Carole Pateman, *The Sexual Contract* (Stanford, Calif.: Stanford University Press, 1988). I thank Sarah Maza for underscoring this point to me.

30. One of the best works along these lines is Mansbridge, *Beyond Adversary Democracy*. A more recent work, although with a different theoretical focus, is Robert Huckfeldt and John Sprague, *Citizens, Politics, and Social Communication: Information and Influence in an Election Campaign* (New York: Cambridge University Press, 1995). The Columbia School was the inspiration for such work, of course. Among other books, see Katz and Lazarsfeld, *Personal Influence*, and Bernard Berelson, Paul Lazarsfeld, and William McPhee, *Voting: A Study of Opinion Formation in a Presidential Campaign* (Chicago: University of Chicago Press, 1954).

31. Mansbridge, *Beyond Adversary Democracy*, 9.

32. Robert A. Dahl and Edward R. Tufte, *Size and Democracy* (Stanford, Calif.: Stanford University Press, 1973).

33. For a summary of James S. Fishkin's work on deliberative democracy, see *The Voice of the People* (New Haven, Conn.: Yale University Press, 1997). For an analysis and critique of Fishkin's experiments, see Daniel M. Merkle, "Review: The National Issues Convention Deliberative Poll, " *Public Opinion Quarterly* 60 (1996), 588–619.

34. A. Phillips Griffiths, "How Can One Person Represent Another?" in *Representation*, ed. Hanna Fenichel Pitkin (New York: Atherton Press, 1969), 133–57.

35. See John Stuart Mill, *Considerations on Representative Government* (London: Parker, Son, and Bourne, 1861).

36. One very good introductory reader in this field is Lawrence Grossberg, Cary Nelson, and Paula Treichler, *Cultural Studies* (New York: Routledge, 1992).

37. The gaps between blacks' and whites' opinions about the case and verdict were large.

In one Gallup poll, taken shortly after the verdict was announced, 89 percent of blacks thought the "not guilty" verdict correct and only 36 percent of whites agreed with them. This differential was apparent throughout the trial period. See Frank Newport, "Wrapping Up the O. J. Simpson Case," *The Gallup Poll Monthly* 363 (November 1995): 24–27.

38. See Catherine Squires, "Black Talk Radio and the Black Public Sphere" (paper presented at the annual meeting of the International Communication Association, Montreal, 1997).

39. Such volumes abound on the public opinion shelves of any university library. One interesting book along these lines is Francis Graham Wilson's fine *Theory of Public Opinion*, which blends philosophical reflection on public opinion and intellectual history (from the ancients through the nineteenth century) with synthesis of existing empirical work on the subject. This work of tremendous scholarship is well worth reading thirty-five years after its publication.

40. In the contemporary historical field there are an enormous number of creative studies that use such documents. In American history, David Nord's work is an excellent example of the innovative use of letters to the editor. See his "Reading the Newspaper: Strategies and Politics of Reader Response, Chicago, 1912–1917," *Journal of Communication* 45 (1995): 66–93. Many historians have turned to popular literature in an attempt to understand public opinion of past civilizations. One example, in keeping with the O. J. Simpson illustration above, is Sarah Maza's *Private Lives and Public Affairs: The Causes Célèbres of Prerevolutionary France* (Berkeley and Los Angeles: University of California Press, 1993). Maza studies legal briefs, a popular form of pamphlet literature, to understand opinion formation and change in eighteenth-century France.

41. Taeku Lee, " 'Dear Mr. President . . . ': Constituency Mail on the Civil Rights Movement as Public Opinion, 1948–1965" (paper presented at the annual meeting of the American Political Science Association, San Francisco, 1996).

42. One study along these lines is Amy Fried's book about Oliver North and the Iran-Contra hearings. She analyzes how various forms of public opinion were used strategically by different actors in this controversy. See her *Muffled Echoes: Oliver North and the Politics of Public Opinion* (New York: Columbia University Press, 1997).

43. Herbst, *Numbered Voices*.

44. There is some good evidence of short-term effects in the laboratory, of course. See Iyengar and Kinder, *News That Matters*, or Iyengar's *Is Anyone Responsible?* Short-term effects are important, but we have been far, far less successful in demonstrating effects outside of the lab.

Appendix A

1. For an introduction to grounded theory methods, see Anselm Strauss and Juliet Corbin, *Basics of Qualitative Research: Grounded Theory Procedures and Techniques* (Newbury Park, Calif.: Sage, 1990).

2. One might argue that this is a source of bias. When the researcher "zeros in" on an informant's point, and therefore is able to conduct a shorter interview, that researcher may be cutting off the interview too early. I was conscious of this problem, however, and there were a

variety of places where the informant could speak in an extended fashion. I did not cut informants off, except in rare cases where they had traveled very far on an unproductive, personal, or irrelevant tangent.

3. Hochschild, *What's Fair,* 24.

4. There is no question that the best qualitative work is often conducted by researchers who understand other methodologies—both quantitative and qualitative. Lazarsfeld is one of our exemplars, of course, but Herbert Blumer is also very thoughtful in this regard. See the excellent discussion of Blumer's methodological struggles in Kenneth Baugh, Jr., *The Methodology of Herbert Blumer: Critical Interpretation and Repair* (New York: Cambridge University Press, 1990).

5. I borrow this phrase, "joint construction of meaning," from one of the most sophisticated and useful texts about depth interviewing, Elliot G. Mishler's *Research Interviewing: Context and Narrative* (Cambridge: Harvard University Press, 1986).

6. Fenno, *Homestyle,* 263–64.

Appendix B

1. For discussion of previous work on deliberation as a concept see Page, *Who Deliberates?* 1–16. See also Robert A. Dahl, *Democracy and Its Critics* (New Haven, Conn.: Yale University Press, 1989).

2. My approach to the question of ideology was very much inspired by one of the premier volumes in this area, Raymond Geuss, *The Idea of A Critical Theory: Habermas and the Frankfurt School* (Cambridge: Cambridge University Press, 1981).

Bibliography

Abramson, Paul R. *Political Attitudes in America: Formation and Change.* San Francisco: W. H. Freeman and Co., 1983.

Agger, Robert E., Daniel Goldrich, and Bert E. Swanson. *The Rulers and the Ruled.* New York: Wiley, 1964.

Allen, Robert C. *Channels of Discourse, Reassembled: Television and Contemporary Criticism.* Chapel Hill: University of North Carolina Press, 1992.

Altschuler, Bruce. "Lyndon Johnson and the Public Polls." *Public Opinion Quarterly* 50 (1986): 285–99.

Antaki, Charles. *Explaining and Arguing: The Social Organization of Accounts.* London: Sage, 1994.

Aristotle. *The Politics.* Edited and translated by T. A. Sinclair. Baltimore: Penguin Books, 1962.

———. *The Nicomachean Ethics.* Edited and translated by H. Rackham. London: William Heinemann, 1975.

Austin, J. L. *How to Do Things with Words.* Cambridge: Harvard University Press, 1975.

Barber, James David. *The Lawmakers: Recruitment and Adaptation to Legislative Life.* New Haven: Yale University Press, 1965.

Barton, Allen. "Asking Why about Social Problems: Ideology and Causal Models in the Public Mind." *International Journal of Public Opinion Research* 7 (1995): 299–327.

Bauer, Wilhelm. "Public Opinion." In *The Encyclopaedia of the Social Sciences*, edited by E. Seligman. New York: Macmillan, 1930.

Baugh, Kenneth, Jr. *The Methodology of Herbert Blumer: Critical Interpretation and Repair.* New York: Cambridge University Press, 1990.

Bennett, W. Lance. "Constructing Publics and Their Opinions." *Political Communication* 10 (1993): 101–20.

Bennett, W. Lance, ed. "Journalism Norms and News Construction: Rules for Representing Politics." *Political Communication* 13 (1996): 371–482.

Bennett, W. Lance, and David Paletz, eds. *Taken by Storm: The Media, Public Opinion, and U.S. Foreign Policy in the Gulf War.* Chicago: University of Chicago Press, 1994.

Bentley, Arthur. *The Process of Government.* Chicago: University of Chicago Press, 1908.

Berelson, Bernard, Paul Lazarsfeld, and William McPhee. *Voting: A Study of Opinion Formation in a Presidential Campaign.* Chicago: University of Chicago Press, 1954.

Berger, Peter L., and Thomas Luckmann. *The Social Construction of Reality: A Treatise in the Sociology of Knowledge.* Garden City, N.Y.: Anchor Books, 1967.

Billig, Michael. *Ideology and Opinions: Studies in Rhetorical Psychology*. London: Sage, 1991.

————. *Arguing and Thinking: A Rhetorical Approach to Social Psychology*. Cambridge: Cambridge University Press, 1996.

Binkley, Robert C. "The Concept of Public Opinion in the Social Sciences." *Social Forces* 6 (1928): 389–96.

Blondiaux, Loïc. "Comment rompre avec Durkheim? Jean Stoetzel et la sociologie française de l'après-guerre (1945–1958)." *Revue française de sociologie* 32 (1991): 753–91.

————. "La Fabrique de l'opinion." Doctoral diss., Institut d'études politiques, Paris, 1994.

Blumer, Herbert. "Public Opinion and Public Opinion Polling." *American Sociological Review* 13 (1948): 242–49.

Bolotin, David. *Plato's Dialogue on Friendship: An Interpretation of the Lysis, with a New Translation*. Ithaca: Cornell University Press, 1979.

Bruner, Jerome. *Acts of Meaning*. Cambridge: Harvard University Press, 1990.

Bryce, James. *The American Commonwealth*. New York: Macmillan, 1891.

Burke, Edmund. "Speech to the Electors of Bristol (3 November 1774)." In *The Works of the Right Honorable Edmund Burke*. Boston: Little, Brown and Co., 1889.

Campbell, Karlyn Kohrs, and Kathleen Hall Jamieson. *Deeds Done in Words: Presidential Rhetoric and the Genres of Governance*. Chicago: University of Chicago Press, 1990.

Cappella, Joseph N., and Kathleen Hall Jamieson. *The Spiral of Cynicism: The Press and the Public Good*. New York: Oxford University Press, 1997.

Carmines, Edward G., and James A. Stimson. *Issue Evolution: Race and the Transformation of American Politics*. Princeton: Princeton University Press, 1980.

Cigler, Allan J., and Dwight C. Kiel. *The Changing Nature of Interest Group Politics in Kansas*. Topeka: University Press of Kansas, 1988.

Cigler, Allan J., and Burdett A. Loomis. *Interest Group Politics*. 4th ed. Washington, D.C.: Congressional Quarterly Press, 1995.

Clark, Carroll D. "The Concept of the Public." *The Southwestern Social Science Quarterly* 13 (1933): 311–20.

Clemens, Elisabeth S. *The People's Lobby: Organizational Innovation and the Rise of Interest Group Politics in the United States, 1890–1925*. Chicago: University of Chicago Press, 1997.

Clinton, Bill. *Public Papers of the Presidents of the United States: Bill Clinton*. Vol. 1. Washington, D.C.: GPO, 1994.

Conover, Pamela Johnston, Ivor M. Crewe, and Donald D. Searing. "The Nature of Citizenship in the United States and Great Britain: Empirical Comments on Theoretical Themes." *Journal of Politics* 53 (1991): 800–832.

Converse, Philip E. "The Nature of Belief Systems in Mass Publics." In *Ideology and Discontent*, edited by David Apter. Glencoe, Ill.: Free Press, 1964.

————. "Changing Conceptions of Public Opinion in the Political Process." *Public Opinion Quarterly* 51 (1987): S12–S24.

————. "The Advent of Polling and Political Representation." *PS* 29 (December 1996): 649–57.

Cook, Timothy E. *Making Laws and Making News: Media Strategies in the U.S. House of Representatives*. Washington, D.C.: The Brookings Institution, 1989.

Bibliography

Crigler, Ann, ed. *The Psychology of Political Communication*. Ann Arbor: University of Michigan Press, 1996.

Crotty, William, and John S. Jackson III. *Presidential Primaries and Nominations*. Washington, D.C.: Congressional Quarterly Press, 1985.

Dahl, Robert A. *Who Governs? Democracy and Power in an American City*. New Haven: Yale University Press, 1961.

———. *Democracy and Its Critics*. New Haven: Yale University Press, 1989.

Dahl, Robert A., and Edward R. Tufte. *Size and Democracy*. Stanford: Stanford University Press, 1973.

Darnton, Robert. "Writing News and Telling Stories." *Daedalus* 104 (spring 1975): 175–94.

Delli Carpini, Michael X., and Scott Keeter. *What Americans Know about Politics and Why It Matters*. New Haven: Yale University Press, 1996.

Dewey, John. *The Public and Its Problems*. Athens, Ohio: Swallow Press, 1954.

Dran, Ellen M., and Anne Hildreth. "What the Public Thinks about How We Know What It Is Thinking." *International Journal of Public Opinion Research* 7 (1995): 128–44.

Dreyfus, Hubert, and Paul Rabinow. *Michel Foucault: Beyond Structuralism and Hermeneutics*. Chicago: University of Chicago Press, 1983.

Eagly, Alice H., and Shelly Chaiken. *The Psychology of Attitudes*. Fort Worth, Texas: Harcourt Brace Jovanovich, 1993.

Edelman, Murray. *Political Language: Words That Succeed and Policies That Fail*. San Diego: Academic Press, 1977.

———. *The Symbolic Uses of Politics*. Urbana: University of Illinois Press, 1985.

Eisinger, Robert. "The Illusion of Certainty: Explaining the Evolution of Presidential Polling." Ph.D. diss., University of Chicago, 1996.

Eldersveld, Samuel. *Political Parties in American Society*. New York: Basic Books, 1962.

———. *Political Parties: A Behavioral Analysis*. Chicago: Rand McNally, 1964.

Emery, Michael, and Edwin Emery. *The Press and America: An Interpretive History of the Mass Media*. Englewood Cliffs, N.J.: Prentice-Hall, 1988.

Entman, Robert. *Democracy without Citizens: Media and the Decay of American Politics*. New York: Oxford University Press, 1989.

Erikson, Robert S., Gerald C. Wright, and John P. McIver. *Statehouse Democracy: Public Opinion and Policy in the American States*. New York: Cambridge University Press, 1993.

Erikson, Robert S., and Kent Tedin. *American Public Opinion: Its Origins, Content, and Impact*. 5th ed. Boston: Allyn and Bacon, 1995.

Everson, David H. "Illinois as a Bellwether: So What?" *Illinois Issues* (February 1990): 9–10.

Everson, David H. "COOGA *Redux*?" In *Almanac of Illinois Politics 1996*, edited by Craig Roberts and Paul Kleppner. Springfield: University of Illinois Press, 1996.

Farr, R. M., and Serge Moscovici, eds. *Social Representations*. Cambridge: Cambridge University Press, 1984.

Fenno, Richard F. *Homestyle: House Members in Their Districts*. Boston: Little, Brown and Co., 1978.

Fishkin, James S. *Democracy and Deliberation: New Directions for Democratic Reform*. New Haven: Yale University Press, 1991.

———. *The Voice of the People*. New Haven: Yale University Press, 1997.

Bibliography

Foucault, Michel. *Power/Knowledge: Selected Interviews and Other Writings, 1972–1977.* Edited by Colin Gordon. New York: Pantheon, 1980.

Fraser, Nancy. *Unruly Practices: Power, Discourse, and Gender in Contemporary Social Theory.* Minneapolis: University of Minnesota Press, 1989.

Fried, Amy. *Muffled Echoes: Oliver North and the Politics of Public Opinion.* New York: Columbia University Press, 1997.

Fuchs, Dieter, and Barbara Pfetsch. "The Observation of Public Opinion by the Governmental System." (Berlin, Wissenschaftszentrum Berlin für Sozialforschung GmbH).

Furnham, Adrian. *Lay Theory: Everyday Understanding of Problems in the Social Sciences.* New York: Pergamon Press, 1988.

Gallup, George, and Saul Rae. *The Pulse of Democracy: The Public Opinion Poll and How It Works.* New York: Greenwood Press, 1940.

Gamson, William. "A Constructionist Approach to Mass Media and Public Opinion." *Symbolic Interaction* 11 (1981): 161–74.

———. *Talking Politics.* New York: Cambridge University Press, 1992.

Gans, Herbert. *Deciding What's News: A Study of the* CBS Evening News, *the* NBC Nightly News, Newsweek, *and* Time. New York: Pantheon, 1979.

Geer, John G. *From Tea Leaves to Opinion Polls: A Theory of Democratic Leadership.* New York: Columbia University Press, 1996.

Geertz, Clifford. *The Interpretation of Cultures: Selected Essays.* New York: Basic Books, 1973.

Geuss, Raymond. *The Idea of a Critical Theory: Habermas and the Frankfurt School.* Cambridge: Cambridge University Press, 1981.

Gierzynski, Anthony. *Legislative Party Campaign Committees in the American States.* Lexington: University Press of Kentucky, 1992.

Glynn, Carroll, and Jack McLeod. "Public Opinion du Jour: An Examination of *The Spiral of Silence.*" *Public Opinion Quarterly* 48 (1984): 731–40.

Gollin, Gillian Lindt, and Albert E. Gollin. "Tönnies on Public Opinion." In *Ferdinand Tönnies: A New Evaluation,* edited by Werner J. Cahnman. Leiden, Germany: E. J. Brill, 1973.

Goodman, Deena. "Governing the Republic of Letters: The Politics of Culture in the French Enlightenment." *History of European Ideas* 13 (1991): 183–99.

Graber, Doris. *Processing the News: How People Tame the Information Tide.* New York: Longman, 1984.

Greene, Steven. "How Convention Delegates Perceive the Political World: A Study of the Delegates to the 1992 National Conventions." Paper presented at the annual meeting of the Midwest Political Science Association, Chicago, April 1997.

Griffiths, A. Phillips. "How Can One Person Represent Another?" In *Representation,* edited by Hanna Fenichel Pitkin. New York: Atherton Press, 1969.

Grossberg, Lawrence, Cary Nelson, and Paula Treichler. *Cultural Studies.* New York: Routledge, 1992.

Habermas, Jürgen. *The Structural Transformation of the Public Sphere: An Inquiry into a Category of Bourgeois Society.* Translated by Thomas Burger. Cambridge: MIT Press, 1989.

Hall, Richard, and Frank Wayman. "Buying Time: Moneyed Interests and the Mobilization of Bias in Congressional Committees." *American Political Science Review* 84 (1990): 797–820.

Hansen, John Mark. *Gaining Access: Congress and the Farm Lobby, 1919–1981.* Chicago: University of Chicago Press, 1991.

Hart, Roderick. *The Sound of Leadership: Presidential Communication in the Modern Age.* Chicago: University of Chicago Press, 1987.

Hartmann, George W. "Judgments of State Legislators Concerning Public Opinion." *Journal of Social Psychology* 21 (1945): 105–14.

Hedlund, Ronald, and H. Paul Friesema. "Representatives' Perceptions of Constituency Opinion." *Journal of Politics* 34 (1972): 732–52.

Heider, Fritz. *The Psychology of Interpersonal Relations.* New York: Wiley, 1958.

Heinz, John P., Edward O. Laumann, Robert L. Nelson, and Robert H. Salisbury. *The Hollow Core: Private Interests in National Policy Making.* Cambridge: Harvard University Press, 1993.

Held, David. *Models of Democracy.* Stanford: Stanford University Press, 1987.

Herbst, Susan. *Politics at the Margin: Historical Studies of Public Expression Outside the Mainstream.* New York: Cambridge University Press, 1994.

———. *Numbered Voices: How Opinion Polling Has Shaped American Politics.* Chicago: University of Chicago Press, 1993.

———. "The Meaning of Public Opinion: Citizens' Constructions of Political Reality." *Media, Culture and Society* 15 (1993): 437–54.

———. "Surveying and Influencing the Public: Polling in Politics and Industry." In *The Cambridge History of Science,* edited by David C. Lindberg and Ronald L. Numbers. New York: Cambridge University Press, in press.

Herrera, Richard. "The Understanding of Ideological Labels by Political Elites: A Research Note." *Western Political Quarterly* 45 (1992): 1021–35.

———. "Cohesion at the Party Conventions: 1980–1988." *Polity* 26 (1993): 75–89.

———. "Are 'Superdelegates' Super?" *Political Behavior* 16 (1994): 79–92.

———. "The Crosswinds of Change: Sources of Change in the Democratic and Republican Parties." *Political Research Quarterly* 48 (June 1995): 291–312.

Herrera, Richard, and Melanie K. Taylor. "The Structure of Opinion in American Political Parties." *Political Studies* 42 (1994): 676–89.

Hibbing, John R., and Elizabeth Eheiss-Morse. *Congress as Public Enemy: Public Attitudes toward American Political Institutions.* New York: Cambridge University Press, 1995.

Hochschild, Jennifer. *What's Fair: American Beliefs about Distributive Justice.* Cambridge: Harvard University Press, 1981.

Holland, Dorothy, and Naomi Quinn, eds. *Cultural Models in Language and Thought.* New York: Cambridge University Press, 1987.

Huckfeldt, Robert, and John Sprague. *Citizens, Politics, and Social Communication: Information and Influence in an Election Campaign.* New York: Cambridge University Press, 1995.

Iyengar, Shanto. *Is Anyone Responsible? How Television Frames Political Issues.* Chicago: University of Chicago Press, 1991.

Bibliography

Iyengar, Shanto, and Donald R. Kinder. *News That Matters: Television and American Opinion.* Chicago: University of Chicago Press, 1987.

Jackman, Robert W. "Political Elites, Mass Publics, and Support for Democratic Principles." *Journal of Politics* 34 (1972): 753–73.

Jacobs, Lawrence R., and Robert Y. Shapiro. "Issues, Candidate Image, and Priming: The Use of Private Polls in Kennedy's 1960 Presidential Campaign." *American Political Science Review* 88 (1994): 527–40.

———. "The Rise of Presidential Polling: The Nixon White House in Historical Perspective." *Public Opinion Quarterly* 59 (1995): 163–95.

———. "The Politicization of Public Opinion: The Fight for the Pulpit." Paper presented at the annual meeting of the Midwest Political Science Association, Chicago, April 1997.

Jamieson, Kathleen Hall. *Eloquence in an Electronic Age: The Transformation of Political Speechmaking.* New York: Oxford University Press, 1988.

Jewell, Malcolm E. *Representation in State Legislatures.* Lexington: University Press of Kentucky, 1982.

Jewell, Malcom E., and Penny M. Miller. *The Kentucky Legislature: Two Decades of Change.* Lexington: University Press of Kentucky, 1988.

Jewell, Malcolm E., and Marcia Lynn Whicker. *Legislative Leadership in the American States.* Ann Arbor: University of Michigan Press, 1994.

Jones, Bryan D. "Competitiveness, Role Orientations, and Legislative Responsiveness." *Journal of Politics* 35 (1973): 924–47.

Käsler, Dirk. *Max Weber: An Introduction to His Life and Work.* Chicago: University of Chicago Press, 1988.

Katz, Elihu. "Mass Media and Participatory Democracy." Paper presented at the Series on Political Communication, Northwestern University, 11 October 1996.

Katz, Elihu, and Paul Lazarsfeld. *Personal Influence: The Part Played by People in the Flow of Mass Communication.* Glencoe, Ill.: Free Press, 1955.

Keeter, Scott. "Public Opinion and the Election." In *The Election of 1996: Reports and Interpretations,* edited by Gerald Pomper. Chatham, N.J.: Chatham House, 1997.

Kelley, Stanley. *Interpreting Elections.* Princeton: Princeton University Press, 1983.

Key, V. O. *Public Opinion and American Democracy.* New York: Knopf, 1961.

Kinder, Donald, and Lynn Sanders. *Divided By Color: Racial Politics and Democratic Ideals.* Chicago: University of Chicago Press, 1996.

Kinder, Donald, and David O. Sears. "Public Opinion and Political Action." In *The Handbook of Social Psychology,* edited by Gardner Lindzey and Elliot Aronson. Reading, Mass.: Addison-Wesley, 1985.

King, Clyde Lyndon. "Public Opinion as Viewed by Eminent Political Theorists." In *The University of Pennsylvania Free Public Lecture Course.* Philadelphia: University of Pennsylvania Press, 1916.

Kingdon, John. *Congressmen's Voting Decisions.* 3d ed. Ann Arbor: University of Michigan Press, 1991.

Kirkpatrick, Jeane. "Representation in the American National Conventions: The Case of 1972." *British Journal of Political Science* 5 (1975): 265–322.

Klingemann, Hans D. "Ideological Conceptualization and Political Action." In *Political Action*, edited by Samuel H. Barnes and Max Kaase. Beverly Hills, Calif.: Sage, 1979.

Krehbiel, Keith. *Information and Legislative Organization*. Ann Arbor: University of Michigan Press, 1991.

Kritzer, Herbert M. "Ideology and American Political Elites." *Public Opinion Quarterly* 42 (1978): 482–502.

Krosnick, Jon A. "Government Policy and Citizen Passion: A Study of Issue Publics in Contemporary America." *Political Behavior* 12 (1990): 59–92.

Krosnick, Jon A., and Shibley Telhami. "Public Attitudes toward Israel: A Study of the Attentive and Issue Publics." *International Studies Quarterly* 39 (1995): 335–54.

Kruskal, William, and Frederick Mosteller. "Representative Sampling IV: The History of the Concept in Statistics, 1895–1939." *International Statistical Review* 48 (1980): 169–95.

Kuhn, Deanna. *The Skills of Argument*. New York: Cambridge University Press, 1991.

Kuklinski, James, et al. "Changing Minds: Political Arguments and Political Persuasion." *American Journal of Political Science* 41 (1997): 88–121.

Lane, Robert. *Political Ideology: Why the American Common Man Believes What He Does*. New York: Free Press, 1962.

Lau, Richard R., and David O. Sears, eds. *Political Cognition: The 19th Annual Carnegie Symposium on Cognition*. Hillsdale, N.J.: Lawrence Erlbaum Associates, 1986.

Lavrakas, Paul J., Michael W. Traugott, and Peter V. Miller, eds. *Presidential Polling and the News Media*. Boulder: Westview Press, 1995.

Lazarsfeld, Paul. "Public Opinion in the Classical Tradition." In *Qualitative Analysis: Historical and Critical Essays*, edited by Paul Lazarsfeld. Boston: Allyn and Bacon, 1972.

Lee, Taeku. " 'Dear Mr. President . . . ': Constituency Mail on the Civil Rights Movement as Public Opinion, 1948–1965." Paper presented at the annual meeting of the American Political Science Association, San Francisco, 1996.

Lemert, James B. *Does Mass Communication Change Public Opinion After All?* Chicago, Nelson Hall, 1981.

———. "Picking the Winners: Politician vs. Voter Predictions of Two Controversial Ballot Measures." *Public Opinion Quarterly* 50 (1986): 208–21.

———. "Effective Public Opinion." In *Public Opinion, the Press, and Public Policy*, edited by J. David Kennamer. Westport, Conn.: Praeger, 1992.

Lincoln, Abraham. "My 'Public Opinion Baths.' " In *Lincoln on Democracy*, edited by Mario Cuomo and Harold Holzer. New York: Harper Collins, 1990.

Lippmann, Walter. *The Phantom Public*. New York: Harcourt, Brace, 1925.

———. *Public Opinion*. New York: Free Press, 1965.

Lipset, Seymour, and William Schneider. *The Confidence Gap*. Baltimore: Johns Hopkins University Press, 1987.

Lodge, Milton, and Kathleen M. McGraw, eds. *Political Judgment: Structure and Process*. Ann Arbor: University of Michigan Press, 1995.

Luskin, Robert. "Measuring Political Sophistication." *American Journal of Political Science* 31 (1987): 856–99.

Luttbeg, Norman R. "The Structure of Beliefs among Leaders and the Public." *Public Opinion Quarterly* 32 (1968): 398–409.

Mansbridge, Jane J. *Beyond Adversary Democracy.* Chicago: University of Chicago Press, 1980.

———. "A Deliberative Theory of Interest Representation." In *The Politics of Interests: Interest Groups Transformed,* edited by Mark P. Petracca. Boulder: Westview Press, 1992.

Mayhew, David A. *Congress: The Electoral Connection.* New Haven: Yale University Press, 1974.

Maza, Sarah. *Private Lives and Public Affairs: The Causes Célèbres of Prerevolutionary France.* Berkeley and Los Angeles: University of California Press, 1993.

McAdam, Doug. *Freedom Summer.* New York: Oxford University Press, 1988.

McClosky, Herbert. *Political Inquiry: The Nature and Uses of Survey Research.* New York: Macmillan, 1969.

McClosky, Herbert, Paul J. Hoffmann, and Rosemary O'Hara. "Issue Conflict and Consensus among Party Leaders and Followers." *American Political Science Review* 54 (1960): 406–27.

McCombs, Maxwell E., and Donald L. Shaw, eds. "Agenda-Setting Revisited" (symposium). *Journal of Communication* 43 (1993): 58–128.

McConnell, Grant. *Private Power and American Democracy.* New York: Vintage, 1966.

McLeod, Jack, Gerald Kosicki, and Douglas McLeod. "The Expanding Boundaries of Political Communication Effects." In *Media Effects: Advances in Theory and Research,* edited by Jennings Bryant and Dolf Zillmann. Hillsdale, N.J.: Lawrence Erlbaum Associates, 1994.

Mead, George Herbert. *Mind, Self, and Society.* Chicago: University of Chicago Press, 1934.

Merkle, Daniel M. "Review: The National Issues Convention Deliberative Poll." *Public Opinion Quarterly* 60 (1996): 588–619.

Merrill, Francis E., and Carroll D. Clark. "The Money Market as a Special Public." *American Journal of Sociology* 39 (1934): 626–36.

Meyer, Philip. *Precision Journalism: A Reporter's Introduction to Social Science Methods.* Bloomington: Indiana University Press, 1973.

Meyrowitz, Joshua. *No Sense of Place: The Impact of Electronic Media on Social Behavior.* New York: Oxford University Press, 1985.

Mill, John Stuart. *Considerations on Representative Government.* London: Parker, Son, and Bourne, 1861.

Miller, Warren E. *Without Consent: Mass-Elite Linkages in Presidential Politics.* Lexington: University Press of Kentucky, 1988.

Miller, Warren E., and M. Kent Jennings. *Parties in Transition: A Longitudinal Study of Party Elites and Party Supporters.* New York: Russell Sage Foundation, 1986.

Minar, David. "Public Opinion in the Perspective of Political Theory." *Western Political Quarterly* 13 (1960): 31–44.

Mishler, Elliot G. *Research Interviewing: Context and Narrative.* Cambridge: Harvard University Press, 1986.

Moscovici, Serge. *Social Influence and Social Change.* London: Academic Press, 1976.

Mutz, Diana C. "The Influence of Perceptions of Media Influence: Third Person Effects and the Public Expression of Opinion." *International Journal of Public Opinion Research* 1 (1989): 3–24.

————. "Mass Media and the Depoliticization of Personal Experience." *American Journal of Political Science 36* (1992): 483–508.

Mutz, Diana C., Paul M. Sniderman, and Richard A. Brody, eds. *Political Persuasion and Attitude Change.* Ann Arbor: University of Michigan Press, 1996.

Neuman, W. Russell, Marion R. Just, and Ann N. Crigler. *Common Knowledge: News and the Construction of Political Meaning.* Chicago: University of Chicago Press, 1992.

New York Times. 12 August 1996; 26 August 1996; 30 January 1997.

Newport, Frank. "Wrapping Up the O. J. Simpson Case." *The Gallup Poll Monthly* 363 (November 1995): 24–27.

Nisbett, Richard E., and Lee Ross. *Human Inference: Strategies and Shortcomings of Social Judgment.* Englewood Cliffs, N.J.: Prentice-Hall, 1980.

Noelle-Neumann, Elisabeth. *The Spiral of Silence: Public Opinion—Our Social Skin.* Chicago: University of Chicago Press, 1993.

Nord, David. "Reading the Newspaper: Strategies and Politics of Reader Response, Chicago, 1912–1917." *Journal of Communication* 45 (1995): 66–93.

Olson, Mancur. *The Logic of Collective Action: Public Goods and the Theory of Groups.* Cambridge: Harvard University Press, 1971.

Page, Benjamin I. *Who Deliberates? Mass Media in Modern Democracy.* Chicago: University of Chicago Press, 1996.

Page, Benjamin I., and Robert Y. Shapiro. *The Rational Public: Fifty Years of Trends in Americans' Policy Preferences.* Chicago: University of Chicago Press, 1992.

Page, Benjamin I., Robert Y. Shapiro, and Glenn R. Dempsey. "What Moves Public Opinion." *American Political Science Review* 81(1987): 23–43.

Paletz, David, et al., "Polls in the Media: Content, Credibility, and Consequences." *Public Opinion Quarterly* 44 (1980): 495–513.

Palmer, Paul A. "The Concept of Public Opinion in Political Theory." Ph.D. diss., Harvard University, 1934.

————. "Ferdinand Tönnies' Theory of Public Opinion." *Public Opinion Quarterly* 2 (1938): 584–95.

Parkin, Frank. *Max Weber.* London: Tavistock Publications, 1982.

Pateman, Carole. *The Sexual Contract.* Stanford: Stanford University Press, 1988.

Patterson, Thomas E. *Out of Order: How the Decline of the Political Parties and the Growing Power of the News Media Undermine the American Way of Electing Presidents.* New York: Alfred A. Knopf, 1993.

Peters, John Durham. "Why Dewey Wasn't So Right and Lippmann Wasn't So Wrong." Paper presented at the annual meeting of the International Communication Association, Montreal, 1997.

Petracca, Mark P., ed. *The Politics of Interests: Interest Groups Transformed.* Boulder: Westview Press, 1992.

Petty, Richard E., and John T. Cacioppo. *Attitudes and Persuasion: Classic and Contemporary Approaches.* Dubuque, Iowa: Wm. C. Brown Co., 1981.

Popkin, Samuel L. *The Reasoning Voter: Communication and Persuasion in Presidential Campaigns.* Chicago: University of Chicago Press, 1991.

Price, Vincent. *Public Opinion.* Newbury Park, Calif.: Sage, 1992.

Bibliography

Putnam, Robert. *The Comparative Study of Political Elites.* Englewood Cliffs, N.J.: Prentice-Hall, 1976.

Putnam, Robert D., Robert Leonardi, and Rafaella Y. Nanetti. "Attitude Stability among Italian Elites." *American Journal of Politics* 23 (August 1979): 463–94.

Reiter, Howard L. *Selecting the President: The Nominating Process in Transition.* Philadelphia: University of Pennsylvania Press, 1985.

Roback, Thomas. "Motivation for Activism among Republican National Convention Delegates: Continuity and Change, 1972–1976." *Journal of Politics* 42 (1980): 181–201.

Romzek, Barbara S., and Jennifer A. Utter. "Congressional Legislative Staff: Political Professionals or Clerks?" *American Journal of Political Science* 41 (1997): 1251–79.

Rosen, Jay. "Making Things More Public: On the Political Responsibility of the Media Intellectual." *Critical Studies in Mass Communication* 11 (1994): 362–88.

———. "The Legislative Institution: Transformed and at Risk." In *The State of the States,* edited by Carl E. Van Horn. Washington, D.C.: Congressional Quarterly Press, 1989.

Rosenthal, Alan. *Governors and Legislatures: Contending Powers.* Washington, D.C.: Congressional Quarterly Press, 1990.

———. *The Third House: Lobbyists and Lobbying in the States.* Washington, D.C.: Congressional Quarterly Press, 1993.

Salisbury, Robert H. *Interests and Institutions: Substance and Structure in American Politics.* Pittsburgh: University of Pittsburgh Press, 1992.

Salisbury, Robert H., and Kenneth Shepsle. "U.S. Congressman as Enterprise." *Legislative Studies Quarterly* 6 (1981): 559–76.

Schattschneider, E. E. *The Semisovereign People: A Realist's View of Democracy in America.* New York: Holt, Rinehart and Winston, 1960.

Schlozman, Kay Lehman, and John T. Tierney. *Organized Interests and American Democracy.* New York: Harper and Row, 1986.

Schudson, Michael. *Discovering the News: A Social History of American Newspapers.* New York: Basic Books, 1978.

———. *Watergate in American Memory: How We Remember, Forget, and Reconstruct the Past.* New York: Basic Books, 1992.

———. *The Power of News.* Cambridge: Harvard University Press, 1995.

Schumpeter, Joseph A. *Capitalism, Socialism, and Democracy.* 3d ed. New York: Harper and Row, 1950.

Shaw, Greg. "Social Policies and the Transmission of Public Opinion in the American States." Ph.D. diss., Columbia University, 1997.

Smart, Barry. *Foucault, Marxism, and Critique.* London: Routledge and Kegan Paul, 1985.

Smith, Tom W. "Trends in Non-Response Rates." *International Journal of Public Opinion Research* 7 (1995): 157–71.

Sniderman, Paul M., Richard A. Brody, and Philip E. Tetlock. *Reasoning and Choice: Explorations in Political Psychology.* New York: Cambridge University Press, 1991.

Soule, John W., and James W. Clarke. "Issue Conflict and Consensus: A Comparative Study of Democratic and Republican Delegates to the 1968 National Conventions." *Journal of Politics* 33 (1971): 72–91.

Squires, Catherine. "Black Talk Radio and the Black Public Sphere." Paper presented at the annual meeting of the International Communication Association, Montreal, 1997.

State of Illinois. *Illinois Blue Book 1995/1996.* Springfield: State of Illinois, 1995.

Stimson, James A., Michael B. Mackuen, and Robert S. Erikson. "Dynamic Representation." *American Political Science Review* 89 (1995): 543–65.

Strauss, Anselm, and Juliet Corbin. *Basics of Qualitative Research: Grounded Theory Procedures and Techniques.* Newbury Park, Calif.: Sage, 1990.

Sussmann, Leila. *Dear FDR: A Study of Political Letter Writing.* Totowa, N.J.: Bedminster, 1963.

Tarde, Gabriel. *Gabriel Tarde: On Communication and Social Influence.* Translated and edited by Terry N. Clarke. Chicago: University of Chicago Press, 1969.

Tocqueville, Alexis de. *Democracy in America.* Edited by J. P. Mayer. New York: Anchor, 1969.

Tönnies, Ferdinand. *Community and Society.* Translated and edited by Charles Loomis. East Lansing: Michigan State University Press, 1957.

Truman, David B. *The Governmental Process: Political Interests and Public Opinion.* New York: Alfred A. Knopf, 1960.

Tulis, Jeffrey. *The Rhetorical Presidency.* Princeton: Princeton University Press, 1987.

Underwood, Doug. *When MBAs Rule the Newsroom: How the Marketers and Managers Are Reshaping Today's Media.* New York: Columbia University Press, 1993.

Van Horn, Carl E. "The Quiet Revolution." In *The State of the States,* edited by Carl E. Van Horn. Washington, D.C.: Congressional Quarterly Press, 1989.

Van Horn, Carl E., ed. *The State of the States.* Washington, D.C.: Congressional Quarterly Press, 1989.

Verba, Sidney, Kay Lehman Schlozman, and Henry E. Brady. *Voice and Equality: Civic Voluntarism in American Politics.* Cambridge: Harvard University Press, 1995.

Walker, Jack L. *Mobilizing Interest Groups in America: Patrons, Professions, and Social Movements.* Ann Arbor: University of Michigan Press, 1991.

Weber, Max. *Economy and Society: An Outline of Interpretive Sociology.* Edited by Guenther Roth and Claus Wittich. Berkeley and Los Angeles: University of California Press, 1978.

Whiteman, David. *Communication in Congress: Members, Staff, and the Search for Information.* Lawrence: University Press of Kansas, 1995.

Wiebe, Robert H. *Self-Rule: A Cultural History of American Democracy.* Chicago: University of Chicago Press, 1995.

Wilson, Francis Graham. "Concepts of Public Opinion." *American Political Science Review* 27 (1933): 371–91.

———. *A Theory of Public Opinion.* Chicago: Henry Regnery Company, 1962.

Zaller, John. *The Nature and Origins of Mass Opinion.* New York: Cambridge University Press, 1992.

———. "Positive Constructs of Public Opinion." *Critical Studies in Mass Communication* 11 (1994): 276–87.

Zaller, John, and Stanley Feldman. "A Simple Theory of the Survey Response: Answering Questions versus Revealing Preferences." *American Journal of Political Science* 36 (1992): 579–616.

Index

abortion, Republicans on, 128, 130
Abramson, Paul R., 225n. 21
activists: ambivalence of, 163–64; background of, 127, 157, 191; connectedness of, 138–39; constituencies conceived by, 166–67; as convention delegates, 126–32; on conversation, 125–26, 133–34, 137–38, 144, 148, 156–58, 177–78; as informants, 30–31, 39–40, 125–26; on interest groups, 125, 139–40, 143–44; interviews of, 44–45, 191–98, 203–5; on media, 125, 132–34, 137–44; and models of democracy, 142–48, 157–58, 160–61, 174, 176–77; motives of, 3, 160–61; on polls, 14, 49, 125, 133–37, 143–44, 157–58, 181; public opinion defined and assessed by, 2, 125, 132, 133–39; on representation, 142–43, 181–82; as representative of public, 142–48; research on, 126–29; role of, 8, 124–26, 126–29, 162; staffers and journalists compared to, 134–35, 139–42, 160, 178–79
affirmative action, Democrats on, 130
African Americans, and Simpson trial, 184
Agger, Robert E., 222–23n. 4
Allen, Robert C., 221n. 23
Altschuler, Bruce, 217n. 1
Antaki, Charles, 26, 27, 214n. 37
anthropology, interview methods in, 195–96
argument: concept of, 27, 218n. 13; context of, 30–31; in conversation, 26–27, 107;

ideology's role in, 29–30; individual's internal, 7, 13, 22, 26–31; persuasive type of, 28–29; political cognition as, 26–31; public opinion constructed in, 62, 78–79; on public sphere by staffers, 62, 72–81, 85–88. *See also* political cognition; rhetoric
Aristotle, 16, 19–20, 177–78, 212n. 9, 213n. 23, 227n. 28
Associated Press, function of, 96
attitudes: ambivalence about, 163–64; based on argumentation, 28–30; concept of, 218n. 13; and media content, 65; and political engagement, 127–29; research on, 28, 183, 195–96. *See also* beliefs
attribution theory, 21, 25–26
Austin, J. L., 107, 221n. 20

Baker v. Carr, 40
Barber, James David, 31, 214n. 47
Barbour, Haley, 130
Bauer, Wilhelm, 1, 209n. 1
Baugh, Kenneth, Jr., 229n. 4
beliefs: ambivalence about, 163–64; inconsistency in, 173–74; and media selection, 183. *See also* attitudes
Bennet, James, 223n. 11
Bennett, W. Lance, 18–19, 213nn. 20–21, 219n. 1
Bentley, Arthur F., 6, 56, 78, 151, 210n. 9, 217n. 4
Berelson, Bernard, 55, 227n. 30
Berger, Peter, 20–21, 150, 213n. 25

governors, influence by, 40
Greene, Steven, 129, 223n. 8, 223n. 10
Griffiths, A. Phillips, 180, 227n. 34
Grossberg, Lawrence, 227n. 36
grounded theory, 74, 87–88, 118, 194–98
groups (general): and issue politics,
    62–64; public opinion represented by,
    6; role of, 55–57, 60; vs. individuals,
    53–54, 56. *See also* focus groups; inter-
    est groups
Gurvith, Georges, 52

Habermas, Jürgen, 2, 107, 210n. 4,
    220–21n. 15
Hall, Richard, 218n. 7
Hansen, John Mark, 217n. 3
Hardy, Thomas, 66
Hart, Roderick, 18, 212n. 12, 213n. 17
Hartmann, George W., 224–25n. 18
health care issue: legislation on, 154–55;
    polls on, 225n. 19; and reform, 185;
    rhetoric on, 17, 18
Hedlund, Ronald, 224–25n. 18
Heider, Fritz, 25, 214n. 36
Heinz, John P., 218n. 8
Held, David, 15, 157, 158, 212n. 5, 212n. 7
Henderson, David, 18
Herrera, Richard, 128–29, 222n. 3, 223nn.
    8–9
heuristics (schemas): context of, 23; in lab
    vs. real world, 26–29; research on, 13
Hibbing, John R., 164, 226n. 10
Hildreth, Anne, 210n. 8
history, research issues for, 184–86
Hochschild, Jennifer, 163, 196, 226n. 9,
    229n. 3
Hoffmann, Paul J., 222–23n. 4
Holland, Dorothy, 214n. 49
Huckfeldt, Robert, 55, 56, 227n. 30

ideology: and elites vs. nonelites, 127–28;
    and media bias, 140–41; and political
    engagement, 129–31; polls influenced

by, 101–2; role of, 29–30, 149. *See also*
    democracy
Illinois: Chicago mayor vs. governor in,
    121; as milieu for study, 42–43. *See also*
    Illinois General Assembly
Illinois Campaign Finance Task Force, 170
Illinois General Assembly: characteristics
    of, 9–12, 89–90; clipping service in, 68,
    71, 171; Congress compared to, 89–92,
    182; institutional memory of, 96; legis-
    lators vs. staffers in, 34–36, 96; news
    coverage of, 37–38, 93–98; and polls on
    issues, 48–52; press corps covering,
    90–92; structure and processes of,
    33–34, 50. *See also* bills (legislative);
    committees; interest groups; journal-
    ists; legislative staffers; legislators
Illinois Legislative Correspondents Asso-
    ciation, 94, 215n. 57
individuals: culture as context for, 23–25;
    internal arguments of, 7, 13, 22, 26–31;
    social reality constructed by, 20–21;
    stereotypes held by, 22; stories focused
    on, 18–19; vs. groups, 53–54, 56; vs. sci-
    entists, 25–26. *See also* citizens; conver-
    sation; knowledge; narrative
information processing: shortcomings of
    focus on, 29–30; study of individuals',
    22–23. *See also* methodology; political
    cognition
Innis, Harold, 219n. 23
interest groups: activists on, 125, 139–40,
    143–44; campaign contributions by,
    170; communication by, 53, 86; com-
    munication directors' attitudes toward,
    82; conflict among, 63–64, 81; as con-
    stituencies, 168–70; critique of, 58–59;
    differences among, 58–60, 140; history
    of, 154–55; honesty of, 54–55, 154; as
    indicators and conveyors of public
    opinion, 6, 52–62, 74–75, 78, 167–69,
    180; and issue politics, 62–64; journal-
    ists' relations with, 97, 159, 219n. 26; in

Index